DESIGN IN AGRICULTURAL ENGINEERING

by

L. L. Christianson
Associate Professor, Agricultural Engineering Department
University of Illinois, Urbana, IL

Roger P. Rohrbach
Professor, Biological and Agricultural Engineering Department
North Carolina State University, Raleigh, NC

An ASAE Textbook
Number 1 in a series published by

American Society of Agricultural Engineers
2950 Niles Road
St. Joseph, Michigan 49085-9659
(phone 616-429-0300)

ASAE Technical Editor: James A. Basselman
August 1986

Library of Congress Catalog Card Number 86-71552

International Standard Book Number: 0-916150-80-1

The American Society of Agricultural Engineers
2950 Niles Road, St. Joseph, Michigan 49085-9659 USA
(phone 616-429-0300)

Dedicated to those who create ingenious
solutions to people's needs—within limits
of practicality

Preface

This is a design text for senior level students in Agricultural Engineering and a reference for design engineers and managers in the agricultural industry. Design techniques and project management methods are explained and supplemented by examples from industry. This book complements technical subject matter books, and can aid design and research efforts in any of the diverse areas comprising Agricultural Engineering. Key design subjects such as safety, cost estimating, project scheduling, time management, patents and drafting are summarized in individual chapters. An annotated bibliography in the Appendix describes the content of each book cited in the chapter references given at the end of each chapter; the chapter references describe additional sources of more detailed information pertaining to each chapter.

This book is based upon the philosophy that engineering design is best taught by focusing design activities on one or more specific projects or products. Our reason is simply that engineers by nature are action oriented and respond positively to the long-established concept of learning-by-doing. The techniques and philosophies of approaching design are most meaningful and become alive when they help solve real engineering problems that are both interesting and significant to the student or practitioner.

Time is your most limiting resource in the design process! Using this text you can glean the information you need quickly so that your focus remains on the actual design problem.

Therefore, this text is organized by parts beginning with Agricultural Engineering Design — An Example, which illustrates all the important steps in the design process. The remaining parts are generally in the order encountered in most design projects continuing with: How Can I Be Effective as a Design Engineer?, How Shall I Start?, How Shall I Develop This Design? and ending with Related Design Topics. Each of these remaining parts have several chapters on topics important to that phase of the design process. Each chapter is concisely written and highlights the most important aspects of that subject. Suitable discussion or homework problems and related design activities for student projects are also provided at the end of most chapters and major parts of the text.

A Special Word to Instructors

We believe the order in which the material is presented in this text is in a logical sequence. However, we recognize that

v

engineering design is an iterative, parallel-activity process which defies organization into a recipe-like sequence guaranteed to produce the desired results. The order of topic coverage should be adjusted to suit project and student needs. Therefore, we have written the chapters so that they can be covered in essentially any order.

Design is an investigative, self-education activity. Instructors should encourage students to read and refer to chapters independent from the class lecture sequence. Effective engineers learn to focus on the activity that is most restricting or progress-limiting.

It is our intent to provide the student with three distinct exposures to the design process. First, Part I is an example case study; second, the student by reading the remaining text is exposed to the details of design; third, the student participates in the systematic application of sound design principles to their problems or projects.

You, the instructor, may suggest that students select and read the chapter most critical to their project and work on the appropriate problems at the end of that chapter. A major portion of class lecture time may be used to discuss student problem solving efforts.

We recognize that there are varied types of agricultural engineering design classes and styles of teaching. This text can be appropriate for courses with all or some of the following objectives:

1. Understand that design is a pragmatic combination of scientific theory, technical skills, people talents and art to create solutions to problems.

2. Develop the time-management, team-effectiveness and motivation skills needed to be an effective engineer.

3. Practice written and oral communication appropriate to engineering design activities.

4. Document each and every step in the design process using an accepted design notebook style.

5. Develop information seeking and sorting talents as required by an engineering design problem.

6. Harness inventiveness and creativity and use these to assist in solving an engineering design problem.

7. Understand the types of design problems that are solved by Agricultural Engineers and recognize how these relate to the Agricultural Engineering subject matter specialities.

8. Enjoy the satisfaction of solving a challenging design problem!

Acknowledgments

Teamwork, the combination of diverse talents and specialized skills, is the theme throughout this textbook. Not surprisingly, many people contributed their expertise so that this textbook is representative of current design and development practice within firms employing agricultural design engineers.

Mylo Hellickson, South Dakota State University, Pat Hassler, N.C. State University and Roscoe Pershing, University of Illinois, as department chairmen, encouraged our writing efforts and made it possible to complete this book while continuing our university work. Brenda Mason, N.C. State University entered the text on word processor with final revisions while Darlene Hofer, South Dakota State University and Sharon Warsaw, University of Illinois typed earlier drafts. Cartoons and line drawings were skillfully prepared by Jerry Barrett, Joan Zagorski and Carolyn Evans, with guidance from Pat Francek of the University of Illinois. Jeanette Rohrbach provided endless hours of proof reading. Linda Christianson designed the chapter logos and cover.

Donna Hull, ASAE, patiently encouraged our writing efforts and Jim Basselman editorially critiqued our final drafts. The entire ASAE Textbook Committee was very supportive of our efforts and recommended publication after a coordinated text review by Dave Smith at Deere and Company. Full text reviews were made by Larry Stikeleather, N.C. State University, Gary Krutz, Purdue University, Bob Sowell, N.C. State University and Jim Ruff, Deere and Company for ASAE. The many valuable observations and suggestions made by these men were gratefully integrated into the text. Ken Finden, University of Arizona and Chuck Peterson, University of Idaho used the text in draft form and provided valuable ideas and critiques.

Many others contributed in special ways. Bob Holmes, Ohio State University, worked with us during the initial text outline and defined topics to be included in various chapters. We appreciate the critical reviews of individual chapters and the contributions of materials by the following individuals to whom we express our personal thanks: Dick Mott, LeRoy Stumpe, John Crowley, Jim Ebbinghaus, Jim Kirchhofer, Keith Pfundstein, John Clark, Dick Paff, Hugh Grow, Frank Abrams, Gerry Baughman, Mike Boyette, Charlie Suggs, Alicia Lanier, Dan McConnell, Jim McCarrville, Rod Devine, Bill Harriott, Walt Lembke, Norm Scott, Bob Fridley, Lyle Shaver, and Al Rider.

And finally, numerous friends, faculty, engineers from industry and former students have provided us with inspiration, ideas, information and critiques. To all of you, we thank you for your help!

LLC and RPR
August 15, 1986

Credits

The following companies, institutions and professional organizations supported our work in significant ways.

Institutions
University of Illinois
North Carolina State University
South Dakota State University
Ohio State University
Purdue University
University of Idaho
University of Arizona

Industries
DuAl Manufacturing
Deere and Company
McCulloch Northco
Butler Manufacturing
Valmont Industries
FMC Corporation
Hesston Manufacturing
3M Corporation
New Holland Inc.
Gravely International
Carrier Corporation

Organizations
American Society of Agricultural Engineers
Farm Industrial and Equipment Institute
Midwest Plan Service
National Society of Professional Engineers

Table of Contents

Preface v
Acknowledgements vii
Credits viii
Table of Contents ix
Part I   Agricultural Engineering Design — An Example 1
Part II   How Can I Be Effective as a Design Engineer? 19
            1. Time Management 23
            2. Team Effectiveness 29
            3. Drawings and Specifications 35
            4. Writing and Speaking 47
            5. Salesmanship and Motivation 59
Part III   How Shall I Start? 67
            6. Engineering Design (Universal Constraints) 73
            7. Problem Definition and Design Specifications 81
            8. Planned Creativity 93
            9. Help from Others 103
            10. Project Scheduling 113
Part IV   How Shall I Develop this Design? 131
            11. Analysis 135
            12. Synthesis 143
            13. User Considerations 151
            14. Materials Selection 159
            15. Product Safety and Liability 165
            16. Cost Estimating 183
            17. Component and Supplier Selection 197
            18. Manufacturing Considerations 203
            19. Standardization and Simplification 215
            20. Testing and Evaluation 223
Part V   Related Design Topics 231
            21. Business Styles and Organizational Structures 233
            22. Patents, Trademarks, Copyrights, and Trade Secrets 243
            23. Futurology 253
APPENDIX I Code of Ethics for Engineers 265
APPENDIX II Related Organizations 273
APPENDIX III Engineering Forms and Formats 281
APPENDIX IV Annotated Bibliography 295
APPENDIX V English/Metric Conversion 303
Index 308

Part I
Agricultural Engineering Design — An Example

*"Important ideas are those that lie within the
allowable scope of nature's laws."*

*"Ignorance is the one thing that cannot be
regained once it has been lost."*

PART I CONTENTS

We begin by looking carefully at one example of a successful
student design project. This case study illustrates the scope and
depth of activities a design engineer might undertake in solving a
problem. In this case, one student participated in all phases of the
design, which was a research and development design and
emphasized the need for creativity. Actual examples from the
student's design notebook show chronologically the design and
associated thought processes for this project. Study the process
and try to anticipate the design engineer's next move.

Recognize the problem

"How can we measure the radii of curvature at a specific point
on the surface of a blueberry?" was the design question faced by
David Coward, an engineering senior at North Carolina State
University. This question originated from a larger research
project which had the objective of developing a means to measure
the firmness of fresh blueberries. Firmness is a key indicator of
how well product quality can be maintained during shipping and
subsequent shelf storage on the retail market. The principal radii
of curvature were needed to calculate berry contact strain during
bruising.

All students in this design class were provided a list of possible design problems, and were asked to select one of interest from the list to pursue. This is typical in that the engineer received the problem from an outside source, and atypical in that the engineer chose from a list of possible design problems. Most engineering design problems are first recognized by product users, sales representatives or others outside of engineering who then bring the problem to the engineers. A practicing design engineer can expect most design projects to begin as an assignment to solve a given problem.

Define the problem in writing

After a few days of library research and consultation, Mr. Coward prepares a letter which vaguely defines the problem but which does estimate cost, time and equipment needs, (Fig I.1). Coward's letter is important in helping him to begin to understand his design problem and plan the solution approach. It is difficult to obtain advice or financial support from others unless you can articulate your problem and explain how you intend to approach the problem. Naturally, the more expensive and complex the problem, the more carefully and thoroughly the engineer must define the problem.

Note that Coward expresses a personal commitment to solve the problem and is enthusiastic about the challenge. Attitude is critical to project success. Secondly, note that he is already sub-dividing the larger problem into parts so that he methodically approaches each part to obtain the completed solution.

Develop ideas

How about placing the berry on a perch and using light sources and fiber optic arrays to measure the curvature (Fig I.2)? Coward's first completed conceptual sketch shows a point of measurement atop the perch with a motor to lower the perch.

Gather information

Coward already has begun asking questions and referring to product catalogs (Fig I.2). McClure provides ideas on a solution and Rohrbach helps him define the problem further. Allied Electronics makes a light emitting diode which might work as a light source for the fiber optics if this first idea is chosen as the idea to develop.

Continue developing ideas

Vertical motion is needed to sense the shadowing of the light beam as the berry is lowered because the relative shadowing is indicative of surface curvature (Fig I.3). Also notice that there is

September 2

Dr. Rohrbach
Biological and Agricultural Engineering
NCSU
Raleigh, NC 27607

Dear Sir,

I am highly interested in tackling the problem of the small
fruit analysis that you have presented. As a senior in
Biological and Agricultural Engineering at NCSU, I am in
the field for this type of challenge. The problem poses
some difficulty, but I believe I can provide you with
a completed project by the spring.
    The solution will include a working apparatus for the
analysis of the radii of the small fruit as well as the interface
and programming required for digital readouts. This early in
the design makes an assessment difficult, but the whole
project should not exceed $3000.
    If you believe I am able to handle your problem
requirements to your satisfaction and are interested in my
services, contact me at my office. I look forward to
the possibility of working for you.

                    Sincerely,

                    David J. Coward

                    Project Designs
                    2520 Clark Avenue
                    Raleigh, NC 27607
                    # (919) 832-4927

FIG I.1 A proposal letter and the first attempt to define the problem.

a concept included which will rotate 90° at the end of the down
stroke so that the *same* fiber optic array can be used to measure
the other radii when the berry is raised.

    Coward has fellow students witness Figs I.3 and I.7 for future
patent protection. All information is dated and ordered
sequentially in a permanently-bound notebook.

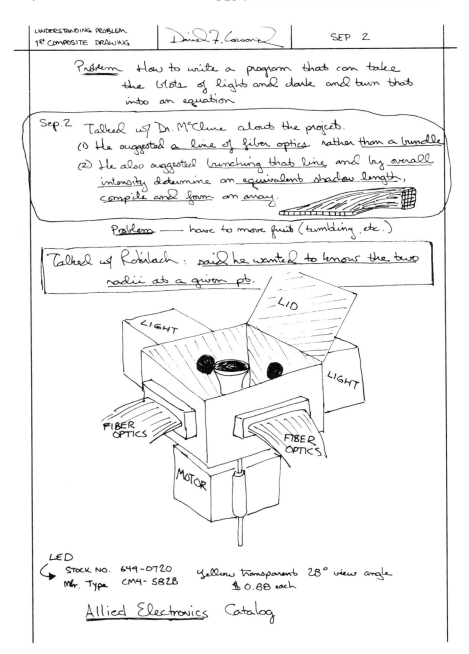

UNDERSTANDING PROBLEM 1ˢᵗ COMPOSITE DRAWING	Daniel F. Cowan	SEP 2

Problem   How to write a program that can take
the blots of lights and dark and turn that
into an equation

Sep.2   Talked w/ Dr. McClure about the project.
(1) He suggested a line of fiber optics rather than a bundle
(2) He also suggested bunching that line and by overall
intensity determine an equivalent shadow length,
compile and form an array.

Problem —— have to move fruit (tumbling, etc.)

Talked w/ Robbach: said he wanted to know the two
radii at a given pt.

LID

LIGHT

LIGHT

FIBER OPTICS

FIBER OPTICS

MOTOR

LED
↳ STOCK NO. 649-0720   Yellow transparent 28° view angle
Mfr. Type CM4-582B $0.88 each

Allied Electronics Catalog

FIG I.2 Ideas and information are combined to produce potential solutions.

COMPOSITE DRAWING	SENIOR DESIGN	David 7. Coward SEP. 8

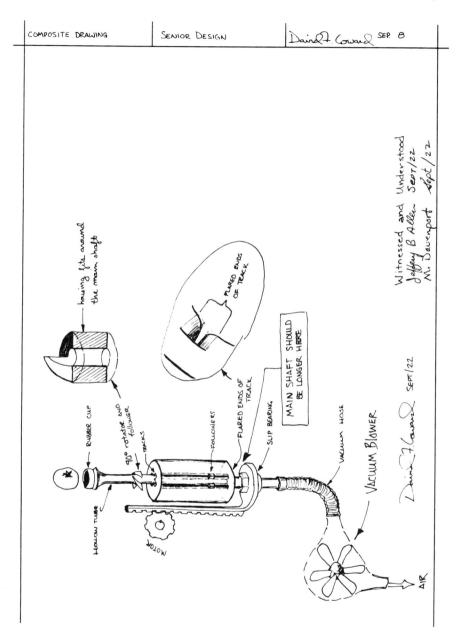

FIG I.3 Some requirements of the problem result in complications.

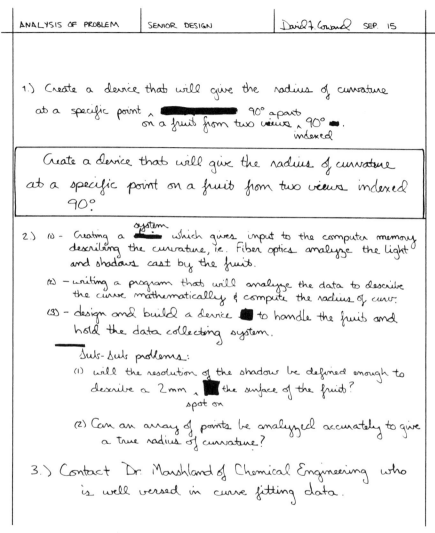

| ANALYSIS OF PROBLEM | SENIOR DESIGN | David F. Coward   SEP. 15 |

1.) Create a device that will give the radius of curvature at a specific point ▬▬▬ 90° apart on a fruit from two views, 90° ▬.
indexed

> Create a device that will give the radius of curvature at a specific point on a fruit from two views indexed 90°.

2.) (1) – Creating a system which gives input to the computer memory describing the curvature, ie. Fiber optics analyze the light and shadows cast by the fruit.

(2) – writing a program that will analyze the data to describe the curve mathematically & compute the radius of curv.

(3) – design and build a device ▮ to handle the fruits and hold the data collecting system.

Sub-sub problems:

(1) will the resolution of the shadow be defined enough to describe a 2mm, ▮ the surface of the fruit?
spot on

(2) Can an array of points be analyzed accurately to give a true radius of curvature?

3.) Contact Dr. Marshland of Chemical Engineering who is well versed in curve fitting data.

FIG I.4 Define the problem, divide into smaller sub-problems and conquer!

Re-evaluate the problem and ideas

Two weeks into the design project Coward steps back in his mind to define the problem more carefully and to evaluate his ideas (Fig I.4). How can these parts be fabricated? Will it work?

By now Coward had assembled 25 to 30 pages of notes from consultations with other engineers and reviews of patents, technical articles and manufacturer's product literature. Coward has a file of information and begins organizing his files accord-

ASAE Standard: ASAE S368.1

COMPRESSION TEST OF FOOD MATERIALS OF CONVEX SHAPE

Reviewed by the ASAE Physical Properties of Agricultural Products Committee; approved by the Food Engineering Division Standards Committee; adopted by ASAE December 1973; revised and reclassified as a Standard December 1979.

SECTION 1—PURPOSE

1.1 This Standard is intended for use in determining mechanical attributes of food texture, resistance to mechanical injury, and force-deformation behavior of food materials of convex shape, such as fruits and vegetables, seeds and grains, and manufactured food materials.

SECTION 2—SCOPE

2.1 Compression tests of intact biological materials provide an objective method for determining mechanical properties significant in quality evaluation and control, maximum allowable load for minimizing mechanical damage, and minimum energy requirements for size reduction.

2.2 Realizing the shortcomings associated with subjective methods, the use of fully automatic testing machines has become popular in recent years. With the use of testing machines, the need for a recommendation for testing, interpretation of data, and reporting of results has become evident.

2.3 Determination of compressive properties requires the production of a complete force-deformation curve. From the force-deformation curve, stiffness; modulus of elasticity; modulus of deformability; toughness; force and deformation to points of inflection, to bioyield, and to rupture; work to point of inflection, to bioyield, and to rupture, and maximum normal contact stress or a stress index at low levels of deformation can be obtained. Any number of these mechanical properties can, by agreement, be chosen for the purpose of evaluation and control of quality.

SECTION 3—DEFINITIONS

3.1 **Bioyield point:** A point such as shown in Fig. 1 where an increase in deformation results in a decrease or no change in force.

3.2 **Force-deformation curve:** A diagram plotted with values of deformation as abscissae and values of force as ordinates.

3.3 **Modulus of elasticity:** A modulus given by the equations shown in Fig. 2. The equations are based on the Hertz problem of contact stresses in solid mechanics and assume very small and elastic deformations. To separate elastic and plastic deformations, an unloading force-deformation curve is required.

3.4 **Modulus of deformability:** A modulus defined by the same equations as those shown in Fig. 2 for modulus of elasticity except that D in these expressions is the sum of both elastic and plastic deformations. No unloading force-deformation curve is required in this case.

3.5 **Point of inflection:** A typical force-deformation curve is first concave up and then concave down (Fig. 1). The point at which the rate of change of slope (second derivative) of the curve becomes zero is called the point of inflection. This point, designated as PI, can be found by using a straight edge to follow the change of slope of the curve and to determine the point at which the slope begins to decrease.

3.6 **Radius of the circle of contact:** The radius of the contact area between the compression tool and the convex-shape specimen at any given load and deformation. For a rigid spherical compression tool on convex specimens and very small deformations (Fig. 2c), the radius of the circle of contact can be approximated by the following formula:

$$a^2 = \frac{D}{\frac{1}{R} + \frac{2}{d}}$$

where
a = radius of the circle of contact
D = elastic deformation
d = diameter of spherical indenter
R = average radius of the convex body

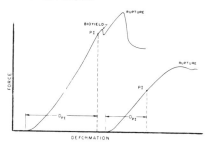

FIG. 1—FORCE-DEFORMATION CURVES FOR MATERIALS WITH AND WITHOUT BIOYIELD POINT. PI = point of inflection, D_{PI} = deformation at point of inflection.

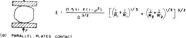

(a) PARALLEL PLATES CONTACT

$$E = \frac{0.531\ F(1-\mu^2)}{D^{3/2}}\left[\left(\frac{1}{R_1}+\frac{1}{R_1'}\right)^{1/3} + \left(\frac{1}{R_2}+\frac{1}{R_2'}\right)^{1/3}\right]^{3/2}$$

(b) SINGLE PLATE CONTACT

$$E = \frac{0.531\ F(1-\mu^2)}{D^{3/2}}\left[\frac{1}{R_1}+\frac{1}{R_1'}\right]^{1/2}$$

(c) SPHERICAL INDENTER ON CURVED SURFACE

$$E = \frac{0.531\ F(1-\mu^2)}{D^{3/2}}\left[\frac{1}{R_1}+\frac{1}{R_1'}+\frac{4}{d}\right]^{1/2}$$

(d) SPHERICAL INDENTER ON FLAT SURFACE

$$E = \frac{0.531\ F(1-\mu^2)}{D^{3/2}}\left[\frac{4}{d}\right]^{1/2}$$

FIG. 2—MODULUS OF ELASTICITY CALCULATED FROM FORCE AND DEFORMATION DATA. E = modulus of elasticity, Pa (psi); F = force in N (lbf); D = elastic deformation at both loading and supporting points of contact, m(in.); μ = Poisson's ratio; R_1, R_1', R_2, R_2' = radii of curvature of the convex body at the points of contact, m(in.); d = diameter of the spherical indenter, m(in.); 0.531 = constant valid for the case where the angle between the normal planes containing the principal curvatures of the convex body is 90 deg and the difference between the curvatures in each plane is small.

FIG I.5 Standards are an important source of reliable information.

ing to sub-problems related to the overall design.

One month into the design Coward is still generating ideas, gathering information, and subdividing the problem into smaller, more clearly defined parts. This clarification, investigation and generation of creative ideas is necessary before you can actually develop the precise design into a working prototype.

Check standards

ASAE Standard S368.1 defines direct contact methods for measuring radii of curvature of convex foods (Fig I.5). This triggers an additional search for alternative solutions to sense fruit surface shape characteristics and three direct contact ideas are conceptualized (Fig I.6).

All three alternatives have significant weaknesses and produce renewed confidence that the fiber-optic shadowing technique is the best solution.

Revise ideas since expenses are often limiting

Fiber optic devices are relatively expensive and Coward has a limit of $300 to use. Therefore, the conceptualized system which would allow an indexed 90° horizontal rotation at the bottom of the vertical stroke and still allow the needed vertical stroke (Fig I.7) remains unresolved.

Re-examine sub-problems

One month later ... light shadowing over the top of the berry will be recorded by a horizontal array of fiber-optics (Fig I.8). Three crucially important sub-problems are clearly identified. (a) How accurately does the light define the surface position? (b) How accurately can the fiber optic grid define the dark/ light shadow interface? (c) Once the spatial coordinates of the surface shape are determined, what calculation algorithm is necessary to produce a radius estimate?

Discover an error in logic

Radius of curvature is a point property not a curve property; only in the case of a circular arc does radius of curvature become both a point property and a curve property. This logic error (Fig I.8) results in several weeks delay. Coward diagnoses the problem only after a detailed computer analysis of the effect of the discrete grid points on the calculated three-point radius estimates.

A design engineer has to expect such errors and plan for them by carefully checking and cross-checking work and by allowing time in the design schedule for such delays. Practical experience and judgments, both the designer's and those who are consulted, should be used to help check for errors.

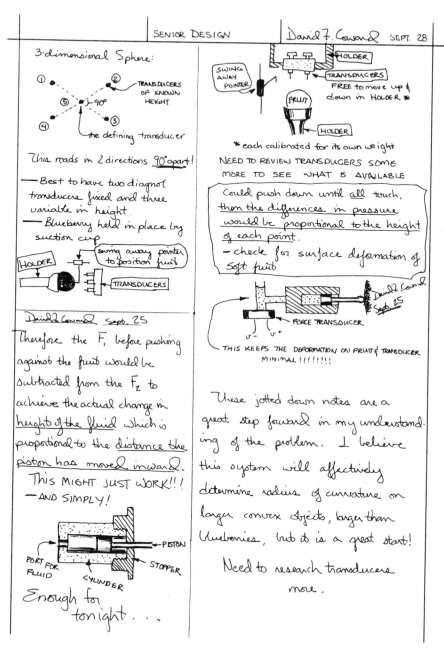

FIG I.6 Are there other ways to solve the problem?

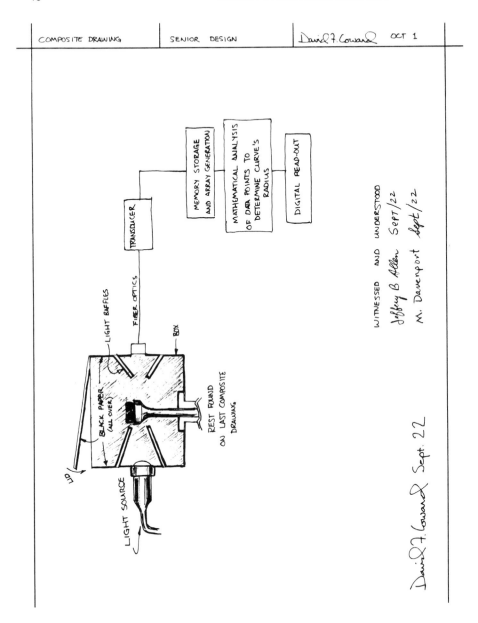

FIG I.7 More details continue to show the emerging problem definition.

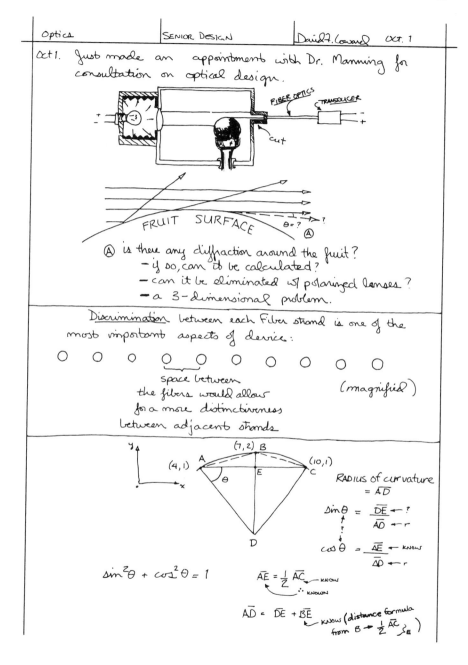

| Optics | SENIOR DESIGN | David J. Coward | Oct. 1 |

Oct 1. Just made an appointment with Dr. Manning for consultation on optical design.

FIBER OPTICS
TRANSDUCER
cut

FRUIT SURFACE $\theta = ?$ Ⓐ

Ⓐ is there any diffraction around the fruit?
— if so, can it be calculated?
— can it be eliminated w/ polarized lenses?
— a 3-dimensional problem.

Discrimination between each fiber strand is one of the most important aspects of device:

O O O O O O O O O O

space between
the fibers would allow
for a more distinctiveness
between adjacent strands

(magnified)

$(7,2)$ B
A $(4,1)$
E $(10,1)$

RADIUS of curvature $= \overline{AD}$

$\sin \theta = \dfrac{\overline{DE}}{\overline{AD}} \leftarrow ?$ $\leftarrow r$

$\cos \theta = \dfrac{\overline{AE}}{\overline{AD}} \leftarrow$ KNOW $\leftarrow r$

$\sin^2 \theta + \cos^2 \theta = 1$

$\overline{AE} = \dfrac{1}{2} \overline{AC}$ ← KNOW
∴ KNOWN

$\overline{AD} = \overline{DE} + \overline{BE}$ ← KNOW (distance formula from B → $\frac{1}{2} \overline{AC}$ ∫ε)

FIG I.8 If the approach toward solving the problem is fixed, what details remain?

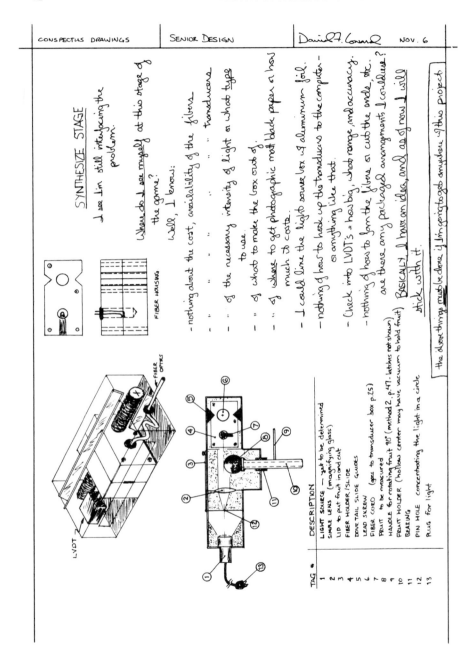

| CONSPECTUS DRAWINGS | SENIOR DESIGN | Daniel F. Conard   NOV. 6 |

SYNTHESIZE STAGE

I see I'm still interfacing the problem.

Where do I see myself at this stage of the game?

Well, I know:

- nothing about the cost, availability of the filters

-    "   "   "   " the necessary intensity of light or what type transducer to use.

-    "   "   "   " what to make the box out of.

-    "   "   "   " where to get photographic matt black paper or how much it costs.

- I could line the light source box w aluminum foil.

- nothing of how to hook up the transducer to the computer - or anything like that.

- Check into LVDT's = how big, what range, and accuracy.

- nothing of how to form the filters or cut the angle, etc. are there any packaged arrangements I could use?

BASICALLY I have an idea, and as of now I will stick with it.

the above things must be done if I'm going to get anywhere in this project

FIBER HOUSING

FIBER OPTICS

LVDT

TAG #	DESCRIPTION
1	LIGHT SOURCE — yet to be determined
2	SIMPLE LENS (magnifying glass)
3	LID to put fruit in and out
4	FIBER HOLDER / SLIDE
5	DOVE TAIL SLIDE GUIDES
6	LEAD SCREW (goes to transducer box p.25)
7	FIBER CORD
8	FRUIT to be measured
9	HANDLE for rotating fruit 90° (method 2, p.47. latches not shown)
10	FRUIT HOLDER (hollow center may have vacuum to hold fruit)
11	BEARING
12	PIN HOLE concentrating the light in a circle
13	PLUG for light

FIG I.9 Where do we stand today?

Fix on a design idea and begin development

Design development takes time and Coward recognizes that after two months he needs to select the most promising idea and begin development (Fig I.9). The fiber optic linear array has been rotated into a vertical position and will be moved horizontally across and behind the berry to sense the vertical component of surface shadowing as a function of horizontal position. Thus, (x,y) coordinate pairs of data will be produced. The fruit holder with sample can now be manually rotated 90° about its vertical axis and the process repeated to produce the second of the two principal radii of curvature.

Build a test prototype

Three months into the project Coward has nearly completed a conspectus design of a prototype that should prove to be adequate for testing (Fig I.10). The problem is defined such that only three data pairs are required. Notice that selected sub-problems are marked with notes as to their present status of development. Coward recognizes that testing will probably help him discover unexpected problems which require changes in the design.

Begin testing

Four months pass while parts are ordered, the first prototype is actually built, and the test apparatus is planned and developed (Fig I.11). The test data in Fig I.11 were obtained using a 14 mm hard rubber ball to represent a berry.

The design has progressed to the crucial testing phase. Clearly, if only three of the data points are fed into the radius of curvature program, the resulting radius will be a function of the three values. But which three points do we select? Look closely at the data in Fig I.11. Examination of the test specimen used reveals a smooth spherical surface in the test region. But why are the data not symmetric? What causes the "bumps and jumps" in the data? Shouldn't the data be more smooth?

The design has made one complete iteration with lots of little reiterations along the way. Faced with the new set of questions arising from the testing, Coward re-focuses and re-opens issues supposedly resolved. Lost motion (play) between the moving fiber-optic array and the guide cause some of the data scatter. Non-uniformity of light intensity from left to right within the viewing field of the fiber optic array cause the major part of the asymmetry. Additional radius extraction algorithms are investigated and developed. A direct, least-squared curve fit of a circle to the data is unsuccessful due to the complexity of the

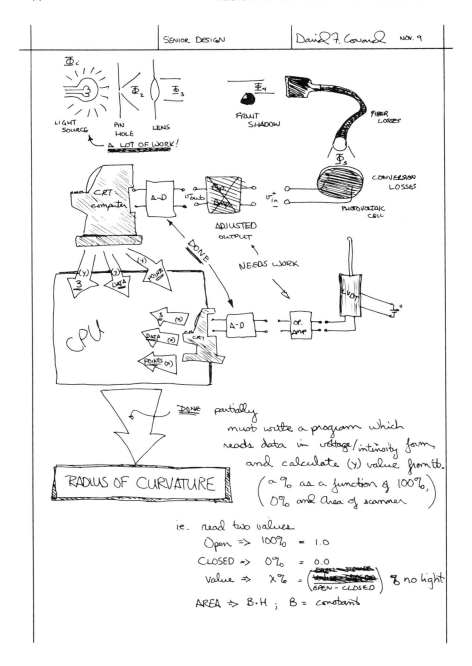

FIG I.10 Here is another way of looking at the total solution. What remains to be completed?

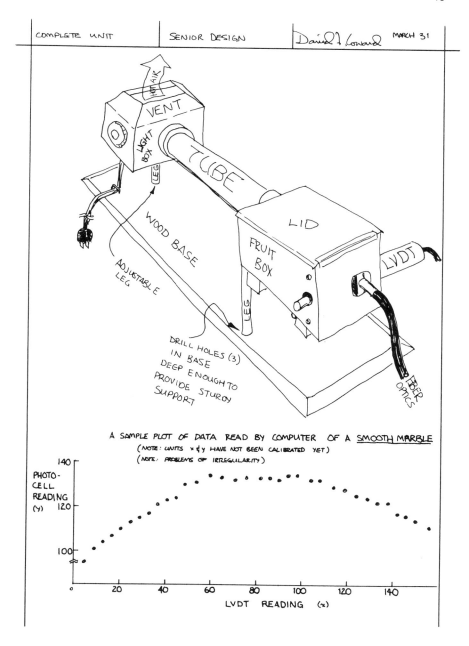

FIG I.11 The final solution and the first results are recorded.

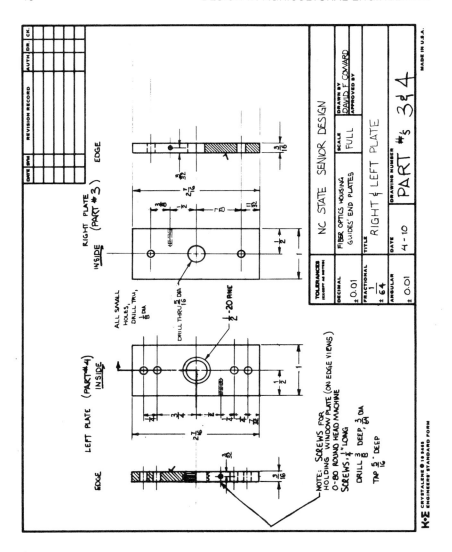

FIG I.12 Design details must be communicated.

resulting equations and computational requirements. The partial differential equations resulting from the least-squared fit are themselves a function of the radius of curvature (r) and the location of the center of the resulting circle (h,l). A Newton-Raphson Method of solving these partial differential equations for r, by successive approximations of h and l, is implemented and results in the timely completion of the overall design objectives.

Document and detail the design

The design concept must be reduced to very specific details including understandable, written descriptions, drawings prepared according to recognized engineering practice (Fig I.12), and vendor specifications. This documentation package may be brief for a one-of-a-kind product or a small product. A complex product which will be mass produced may require specifications comprised of volumes of data, numerous descriptions and hundreds of drawings.

Summary

Coward's approach was typical of that used by successful design engineers. Initially the problem was defined, sub-divided and analyzed. Information was gathered synthesized and combined creatively to develop design ideas. Early decisions and external factors (e.g., costs, time, decisions on materials, options for manufacturing and parts availability) guided the design development.

A working prototype suitable for testing was developed once the design concept was defined. Simultaneously, test plans were formulated and a test apparatus was assembled. During this build-and-test phase old questions were re-opened, re-thought and re-worked. New ideas were generated and integrated into the design, where required by the test results, until a final acceptable solution emerged.

Throughout the design process carefully written records were maintained in a bound and numbered book. Safety considerations, standards, test procedures and results were documented in this book. Consultations and drawings were witnessed and dated. No details that could later prove useful were left to memory.

Working drawings, descriptions and vendor specifications were prepared to complete the design.

Discussion Problems

1. After reading Part I, can you list and explain the five most important activities that a design engineer will be asked to accomplish?

2. Discuss the point at which the Coward design problem becomes "completely defined."

3. Discuss why written design documentation is important and why it is preferable that a written record be made in a *bound* notebook. If your instructor permits a loose leaf binder, what are its advantages and disadvantages?

4. Estimate the relative amount of time required for each phase

of the example design project. Discuss your estimates and justify your choices.

Project Problems

1. Write a proposal letter to the most knowledgeable person in your project area defining as clearly and as completely as you can what you believe is the definition of your design project.

2. As you shall see in later chapters, a written record of your design efforts should be recorded in a *bound* notebook. Depending upon your instructor's directions, obtain a bound or three-ring binder to maintain written documentation of your design project activities. Prepare a table of contents or some other means indicating how material is to be organized and entered into your notebook.

Part II
How Can I be Effective as a Design Engineer?

*"Engineering Design is a **People** Process."*

"No one succeeds today by putting off for tomorrow."

CHAPTER CONTENTS

1. Time Management

Make a written record of your goals, both personal and professional; then allocate your time accordingly. Anticipate opportunities to choose; then decide in a careful but timely manner. Focus your energy toward one thing at a time.

2. Team Effectiveness

Team work and cross-discipline cooperation are essential in this era of exponential growth in our knowledge base, complex economic structures and diverse social systems. Promote understanding of goals, delegate responsibilities, be sensitive to other's concerns, use progress reports properly and respect deadlines.

3. Drawings and Specifications

An assembly parts list summarizes which parts and how many of each are needed to make a product and explains the order of assembly. Each part drawing, specification or assembly drawing communicates that step in the design to those responsible for production.

4. Writing and Speaking

Effective informal conversation as well as polished, but sincere, writing and speaking skills are important in all types of engineering work. Plan for your audience, prepare in advance and practice to be an effective speaker. For effective writing, know the audience, define objectives, develop an outline, draft the material, review and edit.

5. Salesmanship and Motivation

Selling is an inescapable part of engineering. Recognize that most people want to contribute and will if they understand the value of the project and if the engineer communicates exactly what is desired and needed.

Your success as a design engineer will be directly proportional to your abilities to be a "self-starter", manage your time wisely, communicate effectively and motivate others to cooperate with you. No doubt you have already worked to develop these abilities, but you probably are not aware of how important these are; so, you can benefit from a discussion of techniques for improvement.

Definition of personal goals and critical evaluation of your strengths and weaknesses is a good first step toward developing your people skills (Fig II.1). An informal plan for personal development can aid your efforts. Consult and update your development plan on a regular basis. Remember, the future belongs to those who plan for it.

Do not underestimate the importance of spending your time wisely. If you don't feel your design activities are producing the results you think your efforts should; stop, decide why. Ask your peers, teammates or instructor. Each activity should produce a detectable and tangible result. If you feel that you are "spinning your wheels" it is an almost certainty that you are. Develop a sense of when you are being productive and contributing to the design effort. If things are not progressing well — get help! At some time or another everyone will get involved in a totally non-productive design activity, but it is the *effective* design engineer who can recognize the situation, cut short the losses and move on with the work to be done. The best rule to manage your design activities is to ask, before you start the task, "If I can accomplish this task that I am about to start, will its completion really contribute in a meaningful way to the overall design project objectives?"

GOALS

Five-year goals:	
Twenty-year goals:	

DEVELOPMENT PLAN

Knowledge/Skill	Current Ability	Plans for Development
Speaking and Writing a) Formal presentation b) Informal/conversational		
Mechanical Skills (e.g. electronics, machine shop, welding)		
Engineering Practices (e.g. manufacturing methods, drafting, design tricks)		
Computer Skills (e.g. CAD, graphics, home computing)		
Business Skills (e.g. finance, management, accounting, marketing)		
Current Affairs (e.g. business, politics)		
Social/Cultural (e.g. Japanese culture, French language, travel experiences, international programs)		
Humanities/Arts (e.g. art, theater, music, aesthetics)		
Motivational/Salesmanship		
Leadership		

FIG II.1 A self-development plan including a personal self-analysis and statements of five and twenty year goals.

Discussion Problems

1. Define, by listing specific design projects and activities, what constitutes an Agricultural Engineering design. Hint — look in a recent issue of Transactions of the ASAE. On what projects are Agricultural Engineers presently working?

2. Develop a comprehensive list of the attributes of an effective design engineer. Explain why you feel each attribute listed is important.

Project Problems

1. Make a list of the project activities that you believe are important to achieve your overall project objectives.

2. In your project notebook develop Fig. II.1 with sufficient space to write in the results of your self analysis and develop your personal five and twenty-year goals.

# Chapter 1
Time Management

"Plan the work, work the plan."

"People don't plan to fail, they fail to plan."

Organize and concentrate

Remember how effectively you worked the day before the term paper was due? You concentrated. Look at the guy in your class with a perfect 4.0 gradepoint average. Does he study more? Probably not. Is he innately brilliant? Probably no more so than you. Odds are that he is organized and he concentrates.

Concentration can yield tremendous improvements in quality and quantity of personal productivity. None of us works near our potential on a sustained basis, as scientists who study the human brain and note its superior capacity compared to even the largest man made computers can document. Improved organization achieved through personal time management can enhance your concentrational ability.

Being organized frees you from spending as much time and effort monitoring deadlines. Decide which activities need attention and their relative priority. Invest your efforts in high-priority work, not in worrying. Time management is simply an organizational tool that helps you actively choose direction rather than passively react to events in your life.

Schedule for short and long-term activities

Can you discipline yourself to work on an engineering design due 18 months from now while facing numerous immediate problems? Time management is a necessity for engineers because most engineering design work has long-term deadlines with, at best, vaguely defined intermediate deadlines. Meanwhile, there are virtually unlimited diversionary opportunities, many of which are good things to do and relevant to your job responsibilites, that seem to require immediate attention.

Interruptions are inevitable, and this should be considered as you plan your time for both short and long-term projects. It is unrealistic to budget your time on a long-term design project without considering that a portion of almost every day will be spent on unforeseen interruptions. Phones will ring, equipment will fail, health problems will interfere and, of course, the weather will not cooperate.

You can control the timing and extent of some interruptions through time management. Recognize that each person has an inherently more productive time in each day. For some it is early morning, for others it is late afternoon, but seldom is it after a big lunch. Identify your productive periods of the day and reserve your most difficult work for these periods. Less productive times of the day should be spent on more routine activities or recreational endeavors.

A former Avis Chief Executive Officer, Townsend (1970), controlled his interruption by grouping all his incoming and outgoing phone calls into a two-hour block each day. The remainder of each day was reserved for other business activities, relatively free of interruption.

Time for creativity and renewal is important

It is tempting, when defining short and long-term projects, to decide that there is just too much to do; so, you will have to work harder. Sometimes, especially for short periods, this is a reasonable solution. Most often, the only reliable long-term solution is to work smarter, partly by improving your efficiency and partly by choosing not to do some of the "worthwhile" activities on your list of projects.

One serious mistake can be to eliminate personal time for entertainment, creative activity, learning activity and personal relationships. Self sacrifice is not the answer — it may lead to "burn-out," professional obsolescence and personal tragedy. Take time to read, draw, attend a play, participate in coursework, learn a new sport and relax with family and friends! Assess your life periodically to make sure that you do not allow the tyranny of deadlines and good causes to usurp self-renewal activities.

Coffee-breaks, golf or fishing outings, after-hours parties and other social occasions are tremendous opportunities for creative thought and idea exchanges. Try describing a problem of concern that you are experiencing with a current design and getting friends to give you ideas on an informal basis while participating in social activities. Don't make the mistake of regarding these as frivolous wastes of time; rather, strive to achieve a reasonable balance.

Work on the top priority

Ivy Lee, an industrial consultant, once handed a blank sheet of paper to the president of Bethlehem Steel, Charles Schwab, and advised him: "Write on this paper the six most important tasks you have to do tomorrow. Now number them in order of importance. The first thing tomorrow morning look at item one and start working on it until it is finished."

Lee suggested that Schwab try this, and that if he became convinced of the systems value, "then send me a check for what you think it is worth." Schwab responded in writing a few weeks later stating that this was the most profitable lesson he had ever learned. Enclosed was a check for $25,000.

The point is simple. Define your objectives as best you can considering both short and long-term priorities. Expect these objectives to change and be prepared to review and redefine objectives as your priorities shift.

Work on the top priority objective. You can only do one thing at a time-that is why you defined and prioritized objectives. Now concentrate on your priority objective. Successful design requires that kind of intense focus. One way to identify the top priority task is to ask yourself, "What is it about this project that I *least* want to be doing?" For some it is a telephone call to someone you don't really know to ask about a subject that you don't understand well. For others it is a trip to the library, an unwritten letter for specifications on purchased parts, or simply a sit-down conversation with your supervisor. Chances are the activities that you *least* want to do are precisely the activities that you *should* be doing.

Delayed decisions waste time

Do you know who has to make which decisions on your design project? What information are they (or you) going to need or want in order to make those decisions? Do you already have that information, and if so, why have you not decided?

These questions are critical to any design project, and part of the design engineer's responsibilities are to anticipate and plan for them. As the design process moves forward, a number of decisions must be made. The timeliness of these decisions is often delayed because the need to make a decision is not recognized, the correct decision maker has not been identified or there is the belief that insufficient information exists upon which to base a decision. Unnecessarily delayed decisions waste time and cost money.

Recognize that there is seldom *enough* information when making a decision. The trade-off is between the delay caused by the need to get more information (Chapter 10) and the increased utility of the decision due to enhanced information (Chapter 9). Ask yourself, "What additional information do I want before I make a decision? Does the value of this information justify the costs and delay?"

Tips for improving your organization style

1. **Use one pocket appointment calendar** — You cannot be effective if you spend half of your time trying to remember what you need to do and when. Missed appointments and deadlines cause others to lose confidence in you. Equally important is to limit yourself to one scheduling calendar, otherwise you will discover conflicts between calendars and spend extra time keeping all calendars current.

2. **Organize each day** — Spend a few minutes at the start of each day, or the end of the previous day, and decide what needs to be done that day. List those in priority. Look at your calendar and make sure that you are ready for each activity.

3. **Be good to yourself** — Allow time for play and exercise. This keeps your creative abilities alive and renews your enthusiasm. If you try to work non-stop you lose perspective on the world and the problem.

4. **Set personal goals and objectives** — Write them down! Do this on a regular basis. Set goals for the month, the year and 5 years from now. Sure they will change and true, no one can know what they will want 5 years from now. But, you do need a sense of direction for now (Fig II.1).

5. **Pause before you make commitments** — There are millions of worthy causes and activities that can use your help. You can only do a few well. Think before you say yes to an opportunity. Does it further your personal goals and your work objectives?

6. **Analyze a situation before you start** — Engineers often find themselves in the role of a fireman. Thinking before you dash into a problem may save a lot of time and trouble. Look for means of preventing future fires. Your main responsibility is not to dash about madly putting out fires and appearing needed; it is to prevent those fires from recurring.

7. **Develop an effective filing system** — You cannot afford

YOU KNOW FICKSWALD THEY SAY A TIDY DESK
IS A SIGN OF A SICK MIND. SO STOP SMILING!

very many half-days looking for the document you mislaid, nor the mental effort of trying to keep track of everything in your mind in lieu of a filing system.

8. **Keep a clean desk** — This really means: work on one project at a time. Keep the other projects put away so they do not distract you and cause confusion with the project upon which you are working.

9. **Handle routine paper work once** — Every time you pick up that piece of paper you think about it and it takes time. It also detracts from your ability to concentrate on other things. If you need to act on something, do it. If not, throw it away or file it.

10. **Maintain a card file of professional contacts** — Professional colleagues are your number one resource. Maybe you can remember them now, but as time goes on you may not recall an important source. Keep a card with name, address, phone number, job position and reason for acquaintance for each person that you meet professionally.

Tips for improving your concentration skills

1. **Be organized** — Then you do not need to worry about what else you should be doing at the same time.

2. **Block other things out of mind** — You can only do one thing at a time. You have selected your priority activity. Work on that activity only.

3. **Minimize distractions and interruptions** — This may mean having a secretary stop calls for certain periods of the day. It may mean limiting visitors at certain periods. An engineer

cannot be a recluse, but you do need time free from distractions and interruptions.

4. **Keep your work area pleasant** — There is nothing noble about being Spartan. If you work in a bleak space, that affects your mood and diminishes productivity. If you work in pleasant space you feel good and productivity improves.

5. **Keep your enthusiasm** — Psychologists say that if you act happy, you start to feel happy; if you act enthusiastic, you start to feel enthusiastic. If you are unhappy, you think about why you are unhappy and not about the project upon which you are trying to work.

References

1. Bonoma, T V and Dennis P Slevin. 1978. Executive survival manual. CBI Publishing Boston. 234 pp.

2. Hill, P. 1970. The science of engineering design, Holt, Rinehart and Winston, New York. 372 pp.

3. Nilsson, W D and P E Hicks. 1981. Orientation to professional practice. McGraw Hill, New York. 372 pp.

4. Von Oech, Roger. 1983. A wack on the side of the head: How to unlock your mind for innovation. Warner Books, New York. 141 pp.

Discussion Problems

1. Consult your list of short and long term personal and professional goals. Prioritize the top three long term goals and develop or improve plans to achieve these.

2. Keep a daily diary for one week. Estimate at the end of each day the time spent on each significant activity. Are you investing your time consistent with your personal goals? If not, why not?

Project Problems

1. Categorize the various ways you have spent your time on your present project with % of time spent on each objective. Has this time been productively spent? Explain.

2. Budget the time that you can invest in your design project. Prepare a weekly schedule with specified times allocated to the project.

3. Predict the major decisions that you will need to make or have made on your project. What information will be needed and when should these decisions be made?

Chapter 2
Team Management

"Silicon Valley's brilliant success results from the team approach."

*"Very few problems have **never** been considered by others."*

Designers are generalists

Thomas Jefferson 200 years ago was a statesman, inventor, lawyer, scientist, diplomat, farmer, writer, architect, musician and philosopher. We remember Jefferson for all those talents. He was a generalist, yet he *excelled* in each of those fields.

Today we live in a different world. We still need generalists, but their styles must be different. Society has grown more complex and individual disciplines have progressed tremendously. The great leaders of today are "team people" by necessity.

Being a design engineer requires that you be a generalist. Design problems never fit neatly into disciplines. Besides, the solutions always affect and involve people. Charles Kettering, perhaps the most successful engineer of the 20th century, had an interesting way of describing engineers. One could visualize a hammock with each twine running the length of the hammock representing a scientific or other type of academic discipline. Inventors (engineers) represent the cross threads in the hammock. They draw from all disciplines and hold the hammock together.

Once it took an individual with an idea and capital to cause a major engineering change. Money was the key ingredient. Today, things have changed. Brain power is the key ingredient. People with money go looking for a team that can develop an idea. Venture capital has become a major force in our economy—firms specialize in helping money find a project.

Developing a product requires a team effort, and it requires the brains of everyone involved. Some projects are assigned to only one design engineer or student, but, if meaningful results are to be achieved, many people will be drawn into the design effort before the project is completed.

Promote understanding of the project goals and needs

The first step in soliciting hearty cooperation is to make sure that everyone understands the situation. Discuss the goals. Agree on the goals of the project with everyone involved having a chance to have input. Discuss the needs. Know why you are doing this in the first place and know what is required to solve the problem. The surest way to destroy team morale is for each individual to have a different understanding of the problem and goals. People who work at cross-purposes frustrate one another. Another version of the same situation is for one or a few people to understand the problem and then delegate different parts to lower-ranking team members. Those with a partial understanding feel frustrated, not trusted and under-utilized. They bypass relevant ideas and information because they do not have a comprehensive understanding of the problem.

You are not a chess player skillfully manuevering pieces. You are a team member, perhaps a team leader, trying to draw out the skills and abilities of each team member.

Understand the personal motivations of others

If you understand a problem, know what needs to be done, have a good team working with you, and are motivated, you, like most others, will work diligently and effectively toward a solution. But, if you understand that solving this problem fits into your personal goals and needs, it is like having a fire lit under you! Now this is an exciting and important problem. Now you can bounce back from the set-backs. Now your enthusiasm keeps the team morale high. Anyone who watches or participates in team sports has seen the phenomenal results of an inspired team.

Be sensitive to the personal concerns and motivations of fellow team members and others who you draw into the design effort for advice and help. Do you know what motivates your team members and are you aware of some of their idiosyncrasies? Can you present your problem to someone outside of your design team in such a manner that they have a personal interest in helping you?

Delegate responsibility

Now that your team understands the whole picture you can afford to delegate responsibilities. Identify the tasks that must be done first using the design schedule (Part III, Chapter 10). Decide who is best suited for and most interested in working on these different tasks.

The best way to delegate is through consensus and agreement. If the team plans the work and the individuals feel that they can influence their assignments, they work better.

Use the team for brainstorming, critical reviews of progress and coordination of efforts. Gather information, calculate, analyze, draw and think as individuals between group meetings. Make use of coffee breaks, lunches and other informal periods to bounce ideas back and forth.

Do not try to be right

The biggest inhibition to team effectiveness is the desire to not say something stupid. Talk! Everyone is stupid about a *new* problem! If you do not talk you are no better than a collection of individuals working independently to achieve a goal.

Respect your colleagues' opinions no matter how ludicrous they seem to you. A good team member can tactfully criticize ideas (including your own) without causing others to stop advancing ideas for fear of ridicule. Also, be sensitive in timing your criticism so that it does not inhibit generation of ideas.

Use deadlines and progress reports

When faced with a major yet distant goal (e.g., designing a planter), most people do not know how to begin. They spend more time worrying than actually working toward a solution. Intermediate deadlines help people start more quickly. They can work effectively when they have a clear objective and a straight-forward path by which to meet that objective.

To many engineers, weekly progress reports are one of the most despised devices ever conceived. Yet these progress reports can be tremendously effective if taken seriously. No one wants to stand up and say that the day-to-day activities prevented doing anything important to the design. The best way to do anything is to start—progress reports help people start.

Question to draw out ideas

Asking questions is usually more effective than criticism or statements. You can use questioning to get your points across in a non-threatening manner and to draw out ideas from others. Questioning can be a diplomatic way of saying no (e.g., "I will be glad to help with project x. Can we extend the deadline on project y so I will have the time?"), a tool for helping others say what they mean succinctly (e.g., "I want to make sure that I understand. What is your main objection?"), or a means for overcoming a difference of opinion (e.g., "Why do you feel that way?" can be a better alternative than an argument).

There are two types of questions: closed-ended, which require a simple "yes", "no" or statement answer, and open-ended, which require more thought and a more detailed answer. "Do you understand the objectives?" is closed-ended and "How should we revise our objectives? is open-ended. Phrase your question according to the length and type of response that you want.

You can be effective with a questioning technique if you remember four simple rules (Grassell, 1984):

1. **Start with easy questions** — Relax the other person by beginning with non-controversial questions that you know they can answer.

2. **Keep your questions short** — Long questions with qualifying statements confuse the other person and leave the impression that you are setting them up.

3. **Remain silent after asking each question** — A pause after a question is an invisible force which compels most people to respond. Also, this gives them time to formulate their ideas.

4. **Demonstrate you heard and understood what was said** —

Repeating or rephrasing an answer in a questioning, sympathetic way will encourage individuals to explain or justify their answer. This method can be effective in causing others to reevaluate their opinions.

References

1. Burgess, John A, 1984. *Design assurance for engineers and managers.* Marcel Dekker, Inc. New York, 303 pp.

2. Grassell, Milt. 1984. *The power of questions.* The Toastmaster, April, pp. 4-6.

Discussion Problems

1. How does the NIH (Not Invented Here) syndrome affect team approach?

2. How should the relative contribution of each team member be evaluated and quantified?

3. Decide what kinds of people can best complement you on a design project team and explain.

Project Problems

1. Define your own project and recommend an approach to solve your most critical problem.

2. How do you view your design role as a team member? (Even"individual" projects require teamwork.)

3. Develop a written form for measuring the relative contribution by each team member toward the project goals. (Your instructor may wish to use this form for a component of your final grade!)

Chapter 3
Drawings and Specifications

*"Drawings and specifications are the language
and luggage of design."*

*"If you think you understand your problem,
draw a picture of it!"*

The design engineer does not begin developing detailed part drawings and planning the sequence of assembly at the beginning phases of a design project. The engineer should, however, understand the exactness of details needed from the design effort at the project beginning. Thinking "how will this actually be built" is a good exercise for evaluating design alternatives, and is especially critical when the design assignment is to reduce the cost of a given component already in production.

Computer-aided design is changing the design approach

Computer-aided design (CAD), computer-aided manufacturing (CAM) and computer-aided engineering (CAE) are powerful new tools for the design engineer. You can create design alternatives in three dimensions on computer screens and rotate, shift and change components. Standard material dimensions can be pre-programmed so that the designer simply calls the component and the design location to study the physical relationships.

Analytical programs allow the engineer to estimate stresses, fatigue problems and deformations as functions of loads and without physically constructing and testing models. The result is shortened design development times and better designs. Designers can try out the manufacturability of an idea using combinations of CAD-CAM. Some firms specialize in custom manufactured products in which the design engineer controls both design and manufacture from computers.

These advances aid design development, evaluation and record keeping. However, computers do not change the need for the design engineer to understand the logic and requirements of engineering specifications.

The assembly parts list includes all pieces

The assembly parts list (APL) (or the indexed parts list) provides the part number, part description and quantity of parts required to build a product (Fig 3.1). Often the APL is combined with the bill of materials, and the latter describes the material types and quantities used to make each part (Fig 3.1). Additionally, the APL tells the manufacturing sequence during production. The APL is the most important document in a set of engineering specifications.

Every step in the manufacturing process is represented by an engineering part and is listed in the APL. Engineering parts include five basic types:

1. **Standard items** — Standard bolts, grease zerks, cotter pins, roller chains, electrical supplies, belts and other items which can be clearly specified with standard terminology without the necessity of a drawing. These can include standard lumber, metal and pre-manufactured materials available from other sources and not requiring modification.

2. **Prime manufactured parts** — Steel, plastic or some other material is cut, punched, cast, bent and/or machined to form a shape. This requires a part drawing showing the finished part, denoting tolerances and specifying material type.

3. **Weldments** — Two or more prime, standard or other weldment parts are brought together for welding, brazing or some similar permanent assembly process. Each part which goes directly into the weldment is listed on the weldment. (If, for example, parts A and B are welded together in weldment C, parts A and B will be listed on weldment C. Then if weldment C and part D are assembled together in assembly E, parts C and D will be listed on assembly E. Parts A and B will not be listed on assembly E because they go into E indirectly through Part C.) The APL denotes parts going into the weldment by the part

Indexing scheme to show the order of assembly.

Bill of materials, which if completed, would show the quantities of steel, welding rod, paint and other manufacturing material required to make each part.

Column 2 weldments 5782 (row 3), 5786 (row 9), and 5787 (row 19) are combined in column 1 assembly 5800 (row 1).

Column 3 prime parts are combined in column 2 weldment 5782 (row 3).

These numbers are the quantity of each part required per assembly.

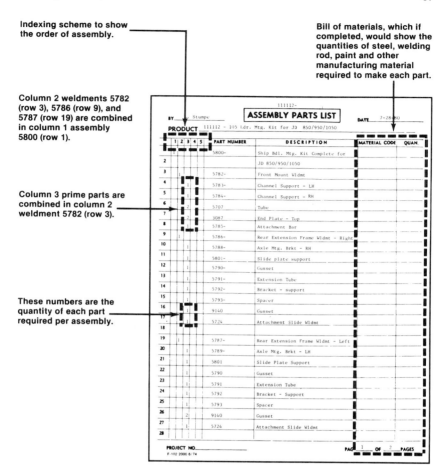

	1	2	3	4	5	PART NUMBER	DESCRIPTION	MATERIAL CODE	QUAN.
1						5800-	Ship Bdl. Mtg. Kit Complete for		
2							JD 850/950/1050		
3						5782-	Front Mount Wldmt		
4						5783-	Channel Support - LH		
5						5784-	Channel Support - RH		
6			2			5707	Tube		
7			2			3087	End Plate - Top		
8						5785-	Attachment Bar		
9		1				5786-	Rear Extension Frame Wldmt - Right		
10		1				5788-	Axle Mtg. Brkt - RH		
11		1				5801-	Slide plate support		
12		1				5790-	Gusset		
13		1				5791-	Extension Tube		
14		1				5792-	Bracket - support		
15		1				5793-	Spacer		
16		1				9140	Gusset		
17		1				5724	Attachment Slide Wldmt		
18									
19	1					5787-	Rear Extension Frame Wldmt - Left		
20		1				5789-	Axle Mtg. Brkt - LH		
21		1				5801	Slide Plate Support		
22		1				5790	Gusset		
23		1				5791	Extension Tube		
24		1				5792	Bracket - Support		
25		1				5793	Spacer		
26		2				9140	Gusset		
27		1				5724	Attachment Slide Wldmt		
28									

111112-

ASSEMBLY PARTS LIST

BY Stumpe   DATE 7-28-80

PRODUCT 111112 - 105 Ldr. Mtg. Kit for JD 850/950/1050

PROJECT NO.
F-102 2000 6/74

PAGE 1 OF 2 PAGES

FIG 3.1 Assembly parts list (APL) for a DuAl model 105 loader mounting kit; the materials portion of the form is not completed (Courtesy of DuAl Manufacturing).

level coding (see notation, Fig 3.1).

4. **Treatments** — This is a painting step, a quenching step or some similar step.

5. **Assemblies** — Two or more prime, standard, weldment or assembly parts are brought together for assembly. Assembly may be bolting, screwing, pinning, other means of combinations of means for putting together. Each part which goes directly into the assembly is listed on the assembly.

Engineering drawings clearly and completely specify each part

Every prime part drawing should indicate the material from

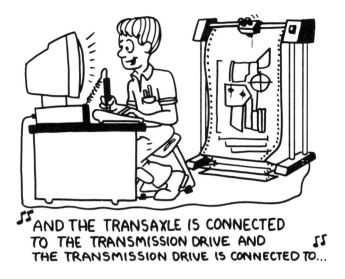

♪♪AND THE TRANSAXLE IS CONNECTED
TO THE TRANSMISSION DRIVE AND   ♪♪
THE TRANSMISSION DRIVE IS CONNECTED TO...

which the part is made, the dimensions of the finished part, any special part treatment such as carburizing, the tolerances, the part name and number, the date drawn, the draftsman's name, the date approved and the person approving the drawing (Fig 3.2). Conventional practice is to note most of this information in the bottom right-hand corner of the part drawing in a "title block". Essentially all manufacturers use title blocks, though the location on the drawing and the details included vary somewhat. Appendix III contains blank sample drawing plates.

Dimensions should be referenced from the most critical points to avoid compounding tolerances. For example, if you begin referencing dimensions from the end of a loader bucket, and continue referencing each location from the nearest preceeding location along the back of the bucket, the total bucket width may vary by the sum (positive or negative) of the allowable tolerances for all dimension points (Fig 3.3). Variation in the bucket width of 2 cm may be inconsequential to the user, but a variation of 0.5 cm in mounting bracket location means that the bucket will not attach to the loader frame without modification.

Heavy, solid lines should show visible part lines. Heavy dashed lines should show hidden part lines. Dimension lines should be lighter, solid and with arrows at the end points. Note that the most important requirement for a drawing is that it produces a distinct, readable print.

Show the part from as many section views as needed to communicate the requirements. Use section views or cut-aways

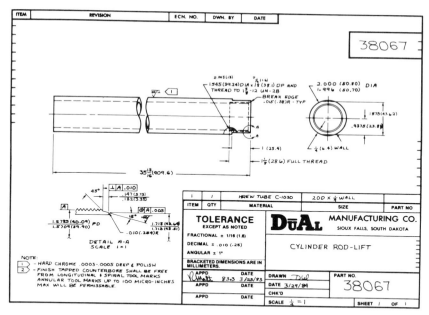

FIG 3.2 Prime part drawing for a cylinder rod. (Courtesy of DuAl Manufacturing).

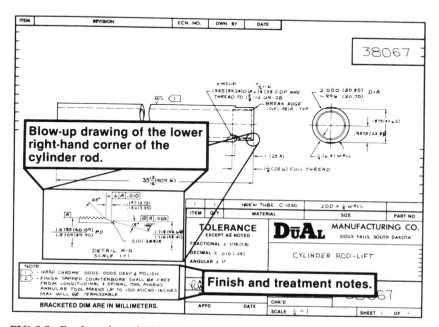

FIG 3.2a Explanation of FIG 3.2.

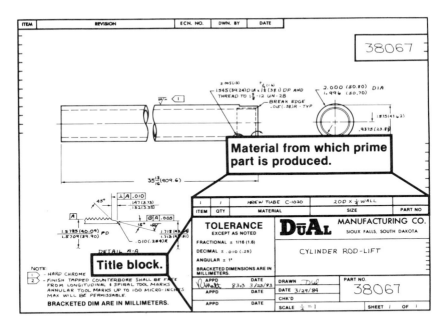

FIG 3.2b Explanation of FIG 3.2.

where needed. Use standardized symbols for denoting surface finishes, hardening specifications, welds, electrical components, etc. (Fig 3.4). The American National Standards Institute (ANSI) and the International Organization for Standardization (ISO) [ANSI is the U.S. representative to the ISO] have standardized drafting symbols for most common, generic parts and manufacturing procedures (Table 3.1).

Weldments and assemblies show the details of assembly, not of each prime part

Weldments and assemblies (Fig 3.5) are like prime part drawings with the following exceptions: (a) every part directly used in the weldment or assembly should be listed in tabular form above the title block, (b) the location of each direct part in the weldment or assembly should be noted on the drawing, and (c) details of each part need not be so inclusive except as necessary to show the inter-connecting process. (You already have a drawing to show you how to make the prime parts.)

It helps to understand that a shop foreman or construction site foreman will hand the appropriate part or assembly drawing to the individual responsible for that part or assembly. That may be all the people producing and assembling the part have

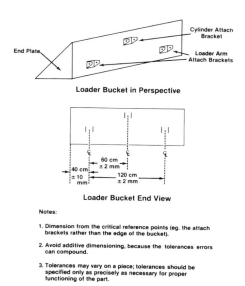

Loader Bucket in Perspective

Loader Bucket End View

Notes:

1. Dimension from the critical reference points (eg. the attach brackets rather than the edge of the bucket).

2. Avoid additive dimensioning, because the tolerances errors can compound.

3. Tolerances may vary on a piece; tolerances should be specified only as precisely as necessary for proper functioning of the part.

FIG 3.3 Partial tolerancing and dimensioning for a loader bucket.

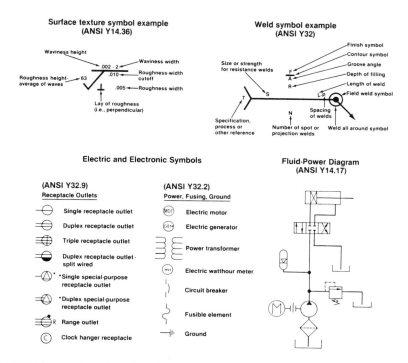

FIG 3.4 Examples of engineering drafting and specification standard symbols and methods according to American National Standards Institute standards.

Table 3.1 Engineering drawings — standard symbols and specifications standards from the American National Standards Institute (ANSI).

ANSI standard number	Standard title
ANSI Y14.1	Drawing sheet size and format
ANSI Y14.2M	Line conversions and lettering
ANSI Y14.3	Projections
ANSI Y14.4	Pictorial drawings
ANSI Y14.5M	Dimensioning and tolerancing for engineering drawings
ANSI Y14.6	Screw thread representation
ANSI Y14.7	Gears, splines, and serrations
ANSI Y14.7.1	Gear drawing standards — part 1, for spur, helical, double helical and rack
ANSI Y14.9	Forgings
ANSI Y14.10	Metal stampings
ANSI Y14.11	Plastics
ANSI Y14.14	Mechanical assemblies
ANSI Y14.15	Electrical and electronics diagrams
ANSI Y14.15A	Interconnection diagrams
ANSI Y14.17	Fluid power diagrams
ANSI Y14.36	Surface texture symbols
ANSI Y32.2	Graphic symbols for electical and electronics diagrams
ANSI Y32.9	Graphic electical wiring symbols for architectural and electrical layout drawings
ANSI B1.1	Unified screw threads
ANSI B4.2	Preferred metric limits and fits
ANSI B18.2.1	Square and hex bolts and screws
ANSI B18.2.2	Square and hex nuts
ANSI B18.3	Socket cap, shoulder, and setscrews
ANSI B18.6.2	Slotted-head cap screws, square-head setscrews, slotted-headless setscrews
ANSI B18.6.3	Machine screws and machine screw nuts
ANSI B17.2	Woodruff key and keyslot dimensions
ANSI B17.1	Keys and keyseats
ANSI B18.21.1	Lock washers
ANSI B27.2	Plain washers
ANSI B46.1	Surface texture
ANSI B94.6	Knurling
ANSI B94.11M	Twist drills
ANSI Z210.1	Metric practice

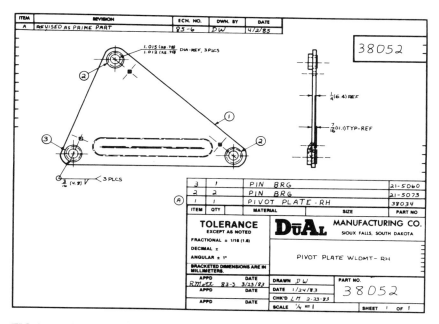

FIG 3.5 Weldment drawing of a pivot plate (Courtesy of DuAl Manufacturing).

to guide their work. This will tell them how to build your product. Certain parts or assembly steps may be performed by a different company, or even in a different country, and they may not even know the intended product use.

Product changes are noted on the drawings or assembly parts list

Once you begin manufacturing and selling a product you have established the Xth model of that product. (A new model is required when parts are not interchangeable or the change cannot be simply recorded.) Often you will find weaknesses which can be improved with a slight change, yet are not worthy of a completely new model. There are two types of such changes: (a) new part or deleted part and (b) change in part shape. The document which records specification (parts added or deleted) or drawing changes is often titled an "Engineering Change Notice" (Fig 3.6).

A parts addition or deletion is noted and dated on the APL. A part revision is noted and dated on the original part drawing conventionally in the upper left-hand corner. Historically it has been desirable to document the reason for the change to serve as a guide for future design decisions. Model changes and

Explanation of the first change including when effective, who requested, why and what the specific changes are.

Departments within the company who are notified of changes.

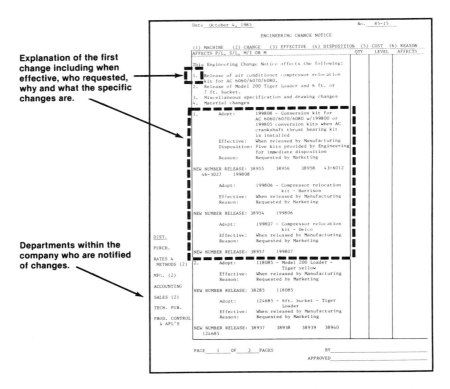

FIG 3.6 Engineering change notice for a Tiger Loader (Courtesy of DuAl Manufacturing).

engineering change notices combined with explanations for the changes serve as a product history, and it is desirable from the design engineer's view to maintain such company records for a minimum of 20 years.

Product liability concerns have changed attitudes about record keeping

When a product becomes involved in a lawsuit, the plaintiff's lawyer will usually request the complete history of the product, including changes and the reasons for these changes. Manufacturers differ in their response to this concern — some continue to maintain all the details that they believe may aid engineering, manufacturing or servicing needs.

Other manufacturers choose to limit retention time for certain records and maintain a product file restricted to the necessary drawings and records to produce replacement parts. These companies believe that the details associated with design development are likely to be misunderstood or deliberately distorted should such detail become available in a product liability suit.

Clearly the issue of record keeping has important legal and ethical consequences in addition to the obvious relationships to future design efforts. Regardless of company policy on long-term record retention, it is critical that a design engineer maintain detailed records for the purposes of aiding the design development and patent protection. Additionally, the engineer must remember personal ethical responsibilities to society by ensuring that both positive and negative concerns are expressed to decision-makers within the company and by ensuring that problems are corrected rather than covered-up.

Emphasize detailed records

Keep dated, signed, witnessed records of all drawings, analyses, test results and changes. This cannot be overemphasized. These records are important to you because you and others on the design team will forget or be unaware of important facts just over the course of the design. Dating records is especially important to aid the design team during the design process. Additionally, these records are important for sharing information within the company, for obtaining patents and for defending patents in court.

References

1. French, Thomas E., Charles J. Vierck, and Robert J. Foster. 1986. Engineering drawing and graphic technology. 13th ed., McGraw-Hill, New York, 737 pp.

2. Jensen, C. and J. D. Helsel, 1985. Engineering drawing and design, 3rd ed. McGraw-Hill, New York, 788 pp.

3. Shoup, Terry E., Leroy S. Fletcher, and Edward V. Mochel. 1981. Introduction to engineering design with graphics and design projects. Prentice-Hall, Englewood Cliffs, NJ 07632, 391 pp.

Discussion Problems

1. Obtain a set of selected parts and their respective parts drawings from a local manufacturer. Develop a parts drawing for each part from veiwing the part, and without looking at the manufacturer's drawing. Compare your part drawing with the manufacturer's part drawing.

2. Obtain a set of "standard parts." Discuss how to specify each part so that the specification cannot be confused when submitted to manufacturers for bidding.

Project Problems

1. Develop an assembly parts list with representative engineering drawings as required by the instructor. (Obviously this is done after your design concept is developed.)

2. Specify materials and methods for each part or step in your design alternatives. (This can be excellent for helping you think through alternatives as you develop them and aiding your selection of a particular alternative on which to focus.)

Chapter 4
Writing and Speaking

"Thinking cannot be clear till it has expression. We must write, speak or act our thoughts or they remain in a half torpid form." H.W. Beecher.

"I believe you understand what you think I said, but I'm not sure you realize that what you heard is not what I meant."

Writing and speaking are deficient skills for most graduating engineers

Writing, drafting and speaking were ranked as the first, second and third greatest skill deficiencies for new engineers by their manufacturing employers (Design Engineering, 1982). In fact these deficiencies were ranked more than five times more critical than any other skill deficiencies.

Tweedy (1982), past president of ASAE, held the same view but with a twist. He agreed that writing and speaking skills are deficient for graduating agricultural engineers. He went on to say that one cannot expect full development of all needed skills during 4 to 5 years of college. Tweedy stated that writing and speaking skills could be developed outside college, and that he, as an employer, was most concerned that the new engineer recognize these weaknesses and work to improve them. He specifically suggested the Toastmasters International speaking program and the Dale Carnegie course as two answers for this development after graduation.

The point is that two to four university level writing and speaking courses do not make you a skilled writer or speaker. It takes practice and effort throughout your life. As a professional employee, you will be expected to develop these skills. Reports you write will be read by extremely busy people including senior engineers, corporation VP's, marketing managers, chief executive officers, and your customers. You must learn to write concise and accurate reports.

General writing considerations

1. **Determine the appropriate style** — Who is the audience? What is your purpose? How much detail do they need? Are you writing a technical paper, an executive summary, a press release, a sales brochure, an operations and maintenance manual or something else?

2. **Develop an outline of key points** — Do not try to write everything you know about a subject. That is the shotgun approach and it is totally ineffective. Decide which points you need to communicate and how to lay the proper groundwork for the reader to understand your message. You want your reader to understand why you did what you did, why they should do what you recommend or why you believe something is true.

3. **Develop transitions for the outline** — How do you easily move from point A to point B on your outline? If there seems no logical connection, perhaps the outline order should be altered.

4. **Write the first draft as fast as you can** —Do not worry about perfection. The hardest thing about writing is to write that first draft. You can correct style and grammar later. Others can give you helpful critiques when they have something specific to review. Without a draft, no reviewer comments are possible.

5. **Proof, solicit critiques and rewrite** — Writing is like design in that you write, proof, critique, then rewrite, reproof and recritique as many times as needed to achieve a satisfactory manuscript.

Technical report writing

There are two main technical report styles. A common style for within a business organization is: object, scope, recommendations, data and data analysis. This business style is most suited to an inter-organization report submitted to your boss. The object, scope and recommendations sections are brief and explain what you did, why and which course of action you recommend. The data and data analysis sections provide the detail which supports your recommendations. Write with sufficient detail that readers can understand your methods and logic if the subject of the report becomes more important in the future.

Technical papers are a second report style, are used for communication with peers or with technical personnel outside your organization and are usually written in the following outline.

1. **Abstract** — Explain what was done, the conclusions reached and the limitations of the results. This may be titled, "Executive Summary" when the audience is primarily internal management.

2. **Introduction** — Briefly explain the problem and the purpose of your work. This should end with the specific objectives of the paper.

3. **Literature review or state-of-the-art** — Explain the relevant technical literature and personal expertise from others which pertain to your work. This should not be an all purpose discussion of related information. Rather it should discuss the technical information directly related to your work and it should be written so the reader understands the need for your work after reading this section. Be sure to attribute data and statements using reference styles which can be traced — don't expect the reader to accept your unsupported statements.

4. **Procedure** — Explain what you did in detail. Fully develop all relevant analyses. Note instrumentation used and their specified accuracies, test times and test conditions.

5. **Results and discussion** — Include analyses and test data in a summarized form (raw data can be in appendices.) Explain the implications of your work. Include judgments in this section, indicate the bases of those judgments and note the limitations.

6. **Summary/conclusions** — State clearly and accurately what you learned. Answer the objectives.

7. **List of references** — Note all sources, including personal contact, directly used to conduct your work and prepare the report. Include author name, date, title of paper and the source from which it can be obtained (Table 4.1). For personal conversations or letters state the name, date, person's qualifications and indicate how that person can be reached.

8. **Appendices** — Include data, information, computer programs and similar material which were important to you in reaching your conclusions, but which are not directly relevant to the reader. The reader refers to the appendices when a very detailed understanding of your work is important.

Table 4.1 Reference style manual for ASAE publications.

Books

1. Kunii, D. and O. Levenspiel. 1969. Fluidization engineering. John Wiley and Sons, New York 65211. 431 pp.
2. Hudson, N. W. 1981b. Soil conservation, 2nd ed., Cornell University Press, Ithaca, New York 65203. pp. 48-61.

Transactions Articles

3. McKyes, E. 1978. The calculation of draft forces and soil boundaries of narrow cutting blades. *TRANSACTIONS of the ASAE* 21(1):20-24.
4. McKenzie, D.W. and B.Y. Richardson. 1978. Feasibility of self contained tether cable system for operating on slopes of 20 to 75%. Journal of Terramechanics. 15(3):113-127.

Technical Society Papers

5. Sides, S.E. and N. Smith. 1970. Analysis and design of potato-stone separation mechanisms. ASAE Paper No. 70-673, ASAE, St. Joseph, MI. 49085.
6. Bals, E.J. 1969. Design of rotary atomizers. Proceedings 4th International Agricultural Aviation Congress, Kingston, U.K.

Monograph Articles

7. Taylor, H.M. 1971. Effects of soil strength on seedling emergence, root growth and crop yield. In: Compaction of Agricultural Soils (Editors, K.K. Barnes et. al.) ASAE Monograph No. 1, ASAE, St. Joseph, MI 49085.

Dissertations and Theses

8. Solie, J.B. 1982. Development of a subsurface jet injector for herbicides. Unpublished PhD dissertation. University of Nebraska, University Microfilm International, Ann Arbor, MI 46211.
9. Abbott, K. 1982. Performance and evaluation of a variable-speed darrieus wind turbine. Unpublished M.S. Thesis, South Dakota State University, Brookings.

Standard Books

10. Agricultural Engineers Standards. 1984. Wet bulb temperatures and wet bulb depressions (D309). ASAE, St. Joseph, MI 49085.
11. American Society For Testing Materials. 1981. Annual Book of ASTM Standards. Part 37. Philadelphia, PA 35021.
12. Midwest Plan Service. 1975. Pole design. TR-5, Iowa State University, Ames.

Conferences

13. Wilson, G. 1976. Heat pumps for drying grain. Proceedings, 1976 Grain Conditioning Conference, University of Illinois, Urbana.

Government Documents

14. Hogan, M.R., D.L. Ayers, P.F. Schweizer, D.C. Doering and G.H. Foster. 1979. The development of a low-temperature heat pump grain dryer. Project Report, Contract No. EC-77-0-01-5026A002, U.S. Department of Energy, Washington, DC 20011.
15. Palm Beach County Health Department. 1968. Annual progress report-air-pollution project. Mar. 1, 1967 — July 1, 1968. Prepared by Palm Beach County Health Department, West Palm Beach, FL 80165. 67 pp.
16. U.S. Department of Agriculture. 1976. Energy and U.S. agriculture 1974 data base. Vol. 1. Federal Energy Administration FEA/D-76/459.

Company Literature

17. Chuo Boeki Goshi Kaisha. 1981. CeCoCo Oil Expeller. Advertising literature and communications. "CeCoCo" Exhibition and Demonstration Farm Center, Ibaraki City, Osaka-Fu, Japan.

(continued)

Patents

18. Beckman, G. 1983. Reaping or mowing machine. U.S. Patent No. 490,781.

Test Reports

19. Leviticus, L.F., F.W. Steinbruegge, W.E. Splinter and K. Von Bargen. 1977. Nebraska Tractor Test No. 1256. Agricultural Experiment Station, University of Nebraska, Lincoln.
20. Works, D.W. and L.L. Erickson. 1963. Infrared irradiation — on effective treatment for herd seeds in small seeded legumes. Idaho Agricultural Experiment Station Bulletin No. 57, University of Idaho, Moscow.

Correspondence

21. Lytle, W.F. 1984. Personal correspondence with W.F. Lytle, Climatologist. Agricultural Engineering Department, South Dakota State University, Brookings.

Agricultural Experiment Station Bulletins

22. Sorenson, J.W. and L.E. Crane. 1960. Drying rough rice in storage. Texas Agricultural Experiment Station Bulletin B-952, Texas A&M, College Station 10 pp.

Proposal writing

Proposals are an inducement for a sponsor to spend money on your ability to turn an idea into a useful or marketable product. What will convince a sponsor to invest money in the work of a design engineer? Probably three factors are the most important. (a) Can you *convince* the sponsor that you understand the problem? (b) Are you *qualified* to solve the problem? (c) Can you identify the resources (help) that you require to develop a workable solution? Good proposals, whether a letter or a detailed report, will address these three questions.

Outlines for detailed proposals are typically: Introduction, Review of Literature, Justification, Procedure, Schedule, Budget, and Personnel. The introduction, review of literature and procedure sections are similar to those of general technical reports. The justification explains why the design or research effort is needed in more detail than the introduction; the introduction may be as brief as a one paragraph problem statement. A one-page table or figure often is the schedule, and may be similar to those described in Chapter 10. The budget details costs by major item and explains the need for those costs, usually according to salaries and wages, fringe benefits, materials and supplies, equipment, travel, computers, other and overhead. Overhead may be more than 50% of the budget and accounts for building, facilities, and management costs that are not easily identified as related to the specific project, but are nevertheless costs of the business. Finally, the personnel section explains the experience and capabilities that you, your colleagues and your company have as related to the problem identified in the proposal.

Design notebook writing

Following are suggestions for record keeping as your design progresses. The test of a design notebook is whether someone not totally familiar with the project can understand from the notebook what you did and why.

1. Keep an index at the front of the notebook. This can be an index by subject or project activity.

2. Make entries in ink at the time you do the work. Cross out where necevssary, but do not tear out pages or erase.

3. Include data in the original form (on charts), not after analyzed and recalculated.

4. Include graphs and plots that you develop from refined data.

5. Reference completely books, journals, oral communication and any other sources of information used in the design.

6. Write all ideas in your notebook and explain why ideas were accepted or rejected.

7. Periodically summarize progress and your views on the design.

8. Have your notebook witnessed, signed by two individuals and dated for any ideas which may be patentable.

9. Include all calculations with an explanation of assumptions.

10. Include photographs taken during design and testing with notes describing the photographs.

General speaking considerations

The only reasons for speaking formally are to entertain and to facilitate audience interaction. Audiences want to be entertained and are far more responsive to your message, so don't neglect entertainment. Enthusiasm, visuals, novel approaches, and, of course, humor are entertaining tools. Audience interaction can be as simple as reading audience response and adjusting your style accordingly or as complex as questions and answers between the audience and the speaker.

The weakness of speaking as a communication tool is that an audience can read far more rapidly than you can speak, plus they can do this on their own schedule. Remember both the reasons for and weaknesses of speaking when you plan your presentation. Following are some guidelines:

1. **Determine the appropriate style and time** — Who are the audience? What is your purpose? How much detail do they need? How long can you reasonably expect their attention? Seldom

speak longer than 30 minutes and almost never an hour. This holds regardless of the time available.

2. **Develop an outline of a *few* key points** — Try to build around anecdotes and examples. Unless you have written material to hand-out or you expect them to take notes, limit yourself to fewer than five main points. People seldom remember even five main points.

3. **Remember that people read faster than they listen** — Do not read. Do not tell them things they can read and understand more quickly. This is an opportunity for audience feedback and for handling complex or sensitive topics which are difficult to handle by writing. Plan your presentation to augment, not substitute for, a technical report.

4. **Develop visuals** — If you speak for more than 10 minutes you need audio visuals to keep audience attention. Do not put too much information on audio visuals. A simple graph or three to five short phrases are right for a slide or poster.

5. **Speak from an outline** — Do not take a text to the podium. Nobody wants to listen to someone read a speech, or to someone who memorizes a speech and uses the text for a prop.

6. **Rehearse** — Check for time. Rehearse at least once so that you

THE TELEVISION RECEIVER WE ARE
DESIGNING WOULD GO HERE.

feel comfortable with your outline. If you forgot something or had trouble at some point, note that on your outline.

7. **Start and end on time** — When you go 30 seconds over your allotted time people start to resent you. Once you are a few minutes over they have completely forgotten your message and are starting to hate your presentation.

Good visuals are critical in both writing and speaking

Visuals break the monotony of written or spoken words. The cliche', "a picture is worth a thousand words," is often true for explaining methods, data, and findings. Most importantly, visuals help your audience remember the most critical points, *and this is your main purpose for writing and speaking!*

Almost *never* will illustrations that you use in your written reports be suitable directly as visuals for use in oral reports (Figs. 4.1 to 4.5). Why? Illustrations used in written reports contain a large amount of information or important points and are complete in themselves or the text. There are no audience questions to clarify points. Speaking visuals are not intended for careful study, but do benefit from speaker explanation and audience interaction.

References

1. ASAE. Information for speakers on meeting programs. ASAE St. Joseph, MI. 49085.

2. Design Engineering. 1982. Getting ahead - What do employers want. Design Engineering, Jan., p. 91.

3. Nilsson, W.D. and P.E. Hicks. 1981. Orientation to professional practice. McGraw-Hill. New York, NY. 372 pp.

4. Strunk, W. Jr. and E. B. White. 1979. The elements of style., 3rd ed. Macmillan Co., New York. 85 pp.

5. Toastmasters International. 1984. Communication and leadership program. Toastmasters International Box 10400 Santa Ana, CA 92711. 71 pp.

6. Tweedy, R. 1982. Agricultural engineering and future issues. *Agricultural Engineering* 63(7):21-23. ASAE St. Joseph, MI.

Discussion Problems

1. Discuss the importance of practice in preparing an oral presentation.

2. Select a recent assignment of about one page in length and reduce the length by 50% without sacrificing information content.

Project Problems

1. Prepare a detailed outline for your final report. Phrase topics as short thoughts and suggest transistions.

2. Prepare and deliver an oral progress report on your design.

3. Develop three or more visuals suitable for an oral presentation.

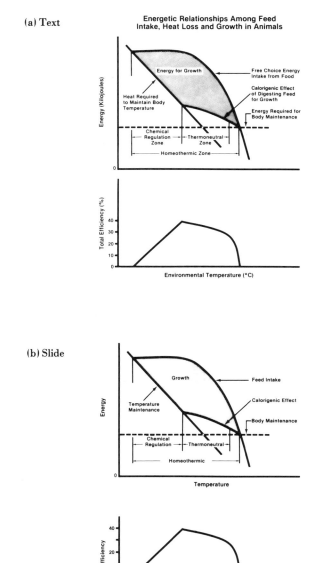

FIG 4.1 Illustrations in texts and reports may require detailed captions and explanations to minimize the chances of incorrect reader interpretations (4.1a). Fewer and simpler captions are important for visuals because the details are less legible (4.1b). By separating a complex text illustration into two or more slides, better visuals can be produced (4.1b).

(a) Text

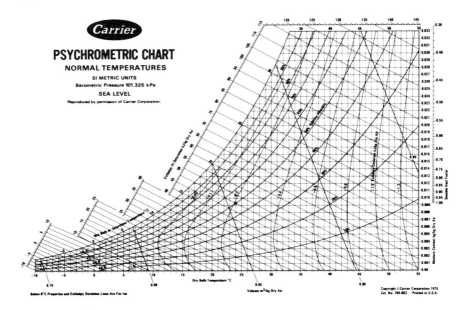

(b) Slide

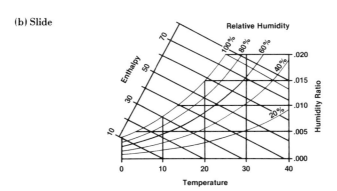

FIG 4.2 Data are often graphically displayed in a technical report or standards document in sufficient detail for the user to work problems from the graph(4.2a). To present as a slide or visual, reduce the scale detail, increase lettering size, remove notes with explanatory detail and condense axes ranges (4.2b) (Courtesy of Carrier Corporation).

(a) Text

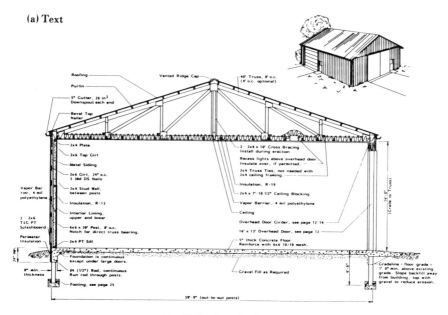

40' x 48' Shop Cross Section

(b) Slide

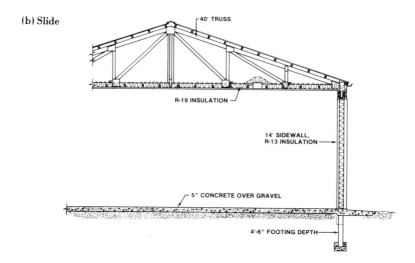

FIG 4.3 Building, machine part, electrical circuit and hydraulic circuit blueprints are prepared for the user to study in detail. Slides explaining blueprints should be simplified and emphasize only the information which needs to be communicated in the intended presentation (Courtesy of Midwest Plan Service).

(a) Text

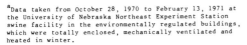

COMPARISON OF WINTER[a] SWINE PERFORMANCE WITH THAT
PREDICTED BY THE NEBRASKA MODEL[b]

Time Interval (days)	Feed Consumption (kg)		
	Simulated		Actual
	$A = 1$ [c]	$A = .9$ [c]	
0 to 20	56.4	48.9	43.7
20 to 40	83.4	69.9	71.4
40 to 60	107.7	101.7	94.9

[a]Data taken from October 28, 1970 to February 13, 1971 at the University of Nebraska Northeast Experiment Station swine facility in the environmentally regulated buildings, which were totally enclosed, mechanically ventilated and heated in winter.

[b]These results adapted from DeShazer and Teter (1974).

[c]"A" is the feed intake adjustment; A = 1 represents the original Nebraska model and A = .9 represents a 10 percent reduction in feed intake.

(b) Slide

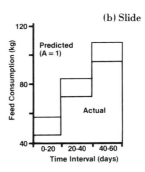

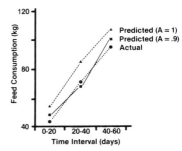

FIG 4.4 Bar graphs, line graphs or pie charts are usually better than tables for visuals (4.4b). Tables with footnotes may contain more information and are useful in written reports (4.4a).

(a) Text

The principal objectives were:

(1) Design a Darrieus system suitable for variable-speed operation.

(2) Construct a Darrieus according to the proposed design.

(3) Develop a suitable testing procedure for a variable-speed Darrieus system.

(4) Test and evaluate the performance of the variable-speed Darrieus system.

(5) Compare the efficiency measured during variable-speed operation with the theoretical efficiencies of constant-speed operation.

(b) Slide

Objectives

☐ **Design variable-speed Darrieus**

☐ **Construct system**

☐ **Define test procedure**

☑ **Test and evaluate performance**

☐ **Compare measured to theoretical efficiencies**

FIG 4.5 Visuals with objects, not words only, are usually best. However, word slides may be best for objective, conclusion, title and heading slides. A checklist, highlighting, backgrounding, and changes in type style are effective means for drawing viewer attention to phrases within the visual aid (4.5b).

Chapter 5
Salesmanship and
Motivation

"About the only resource of any consequence is people." Dr. Gene Amdahl, founder of Amdahl Corporation, Chairman and Chief Executive of Trilogy Systems Corporation.

"Two foes of human happiness are pain and boredom."

Design engineers are salesmen

You have to understand and accept that design engineers are all salesmen if you intend to be an *effective* engineer. You are selling your colleagues on cooperating with you, you are selling your management on supporting you, you are selling other groups on providing financial support and you are selling suppliers on your firm so that they will provide information and materials. You are selling ideas, selling yourself and selling your firm. Selling is inescapable.

Most of the time you speak or write you are in a selling situation. This is true of most formal presentations and progress reports. You are also in a selling situation during many impromptu conversations with your boss, co-workers and others you deal with in a work-related situation. There is nothing morally wrong with selling.

A good salesman does a favor to the person he is selling and to himself. A good salesman sells a product that will help the buyer for a price that will earn the seller a reasonable profit. As a good engineer, you sell your managers and peers on a design approach which will benefit them as well as you. If you are doing good work, you ought to have enough pride in the design to sell it. If you do not have enough pride in your design to sell it in good conscience, you should re-evaluate the quality of your design work.

Attributes common among effective engineers and good salesmen

1. **Honesty** — A good salesman is honest. You do a favor to everyone involved in the selling transaction. You cannot afford to do otherwise, because your reputation is at stake.

2. **Enthusiasm** —The best idea presented unenthusiastically almost always fails. People respond to enthusiasm. Lack of enthusiasm sends the nonverbal message that you have a bad product.

3. **Self confidence** —You have to believe in yourself to sell anything. It is important for a beginning design engineer to work hard at developing a positive self-image. You need to sell yourself to yourself in order to gain the confidence needed to sell a good idea to someone else.

4. **Empathy** — Think of the other person and their needs and concerns. Sell your idea in ways meaningful to them. That means your sales approach is different for each group of people, because each group is different.

You need each of the above attributes for every selling situation. You will encounter three major types of selling situations as a design engineer: (a) proposing a course of action, (b) motivating fellow employees and others you must work with, and (c) presenting a status report with recommendations to your management.

Use the AIDA four-step technique for proposing a course of action

1. **Attention** — Develop a strong opening that motivates the audience to listen. You have just a few seconds, so do not waste time on thank yous, introductions or small talk.

2. **Interest** — Create word pictures in your audience's minds, show models or pictures and explain how this proposal affects them. Why should they be interested in your project?

3. **Desire** — Dramatize your presentation and help them feel that you have a good idea. Explain the strong features of your design. Tell them why this design should be produced.

4. **Action** — Build to a powerful close with a specific call for action. What exactly do you want them to do? The specific action that you request must be within their power to do or approve.

Deal with conflicts

First, state your proposal clearly and make sure the audience understands. Then confront and eliminate conflicting ideas. Finally, ask for approval or consensus on your recommended plan. Do not try for fast, easy approval by not mentioning important conflicting ideas. You want your audience to stay motivated after they leave or you want to establish an alternative plan which will maintain their continued support.

Status reports appraise your management or co-workers of a situation

Status reports are a tentative type of selling. Your primary objective is to present an accurate, clear and complete picture. Your secondary objective is to provide recommendations regarding the situation. This technique is appropriate when your audience is likely to have information relative to the problem which you do not have. Your goal is to facilitate discussion which brings out additional information and ideas. This new knowledge plus your analysis of the situation and recommendations will then allow the group or an individual present to make an informed decision.

For this type of selling situations there are two major styles: the executive summary style and the object-scope-findings-recommendation style.

1. **Executive Summary Style**
   (a) Explain what the report is about.
   (b) Explain the significance and implications of the work.
   (c) Explain the action you believe most appropriate.

2. **Object-Scope-Findings-Recommendations Style**
   (a) Object — state the purpose of the report.
   (b) Scope — explain the nature and scope of the study, problem areas, depth of research and techniques used.
   (c) Findings — list the findings, describe alternatives, provide your analysis.
   (d) Recommendations — conclude with specific suggestions on a course of action.

Skills used in selling

Selling is a complex process. Good salesmen do not approach selling haphazardly. Good engineers who want their ideas listened to do not approach selling haphazardly. Engineers who wish to advance in engineering or general management must develop the following sales skills:

1. **Speaking and writing** — These are your principal means of communication, and communication is required to sell.

2. **Psychology** — Understand people and understand non-verbal cues. Watch posture and be thoughtful about how close you stand when talking with people. In general, the closer you stand (to within about one meter) the more effective and efficient is the verbal information transfer. Know how to motivate people.

3. **Technical knowledge** — There is no substitute for technical knowledge. That is one area where engineering curricula are highly successful; so, you will not likely have a problem unless you think that education ends with graduation.

4. **Social and cultural knowledge** — Should you abruptly begin with business or lead in with small talk? Do you talk over coffee, lunch or a drink? Do you discuss business in the office and not in the social situations? Do you hard-sell or soft-sell? The answer to each question varies with people and culture.

5. **Networking and social skills** — Develop friendships with your colleagues. There is no substitute for professional ties, especially in selling situations.

Motivation is important

People want to work! People are our greatest resource. They are also our most underutilized resource. It is true of you. It is true of those you work with.

When you identify the strong companies, you are identifying companies that motivate and develop their people. Find a faltering company, and you find a company that has problems with people. The low morale you see is not the result of tough times; it is the cause of bad times.

You can be a good scientist and not be able to motivate people. You can be a good machinest, electrician or technician and not be able to motivate people. But, you cannot be a good engineer if you cannot motivate people. An engineer uses technology to solve problems for people. You must work with the technology people, the financial people, the legal people, the sales people, the management team and the product user.

Three myths about motivation

Myth 1. People hate work.

Myth 2. People must be driven and threatened with punishment to get them to work toward organizational objectives.

Myth 3. People like security, want to be told what to do, do not want responsibility and are not ambitious.

The best you can achieve if you accept these three myths is fractional effort and peoples' time from 8 to 5. That may have been enough when you hired people for their physical working abilities. It is totally inadequate when you are hiring people to think. People cannot compete anymore with machinery, electronic controls, computers and robots for doing purely physical work. It is peoples' thinking, analytic abilities, skills, intuition, and feelings that are needed. Sometimes it is judgment coupled with physical work. The point is that you need peoples' enthusiasm not just their time, and you get their enthusiasm only if they cooperate.

As an engineer you will be in a particularly difficult situation for motivating people. Many of the people you need to work with have no managerial accountability to you. They are often in different divisions of your organization or even in other organizations. An engineer's job is really to secure the cooperation and help from a diverse group of people to solve a problem. To do this, you need to understand the personal concerns and motivations of each individual in that group.

Understanding motivation

Psychologists say that man has a hierarchy of needs and wants. Needs in order of priority are:

1. **Survival** — food and shelter.
2. **Safety** — health, protection from adverse climate and physical threats.
3. **Social/sexual** — belonging to a group, feeling accepted, meeting emotional warmth needs.
4. **Ego** — belief in self-worth, self-confidence.
5. **Actualization** — personal development, growth and change, trying new challenges, exploring new things.

Most people in the United States have the first two needs met. Most adults who do not have serious psychological problems have their social needs reasonably fulfilled. That means people are concerned with ego and actualization needs. They are motivated to do things that help them fulfill their self-confidence and growth desires.

Motivational considerations are also important from within an organization. People really want to work if they are provided challenges which are interesting to them and rewards which are meaningful to them. The work itself must be made interesting. No amount of monetary rewards and job benefits will cause people to put their hearts into their work unless they like the work.

Techniques for providing a positive work environment for others and yourself

First, explain the situation in terms relevant to the listener. No one but you cares about your problem in exactly the same way that you do. No one but you sees the problem from your unique point of view and special angle. Think about the other person's way of looking at things and try to explain it in those terms.

Second, explain why solving the problem (producing the desired results) benefits the listener. Again, the listener does not care about solving your problem. He wants to solve his problem or in some manner satisfy his ego and developmental needs. Tell him how this desired result is going to help him and be meaningful to him.

Take time to understand the listener's perspective. You have told him the problem and why he should want to solve it in what you *think* are his terms. Here is your chance to find out whether you succeeded. If not, you can try to re-explain the problem or desired results in terms that are important to him.

Be willing to share responsibility and credit. You cannot develop a healthy, long-term working relationship with others if you will not share responsibility and credit. Without responsibility, they will lose interest in working with you. Without credit, they will resent you and perhaps actively work against you. The days of the self-reliant engineer who does not need the enthusiasm and cooperation of others are long gone.

Be willing to listen to alternative ideas and concerns. The problem and desired outcome may seem quite clear to you. It may not be that clear and simple. Seriously consider other's views of the problem. You will be a far more effective team if you can capitalize on each other's ideas and maintain the fluidity to change approaches when appropriate.

Understand and remember the difficulty of doing anything new

Technical problems are complicated. Technical problems which involve people are far more complicated. Do not expect success quickly or the first time. Design is a trial-and-error process and the important thing is that you keep trying.

Here are five philosophies that can help you remain enthusiastic and help you continue working when things seem tough:

1. An engineer is successful if he fails 999 times but tries again that 1000'th time and succeeds.

2. Murphy's laws apply to most engineering situations. This is particularly true in the one which says that you double the estimated time and money and then take them to the next higher order of magnitude to find out what will really be required. In

other words a 1 hour project will take 2 times 1 hour, then to the next higher order of magnitude (i.e., 2 days). Similarly, a $100 project will cost $2000.

3. Try to keep a positive attitude with some humor. No matter how bad things look, they can always be worse. Besides, without these bad experiences what would you have to tell your grandchildren when you are explaining how tough things were.

4. Remember that there are no experts or geniuses. Design is an ego-bruising activity. When things look bleak, it is easy to think that there are all kinds of brilliant people out there who could easily solve your problem. If there were, you would not be hired to work on the problem.

5. Have fun!

References

1. Girard, J. 1977. How to sell anything to anybody. Warner Books, New York, NY. 238 pp.

2. Schwartz, D. 1965. The magic of thinking big. Simon and Schuster, New York, NY. 192 pp.

3. Toastmasters International. 1984. Communication and leadership program. Toastmasters International Box 10400 Santa Ana, CA 92711. 71 pp.

4. Townsend, R. 1970. Up the organization. A.A. Knopf, New York. 202 pp.

Discussion Problems

1. Why is it important for engineers to develop speaking and salesmanship talents?

2. Discuss methods of establishing and maintaining productive personal rapport with secretaries and technical help in achieving project objectives and goals.

Project Problems

1. Prepare a statement requesting an interested party to provide modest funding to develop and/or market your project.

2. List and defend the important factors influencing a successful request for funding for your project.

Part III
How Shall I Start?

*"Failure is frequently the path of
least persistence."*

*"One can never consent to creep when one
feels the impulse to soar." Helen Keller*

CHAPTER CONTENTS

6. Engineering Design (Universal Constraints)

People are the reason for engineering design. Design is working within the univeral constraints of teamwork, decisions, costs, acceptability, simplicity and time to solve problems for the customers.

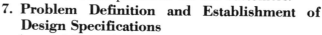

7. Problem Definition and Establishment of Design Specifications

A carefully written definition of the problem along with a quantified set of design specifications, agreed to by all involved parties, are the foundation of a successful project. Examine the customer's needs completely to avoid limiting the solution by an inaccurate definition.

8. Planned Creativity

Creative ability is learned. Systematic approaches and techniques such as brainstorming facilitate and enhance creativity in engineering design.

9. Help From Others

Conversation with the customer, engineering colleagues, company representatives and those who have similar problems, complemented by a methodical review of published materials, allow the engineer to build upon the knowledge of others. Information must be sorted and ranked by the reliability and background of the source rather than simply accepted and accumulated.

10. Project Scheduling

Engineers use scheduling methods to estimate time, money, facility and equipment needs and to provide appropriate deadlines for assessing progress. The goals and accomplishments of research and design efforts are communicated to the management for timely inclusion into the entire organizational missions.

Every design project begins with the recognition of a need. This need may be motivated by humanitarian, philanthropic or economic considerations, but the need *must* be recognized. The need may be to produce a cheaper mechanism to plant seeds, a more accurate means of regulating the water level in a sub-surface irrigation system, a faster response system for process control, or a more easily constructed structural system for farm buildings. Design projects may start as a result of management's decision to increase research and development activities or sale's needs to redesign a user-identified product weakness. Research or advanced planning may have need for a particularly promising idea to be further evaluated for technical and manufacturing feasibility—a process which is called concepting. Someone must recognize the need and articulate it to the design engineer. Notice that a common component of any design problem is that the solution sought is the "best" of all possible solutions. The solution is simpler, cheaper, faster, easier to use, lighter, easier to build, stronger, lasts longer, and the list goes on and on. Thus the design begins with an identification of a need and a statement of how the solution to this need is going to be better than alternative solutions.

Design is an iterative, interactive process requiring the development of specific design strategies where existing textbook methods are not capable of producing acceptable results. The problem is open-ended and no unique solution exists. Thus, design is not a linear step-by-step process that can be laid out totally at the start of any specific design project (Fig III.1). Rather, design is like a merry-go-round, not really any one place to get on, and it may go around and around for a considerable time.

It is often difficult for even an experienced design engineer to know how to start and proceed initially. Most engineers find it necessary to define a series of steps and to proceed logically with these steps, because this helps organize the process, even though they recognize the iterative nature of the design process. The five

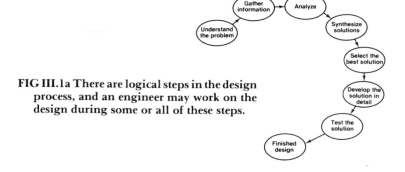

FIG III.1a There are logical steps in the design process, and an engineer may work on the design during some or all of these steps.

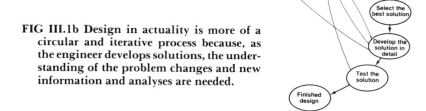

FIG III.1b Design in actuality is more of a circular and iterative process because, as the engineer develops solutions, the understanding of the problem changes and new information and analyses are needed.

FIG III.1c Usually the design is not perfected sufficiently the first time, and testing leads to modification of the solution and sometimes even redefinition of the problem. Most importantly, recognize that design is an optimization process in which the final design is determined by the time and money available. There is no one right answer, and the design can always be improved.

FIG III.2

following chapters will provide you with guidelines and ideas to help you start your own design project and be systematic in the process.

Your ability to think analytically and synthesize creatively will be your most important resources as a design engineer. The human brain is a fascinating computer. More than any other group, engineers are paid for *using* their brains, not *having* them! Consider your development as a design engineer to the plight of the engineer in Fig III.2. Your confidence in your ability to solve problems must be proportional to your resolve to be successful in your design efforts. Working hard is important, but working smart is to be successful. One attribute of the brain is the capability to view a problem from several perspectives simultaneously. Make use of this talent in your conscious and subconscious mind as you develop a thorough understanding of your design problem. Remember that the basic concept of the design must be validated before a meaningful analysis can be undertaken. A second attribute is the capability of logically and methodically approaching a problem. Capitalize on this organizational ability.

FIG III.3 Identification of the design project phases.

Develop individual design strategies that meet your problem constraints. You must be both a dreamer and organizer. Keeping a written record of all your project activities is essential and will assist your organization.

Finally, we view philosophically where to begin by reviewing the engineer in Fig III.3. The recognition of a need and a decision to do something in response to that need must preceed all other activities. It is difficult to speculate his need, a place to fish, a cool spot to relax, a challange to build an earthen dam or whatever. He assembles the resources available to implement his solution. Now the crucial field test! An unanticipated problem? By the last frame one is tempted to conclude that the engineer has proceeded no further than the first frame. Nothing could be farther from the truth! The engineer has successfully completed the *first* iteration of the design process and perhaps only now is beginning to understand the true nature of his design challenge.

Discussion Problems

1. Discuss the relative importance to the design engineer of accurately and completely defining the design problem before extensive effort is invested in solving the problem.

2. For each frame from Fig III.3 discuss which of the design activities from Fig III.1c might be actively underway in the engineer's mind.

Project Problems

1. Develop a completely comprehensive problem definition of your design project and describe clearly how the solution sought will be the best of all possible solutions.

2. Identify one or more individuals whom you think may be familiar with your design project. Before visiting with them, write out a list of questions about your project for them to help you develop answers. Make a written record of their responses.

Chapter 6
Engineering Design
(Universal Constraints)

"He who never made a mistake never made a discovery." Samuel Smiles

"Mathematicians describe and define, scientists discover and predict, engineers create and solve."

Engineering design is the process of creating a solution which is universally constrained by (a) working with others, (b) making decisions, (c) affordability, (d) acceptability, (e) simplicity, and (f) timeliness. Many other constraints apply to any specific design problem. Real design problems have multiple constraints. Consider these universal constraints in more detail.

Engineering design is a "people" process

Your success as a design engineer will be, in general, proportional to your ability to work with others. Design teams are often formed with one or more engineers and other non-engineers. The exact make-up of these teams is based upon the key areas of needed expertise and experience. Members of a design team *share* the responsibility of producing an acceptable solution to their common problem. Many other individuals, groups or companies may productively contribute to the design effort but are not enumerated as members of the design team unless they *share* in the responsibility of the design. Each team member should have a specific area(s) of responsibility and the *authority* to make decisions affecting those responsibilities while remaining within the design team's charge. Thus working with others requires you to interact with both team members (those with direct design or management responsibilities) and anyone else (non-team member) who can impact the design with a meaningful contribution.

The relative importance of the decision making process in the overall design process cannot be overemphasized. The actual process of making design decisions will be covered in Chapter 10. The issue here is that decisions *must* be made in order to further the design process. Decisions will be made by the people who must accept the credit for the good decisions as well as the blame for the bad decisions. People who make or participate in decisions are, in fact, members of the design team. A design team may have only one formal member.

Affordability is important to everyone

Affordable means that the engineering design is a good deal for the manufacturer *and* the buyer. In some special cases the manufacturer and the buyer are the same! As a good engineer, you earn your salary plus a profit for your employer while providing a service to society. The goal of engineering design is to maximize economic benefits for both the buyer and seller and not necessarily to develop the longest-lived or the most technically advanced product. The free market system will automatically select the product that gives the most value for the price.

Acceptable means the customer wants it and your firm supports it

Acceptable means that the design engineer can persuade others to continue to finance the design and, ultimately, the manufacturing of the product. Engineering design is creating something which does not exist. The engineering manager has to decide whether this product, which does not exist, can be sold profitably in an economic climate he cannot accurately foretell. Further complicating the acceptability issue are people. Manufacturing companies are comprised of people with individual likes and dislikes which affect their decisions. The consuming public is notorious for irrational or "trendy" buying habits.

Acceptable also means that the legal, ethical, and social structure will allow the solution. Laws may restrict the solution or favor another solution regardless of merit. People may prevent acceptance, such as the slow-down of nuclear plant construction or the opposition to mechanization of fruit harvesting. Nuclear radiation to preserve fresh fruits, vegetables and meats has been technologically feasible for a number of years. The use of pesticides to control outbreaks of fruit flies in both California and Florida appears technically correct but was opposed by the general public. These actions may be based on economic or other fears from a segment of society which neither manufactures nor buys the product. A considerable amount of design effort is expended to make products conform to safety or environmental standards.

Simplicity is a virtue

Edward R. Murrow once said, "The obscure we see eventually, the totally obvious it seems takes a little longer!" The design process is constantly constrained by the need to keep it simple. We can all recall working with a product that required unreasonably complicated servicing for a frequently recurring problem. Every piece of a design has a probability of failure; so, every additional part or feature is another opportunity for problems to the user. You also are aware of sophisticated computer programs with explanations so complex that the time needed to learn that software package exceeds the total time you will ever spend working that kind of problem using a calculator.

Aesthetics, a term frequently used by artists, writers, and designers, refers to a pleasing appearance with clean, clear and simple methods or forms. Aesthetic engineering design means a clean, simple design that performs the intended function well. When your design has progressed to a point at which you "know it will work," ask yourself "Can I do it more simply?"

Deadlines and time limits are inherent to engineering

Timely means the obvious "on schedule" which is important because money is lost, often at prodigious rates, when production or sales are slowed. Timely also means the subtle "organization confidence in engineering" issue. Late work erodes management's confidence in the designer. There is always a more nearly "perfect" solution to the problem—it is the engineer's job to develop the best solution possible in the time available. Half right, on time, may be better than all right too late!

Engineering design problems have more than one solution

College classrooms and mathematics problems are probably the only situations in which one will likely find problems with one right answer. There are thousands of ways to travel from New York to Chicago; the best way depends on the criteria important to the traveler. There are hundreds of commercially available tractors; the best tractor depends on the needs and concerns of the user in addition to the usual cost, acceptability and timeliness constraints.

Engineering design is an order of magnitude more complex than deciding how to travel or which tractor to buy. You are trying to create something which does not exist and compare it with alternatives, some of which have not been developed. You do not know the technological and economic changes that will take place during the time between design and production, let alone during the product life.

Real problems are complicated

Real engineering problems cannot be solved by simply referring to the appropriate text and finding a comparable example. If they could be, businesses would not hire engineers—they would use computers! Text-book problems are carefully defined so that each problem can be solved with only one right answer. In real-world problems, the assumptions necessary to analyze the problem mathematically are difficult to choose and justify.

Several factors limit the reliability of a mathematical solution to the problem: (a) materials variability, (b) fabrication error, (c) problem assumptions, (d) safety factors and (e) equation assumptions. Notice that most engineering equations are based on rather ideal assumptions. The equations themselves may not be valid in cases different from the experimental situation from which the equations were developed.

Real problems involve people and organizations. People aspects of the problem are usually more important than the technical aspects. Is the design attractive to people? Are the people who will build it accustomed to working with the materials and fabrication procedures that you have selected? These are just a few of the many questions that face a design engineer.

There are optimal solutions

While optimal solutions exist it may be virtually impossible to demonstrate that you have indeed found one. The problem, as perceived by the user, is always changing (e.g., desirable tractor features change with the economics of available technologies and with farming practices). Means for solving the problem are also changing (e.g., technology available to manufacture the tractor changes the relative cost of different techniques and advances in electronics add features which can be designed into the tractor).

Life is change! That's exciting, but it's also frustrating if you are expecting to find the best or optimal solution to an engineering problem. That explains why several brands and types of livestock buildings, grain bins, center pivot irrigators, farm tractors and waste handling equipment are manufactured and sold. Each model has advantages in performance, cost, availability, serviceability, etc. The design engineer must develop design strategies which permit the evaluation of the proposed design to determine whether a good design has been achieved.

Learn from failure

Charles F. Kettering, long-time Director of Engineering for General Motors, is perhaps the greatest design engineer of the 20th century. He was responsible for high-speed, light-weight diesel engines, electronic ignition, fast-drying paint, freon refrigerant and many other inventions. Crucial to his success was his willingness to "cut and try" or in more scientific-sounding terms "experimentally evaluate" new ideas.

According to Kettering it is not important whether we succeed at the first or even the hundredth attempt. What is important is that we learn from each attempt and try repeatedly until we do succeed. Failures should be regarded as practice shots and as opportunities to develop a more intimate understanding of the problem.

This is a different approach from the traditional mathematics-and-science approach used in classrooms. In classrooms one is expected to be right the first time or be penalized in grade. That develops a fear of the trial-and-error approach and stifles creativity.

Your success as a design engineer will be shaped by your willingness to push ahead and try things. That will often be difficult when you are faced with criticism or ridicule for failure during your practice shots. It is far easier when facing a difficult and complex problem to skirt around it and procrastinate. Throughout your design work you need to keep your focus on the problem and keep working toward a solution. But, remember the adage: "Do something! Do it now! or, Someone else will pull the plow!"

Depend upon past experience and proven technologies

While it is important to be willing to try new ideas and approaches, a large number of design problems can be dispatched purposefully with proven technologies and past experience. Often, significant design improvements can be achieved based upon existing product performance and design analysis data. For example, a planter part may have a history of stress-strain related failures in the field when peak stress and cyclic stress analyses suggest no basis exists for these failures. Careful evaluation of in-service conditions may reveal a stress-reversal phenomenon

HAY BALER

PERSON WISHING FOR A NICE BALE OF HAY PUSHES HANDLE ON DETONATOR (A) WHICH SETS OFF DYNOMITE (B) WHICH HURLS BUCKET (C) UP TO HIT CANNONBALL (D) WHICH ROLLS DOWN GUTTER (E) FALLING ONTO MALLET (F) PLUNGING HAY INTO COMPACTOR (G). MEANWHILE THE HANDLE OF MALLET (F) PUSHES AGAINST BULB ATTATCHED TO BUGLE (H) WHICH PLAYS A BATTLE CHARGE. MONKEY (I) DRESSED IN CIVIL WAR COSTUME AND HIRED TO PLAY A FAMOUS GENERAL; HEARS FIRST THE EXPLOSION, THEN THE CLANG OF THE CANNONBALL AND FINALLY THE BUGLE LEADS A CHARGE. THIS MOVES HIS BOOTS WHICH ARE GLUED TO MECHANICAL HANDS (J) WHICH TIE THE WIRES ON THE NOW COMPRESSED BALE (K)

not originally considered in the engineering design analysis. Don't forget that you can benefit from other's experience by communicating your needs to them.

There are 10 truisms of engineering problem solving

1. Most important problems are people related. All design problems of interest to agricultural engineers are ultimately motivated by their impact on people.

2. Most people are afraid of failure and slow to tackle difficult problems. The best way to avoid mistakes is not to take *any* action.

3. Engineering design is really people management, usually through informal channels. It is estimated that engineers spend at least 30% of their careers writing proposals, specifications, reports and results which are ultimately an attempt to bring others into the effort.

4. The most important skill of engineers is to partition the problem into understandable, assignable segments that average people can and will tackle. Small problems can be solved; large

undivided problems will overwhelm even the most experienced designer.

5. You cannot afford to waste anyone's mind. No useful interest is ever served by not providing an opportunity for multiple inputs.

6. People have to plan their work in order to be enthusiastic and effective. Tell them the goal; let them devise the plan.

7. People need to understand the goals and objectives (i.e., have a clear sense of purpose) to be effective. This is the action form of, "Ask me no questions and I'll tell you no lies." To be effective is to be involved.

8. Knowing how to find information and evaluate its reliability is the mark of an experienced professional. Often, free advice is worth what you paid for it.

9. It is your responsibility to communicate and ensure understanding with the user, salesman, repairman, builder and draftsman. The best result in the world is of no value if no one understands or believes it.

10. Most people do not think big enough to tackle a complex or innovative project. Often the engineer's first task is to convince the powers that be that the project is indeed possible.

Quantifying engineering design ability

Your success as a designer cannot be predicted with a high degree of certainty, but in the true spirit of design analysis the following functional relationship appears to be a reasonable approximation.

Design Success = $(I*J*K)^E$,

where,

I = Imagination,
J = Judgment,
K = Knowledge, and
E = Enthusiasm.

Mature designers are strong in all four factors. Engineering students possess analytical skills comparable to many practicing engineers, and certainly no one has a lock on imagination. Notice the exponential role of enthusiasm. As a new engineer, you haven't had the opportunity to develop engineering judgment to the level of an experienced engineer, but you can find someone who has the experience to help you. If you don't know something that is important to your project, find someone who does. The design engineer must work with others to achieve solutions to complex, real problems.

References

1. Boyd, T.A. 1957. The professional amateur, The biography of Charles F. Kettering, Dutton, New York. 242 pp.

2. Herzog, R.E. 1977. Design imperatives. Machine Design, December 8.

3. Jones, J.C. 1980. Design methods — Seeds of human futures, 2nd ed. Wiley & Sons, New York. 407 pp.

4. Koen, Billy Vaughn. 1984. Toward a definition of the engineering method. Engineering Education, December.

5. Leech, D.J. 1972. Management of engineering design. Wiley and Sons, London. 258 pp.

6. Schaumburg, F.D. 1981. Engineering — As if people mattered. Civil Engineering, ASCE, October.

Discussion problems

1. Divide into teams, select the best commercially available tractor for a particular agricultural application representative of your area and present your selections to the class. Discuss the impact of the 6 universal design constraints on your selection process as well as your selection.

2. Discuss as a class the 4 factors needed for design success. Comment on how your present university curriculum has contributed (or not) to strengthening these factors.

3. Do problem 1; however, select the best exterior siding material for dairy milking parlors in your area.

4. Discuss what is meant by a "design failure" according to C.F. Kettering.

Project problems

1. Develop a statement about your design project which explains how your design approach will relate to the "10 Truisms of Engineering Design."

2. Describe three potential solutions to your design project and compare them by listing the desirable and undesirable features.

3. List the six universal design constraints and rank their importance to your design project. Explain why.

Chapter 7
Problem Definition and
Design Specifications

"If the only tool you have is a hammer, you tend to see all your problems as nails."

"Hit or miss methods usually miss."

Clearly defining the problem seems so obvious and simple. Yet, it is the single, biggest source of frustration and wasted time in design projects. Consider the breeders of draft horses who worked industriously to solve the problem of "improved draft animals." They discovered after their horses were replaced with tractors that the real problem was "how to move implements in the field."

Knowing what you want is half the battle

Consider all the design engineers who have worked to improve the moldboard plow. Even Thomas Jefferson made a contribution to this effort! The real problems were to develop methods for loosening the soil and killing weeds at minimal cost. Chisel plows, chemical weed control and several other methods are now competing with the moldboard plow for solving this problem.

Considering the existing solution as the problem itself is perhaps the most common mistake. Are you designing a tractor or a means of powering implements? Are you designing a center pivot irrigator or a means of providing water to crops on uneven terrain? Are you designing a stanchion milking barn or a system for milking cows efficiently? No significant new technology or approach will ever be developed by defining the problem in terms of the existing solutions.

History is littered with companies that failed because they lost sight of the real needs. At one time railroads were the largest, most capital strong industrial sector of the United States. Railroads continued to think that they were in the railroad business. They could have been in the business of transporting people and goods efficiently. They could have been the developers of airline transport and the organizers of a combination rail-truck goods moving system. They could have been pioneers in coupling and decoupling passenger cars for automatic guidance on frequently traveled routes.

Keep purpose in mind, but be alert to unexpected developments

Inventing an answer without a problem is not logical. Yet, we do that often. It happens quite innocently when we redefine the problem to make it easier to solve. The result is a wonderful solution to a problem that does not exist, except in a trivial sense.

However, do not be oblivious to serendipitous results. Penicillin was discovered when researchers were alert to the unexpected. Too often, design engineers stumble across a truism, but get up and move on their way as if nothing had happened. One of the biggest challenges engineers face is evaluating data, especially data from previous design iterations. In almost every situation the design engineer can learn something useful, if not for the present project, perhaps a future problem.

Real problems are tough. Human nature is to avoid tough problems. Carefully defining the problem in the first place helps keep our focus on the real problem throughout the design. The rewards, satisfaction and money, are for solving real problems.

Can you trust anyone?

This is not a commentary on the maliciousness of human nature. It simply means that people sometimes do not know what problem they want solved. They think they want a better tractor when they really want a more efficient means to power implements. Remember this when the manager of sales tells you that your company needs a new model.

Do not take the initial definition of the problem at face value. Ask questions to determine the history, background and the person's relationship to the problem. Then seek others who are familiar with the problem and learn their perceptions of the problem. Visit the problem site and talk with individuals who face the problem daily. Also, if possible, talk with those who have tried to solve the problem and failed. Time spent reaching a clear and agreed upon definition of the problem situation is the most important time spent on the design project.

In most companies market research techniques are relied upon to determine what the customer wants, what the cost must be and what the general market specifications are. The design engineer must then translate the market research results into technical specifications and design concepts that meet those market requirements in the most cost-effective manner considering the company's resources and manufacturing capabilities. Problem definition studies are often initiated to get as many interested people together as possible. Marketing, manufacturing, materials, service, and product engineering people together work out differences, build on each others' specialized knowledge and thus reach a better problem definition.

The perception of the problem situation preconceives its solution

Suppose you are presented with the following problem situation. In the spring of the year farmers are complaining that it is "too wet to plant corn as early as they would like." One geneticist will define the problem as a need for a new "wet tolerant" variety of corn while another geneticist will see the need for a new variety that "can be planted later and matures more quickly." One agricultural engineer will see this as a definite need for "improved drainage means," while another will see a clear need for "higher flotation tires," and a third will see the need for "developing a way to plant in the fall and delay germination until spring."

Don't fall victim to mis-communication (Fig 7.1). Design problems are difficult to solve. Be certain that you are attacking

What contracting quoted-
Leaf rake

What salesman ordered-
Leaf blower

What engineering designed-
Leaf vacuum

What manufacturing produced-
Organic mulcher

What installing delivered-
Leaf refuse collection system

What the customer wanted-
Garden rake

FIG 7.1 What's the problem?

the right one. Ask all the people you can find who have any association with the problem situation what they think the *real* problem is. Integrate all these responses into the final problem statement.

Define the problem in writing

No engineering problems, except the most trivial, are solved by an individual acting independently. Design is complex and usually requires combined efforts. Many others are directly concerned, including the customer, (product user) and those people with sales, management, manufacturing and testing roles within the company. Opportunities for confusion and mis-communication are everywhere.

Oral definition of the problem is totally unsatisfactory. First, the chance of having all parties present when defining the problem is slight. Second, personnel will change. Third, peoples' memories are fickle. Fourth, people interpret the problem to suit their own needs, which are different from everyone elses'.

Writing out the problem gives people a chance to critique, clarify, and concentrate on the problem definition. Better under-standing and more esprit-de-corps are promoted. Actively solicit review and commentary because accurate problem definition is more than half the design. The actual process of putting the design project definition in writing will force you to clarify the true nature of the design task which lies ahead.

Design is also expensive. Managers want a chance to evaluate a project before investing significantly. Each company will use forms, such as those shown in Appendix III, to insure early involvement of sales, manufacturing, finance and engineering. You can use the written problem definition for several purposes. First, you can use it to ensure that everyone agrees what problem you are setting out to solve. Second, you can use it as a foundation for generating ideas for solutions to the problem. Third, you can use it during the design and development phases as a focus for the design team. Fourth, you can use it to avoid future disagreements and to settle disputes regarding the project goals and responsi-bilities.

Remember, the tendency to avoid or disregard the real problem is powerful. A written problem definition helps avoid that tendency. Success as a designer is heavily dependent upon your ability to define the design problems.

List and quantify design variables to help define the problem

Once you have developed a written statement of your design problem, redevelop the statement in engineering terms with appropriate units (i.e., flow rates, speeds, power, cycle times, strengths, motion limits, accelerations, costs, weights, etc). Make a list of all known variables which are believed to be involved in the design problem under consideration. Identify them as independent or dependent in the sense that the designer has control over the values used (independent) or the variable values are functions of other variables within the problem (dependent). Once these lists are complete, existing analytical procedures can be utilized where possible to produce functional relationships which can be manipulated to produce optimal or "best" solutions.

As you quantify criteria, remember that the problem definition, and hence the solution, should be customer focused. Determine what the customer wants and needs; then, develop measurable criteria for the design that will result in a product that the user will buy.

Also, be careful to separate the design criteria for your project from those of the larger project to which your design will be applied. If, for example, you are designing a solar collector for grain drying, it may not be necessary to have a grain dryer design in the problem. The problem may be to produce a solar collector design which results in the lowest possible cost per unit of solar energy captured and delivers that energy in an air stream suitable as an *input* to a grain dryer. The design engineer must understand the drying process sufficiently to determine the necessary heated air conditions.

The black-box approach can help you reach a broader knowledge of your problem

Another tool for defining the problem is the "black box" approach. The solution to the engineering design problem is depicted as a black box (Fig 7.2). "Available resources", which can

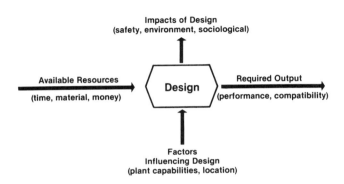

FIG 7.2 Black-box approach to problem definition.

be used to solve the problem, go into the black box. These resources include time, technical capabilities, materials and money. "Required output" comes out the opposite side of the black box. These are the functions which must be performed by the design. "Factors which influence the system" go into the black box. These include customer needs, plant location, market location, available manufacturing equipment, tax laws and numerous other factors which influence the design but are not resources directly used by the design. "Impacts of design on society" come out of the black box. These include potential safety and environmental issues and the economic concerns of people indirectly affected by the design.

The black box technique can be useful because it encourages one to examine each of the four groups of variables independently. It is a method for studying the problem by parts. The technique is not meant to replace reviewing the problem from an overall perspective. Rather it is meant to complement and facilitate your efforts to define the overall problem.

A third technique is to segment the problem into four categories. These are "musts," "must nots," "wants" and "want nots." This technique allows you to distinguish among the essential and desirable aspects of your design problem. Like the blackbox technique, it helps you clarify the problem.

Understand the difference between design objectives and design criteria

Normally the first step in a problem definition effort is to write a set of design objectives. These objectives are statements of goals of the project to which design efforts will be directed. These objectives are then translated into quantifiable design criteria.

The key feature differentiating objectives from criteria is that criteria are a set of quantifiable standards upon which judgments or decisions may be based. If, for example, one is going to design the "least cost method," that is a noble objective. Unless "least cost method" can be quantitatively defined (e.g., cost less than $100), the objective has no parallel criterion statement. Similarly, the objective of the irrigation weir design to provide an accurate measurement of flow rate would have a parallel criterion of providing flow rate measurement within ± 0.5% full-scale accuracy.

Quantify design criteria

After you and other parties have defined the problem and developed objectives or goals, your next step is establishing design criteria. Quantify! Design criteria must have a standard for comparison to be useful. You may describe some design criteria in

Table 7.1. Design criteria check list*.

1. Outputs (forces, flow rates, energy, power).
2. Reliability (cycle-lives, extreme loads, design lives).
3. Compatibility (interchange with..., match with...).
4. Manufacturability (material restrictions, process restrictions).
5. Economics (manufactured costs, tooling costs, life-cycle economics, operating costs).
6. Safety (pass standards, minimal hazards from anticipated misuses).
7. Practicality (weights, ease of use; ease of service).

*Consider carefully your design and check to ensure that you have written quantifiable criteria wherever appropriate.

Table 7.2. Design factors for a low pressure sprinkler nozzle (courtesy of Valmont Industries).

1. Replace existing 24 ft or 48 ft booms with a low pressure nozzle device.
2. Keep the cost/foot system length to the customer at less than normal boom cost. ($8/ft for linear systems and $4/ft for pivot system).
3. Achieve a comparable wetted diameter to boom systems. (For a 48 ft boom an 83.5 ft wetted diameter at 20 psi and a 73.5 ft wetted diameter at 6 psi; for a 24 ft boom a 62 ft wetted diameter at 20 psi and a 52 ft wetted diameter at 6 psi).
4. Develop comparable droplet size to Valley spray nozzles.
5. Minimize wind drift.
6. Achieve uniform application rate in the line of travel.
7. Achieve uniform distribution perpendicular to line of travel (a 92% or better coefficient of uniformity).
8. Design nozzle to have ¾" NPT male base. (Above 20 gpm 1" NPT male base is acceptable).
9. Design nozzle to operate in 6-20 psi range.
10. Develop a system of size increments and flow rates comparable to existing Valley spray nozzles.

relation to an existing product while other design criteria may be absolute (Table 7.2).

Design objectives such as "inexpensive", "long-lived", "easy to operate" and "efficient" are obvious, but difficult to evaluate. Such objectives apply to almost all design problems. Design criteria should be specific and provide the basis for determining when each criterion has been met. A battery design criterion of 1000 cycles at 80% depth of discharge is "long-lived". A seed metering mechanism that "delivers single seeds 95% of the time" is one way of specifying an objective of "singulates".

Design criteria that quantify help in three important ways. First, they cause the design team to analyze the problem carefully in order to formulate specific criteria. This includes some early problem analysis and idea screening. Second, they provide clear, measurable decision points for the design team. This is particularly helpful to inexperienced members in keeping the work focused, coordinated and timely. Third, they improve team morale. People work with enthusiasm and a sense of purpose when they have defined goals that are attainable. Conversely, people are frustrated and reluctant to work when they do not have measurable, clearly-stated goals. In the latter case people may put in their time, but it is poorly used because they cannot grasp the problem or the purpose.

Expect the problem and criteria to change

Now you have carefully and methodically defined the problem and the design criteria. Expect them to change as you work! Your time was not wasted. Tomorrow you will know more than you do today about the problem. Design is not a cookbook recipe process; it is an iterative process. Periodically you will need to rethink your problem definition and criteria.

Once you begin developing and analyzing solutions, you will find you will need to compromise. You will find that some factors enter into the problem that you previously had not expected. You will understand the problem better, and your problem will have changed as in Fig 7.3. Life changes, technology changes, people change and needs change. The problem you set out to solve does not need to be solved; a slightly different one does.

Beware the hazard of problem avoidance! When you review the problem definition and design criteria, be careful not to sidestep the problem to achieve an easier solution. A beautiful solution to a nonexistent problem is priceless, but the cost of reaching the solution is not!

FIG 7.3 **Expect the design project to change.**

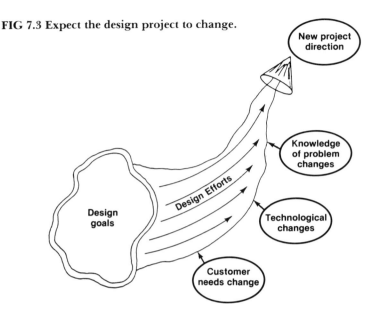

Differentiate among factual, judicial and creative problems

All problems of interest to engineers can be assumed to fall into one of three separate but related groups. Factual problems are those problems that are known to have one, single, unique and correct answer. One should not assume that factual problems are necessarily simple or that the correct answer can be obtained in practice even though the answer is known to exist. For example, "How many hectares of corn were harvested in the USA last year?" is a factual problem. A unique answer is known to exist but is not easily obtained, and some people devote their professional lives in an effort to develop the "correct" answer.

Judicial problems are typically characterized as having a yes, no or maybe answer. Questions on product liability and engineering ethics are, for example, clearly in this group. Their answers depend not only upon the "facts" in the case but upon how those facts are interpreted and applied in light of past (and often incomplete) experience. Asking a series of factual questions can be an important aid for resolving judicial problems. With a specific application in mind, as another example, you may ask, "Is a roller pump better than a gear pump?" To answer this type of question, you first ask factual questions about the specific application such as pump life, power requirements, pressure and flow characteristics, etc., for each pump. After careful assessment as to the relative importance and desirability of each factor, make a judgment.

Creative problems can be solved in more than one way; so, the issue is deciding how the ultimate solution is the "best" of all possible solutions. Problems in this group are of the general form, "In what ways can something be achieved subject to the given optimizing or constraining functions?," where the "something" defines a specific problem. For example, "In what ways might ride comfort for tractor drivers be improved without increasing cost or reducing operator function?" requires you to create possible solutions from which the "best" is selected according to the constraints.

The interrelationships of the three problem groups should be noted. Judicial problems can be broken down into a series of factual problems. To solve judicial problems, you solve all the associated factual problems and evaluate the factual solutions as to their relative importance, thus generating a solution to the original judicial problem. Creative problems require the *generation* of a series of judicial problems in response to the stated optimal or constraining functions. In general, design engineering can be defined as developing ingenious solutions to creative problems.

Advice to students from Ken Finden, University of Arizona and retired Toro engineering manager

"My experience is that the most successful projects have been those where the basic concepts and parameters have been well-defined and established early in the design process. False starts and last minute changes have doomed many great designs. It's my experience that students tend to grab the first concept that comes along and are too anxious to get into the fun part rather than refine the design with rigorous analysis.

"It's particularly critical for students to learn the need for clear definition of the problem and to focus the design on solving that problem. Secondly, it's essential to identify and verify those two or three critical elements (e.g., cost, number of acres or animals, crop power requirements, etc.) that control the entire design. It is also important to identify the sub-issues (e.g., controls, environmental impact, materials, etc.) that can also make or break a project.

The student (with faculty advisor help) should largely resolve these items during an early meeting with the client (industry, faculty or other) who is providing the project problem. Students need to learn how to interrogate clients to determine the real problem to be solved. The client may not even recognize or be aware of the key issue."

References

1. Crosby, P. 1972. The art of getting your own sweet way. McGraw Hill, New York. 182 pp.

2. Leech, D.J. 1972. Management of engineering design. Wiley and Sons, London. 258 pp.

3. Townsend, R. 1970. Up the organization. A.A. Knopf, New York. 202 pp.

Discussion Problems

1. Define the function of a milking barn and develop a problem definition and design objectives appropriate to the function. Does it need to be a building?

2. Consider the existing and potential roles of a lawn-and-garden tractor and attachments. Is there a niche not being filled by present lines? Develop a problem definition and design objectives appropriate to a manufacturer who wishes to design a system that can compete in the market.

3. Analyze the automobile transportation system using the black-box approach. For example, does the automobile have a good refuse management system? Hint: Consider why highways are littered.

4. Write a problem definition, design objectives and design specifications for the steering system on a tractor.

5. Discuss which of the 10 listed items in Table 7.2 are design objectives and which are specifications. For each objective develop a parallel specification.

Project Problems

1. Write a proposal letter to your "superior" to express your interest, abilities and understanding of your present project.

2. Develop lists for your project of your "musts," "must nots," "wants" and "want nots."

3. Develop a list of specific design objectives for your design project.

4. Develop a list of design specifications based upon your answer to project problem No. 2.

5. Develop a conspectus sketch or drawing of your project which you believe meets all objectives and include "black boxes" where necessary. Refer to Fig I.10 for example.

6. Visit a farm equipment dealer and discuss the needs of his customers not met by existing equipment. Also discuss problems related to present equipment that are troublesome to customers.

Chapter 8
Planned Creativity

"Some things have to be believed to be seen."

*"Creativity is 10% inspiration and
90% perspiration."*

Creativity results from hard work

Have you ever written a term paper the night before it was due? Almost everyone has and some of them were outstanding — Creatively outstanding. We have amazing abilities when we seriously confront the situation. Remember all those times you waited for inspiration to strike when the due date was still a week away? It never strikes until you decide, "I have to get this d---- thing done," and sit down, pencil in hand.

Design engineers face a similar problem. Creativity will not strike without a serious effort. Serious, meaning 100% concentration with enthusiasm. The main difference between engineering design and writing a term paper is that the engineering design is usually a lot more complicated. That means it takes a lot more time and you cannot afford to start the night before. That is part of the reason that engineering designers develop project plans with deadlines for each of the design steps.

Understanding engineering design creativity

Bill Harriott, past president of the American Society of Agricultural Engineers, formerly from FMC Central Engineering

Laboratories and currently a research and development consultant, defines creativity as follows: "Creativity is the productive and synergistic interaction between the application of the talents of individuals and the resources of society that produces unique solutions of problems that meet the needs of individuals and society over time." Creativity uses emotion with logic, subconscious with conscious and artistic and aesthetic talents with scientific and mathematical talents. It is complex and exciting!

Creativity is the heart of engineering design. Creativity is the fire which fuels invention and progress. Creativity is the basis of a strong, healthy economy. Perhaps most importantly, creativity is the result of planning and effort. Psychologists and educators agree that creativity is a talent which can be developed.

Enthusiasm is needed

You cannot wait for creativity to happen to you. Engineering is a demanding profession. Successful, creative design requires that you approach the problems with enthusiasm. If you view them with a "ho-hum" attitude your chances of creativity are nil. The engineering profession runs on enthusiasm and bustle; if you do not have those you ought to seek a different career. Furthermore, enthusiasm must be *focused* to be effective (Fig. 8.1).

Creativity as it fits into the design process

Creativity is important during each of the design activities shown in Fig 8.2. Recognizing and defining the problem requires creativity and a sensitivity to needs and problems.

Information gathering is a creative process. Most of the information you need is *not* available in engineering texts. Personal and professional contacts, field trips and meetings, observation and recall, all are avenues for information gathering. This process is a lot like the detective's search for information.

Smoldering charcoal fire- no enthusiasm.	Dynamite explosion- enthusiasm, but no focus.	Space shuttle- focused enthusiasm!
	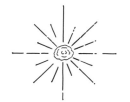	

FIG 8.1 Enthusiasm must be focused to be effective!

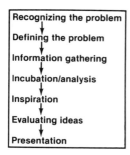

FIG 8.2 Activities in the creative
problem solving process.

Incubation and analysis are the development and screening of
ideas. There are more failures than successes. Inspirations occur
while working at this stage of the creation process. Often these
great ideas occur during non-working hours when the mind is
free from distractions.

By this time several solutions will have emerged. These ideas
must be evaluated carefully to select the best one. A prototype is
built and tested. Creativity is applied to develop ways of testing
and composing the design. The idea is re-evaluated and improved
or rejected.

Finally a workable design is developed. Do not expect your
company to congratulate you on your success. Plan to sell your
idea—it is the only way it will be accepted! Skillful and creative
development of visual aids and wording for effective communication of your results will be essential.

There are techniques for enhancing creativity to solve your problem

It is fine to talk about creativity; now, let us face the design
problem. How are you going to plan creativity into your design
process? Admittedly, planned creativity is difficult, but here are
five techniques that can help.

1. Brainstorming

This is a method for generating ideas in a group. The group
can be your design team. The objective is to develop and record
as many ideas as possible during a one hour session. Criticism
and evaluation of the ideas will come later. Let your imagination
run!

Select a moderator to keep the brainstorming on the subject
and select someone to record the ideas. A blackboard is helpful
so that everyone can see ideas as they are expressed and build
upon them. Planning is important. Pick a time when people

are alert and a location away from interruptions. Provide background information (such as the problem definition and design criteria) ahead of time. Make sure that everyone understands the purpose and realizes that ideas are not to be criticized no matter how outrageous.

Bring the group together at a later date to brainstorm the subject again. The ideas generated will have incubated and your best ideas may result from the second or third brainstorming sessions. Finally, bring your group together to critique and analyze your ideas.

You can brainstorm alone with a piece of paper and an open mind. Do not overlook this possibility of producing meaningful results.

2. Morphological approach

This is a method that is particularly effective when used with the brainstorming technique. It consists of segmenting the problem into required and desired outputs. For example a swine farrowing building should: (a) keep out the wind, (b) maintain a temperature of approximately 20°C for the sows, (c) maintain a temperature of approximately 30°C for the pigs, (d) keep the feed dry, (e) store wastes in a healthful manner, (f) provide for operator comfort, etc. (Fig 8.3). Now generate solutions for each segment of the problem using the brain-

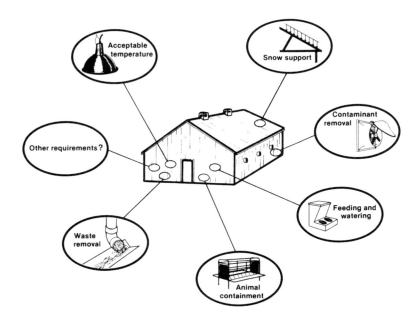

FIG 8.3 The morphological approach applied to farrowing house design.

solutions for each segment of the problem using the brainstorming technique. Look for ideas that can be combined into a package solution to the hog building design problem.

You can use the morphological approach in other ways. You can look at inputs rather than outputs (functions) of the design. List the materials or components that might be alternatives for each facet of the inputs. For example, the building skin could be plywood, fiberglass, particle board, galvanized steel, aluminum or painted steel. The walls could be panelized or site assembled. Now evaluate the alternative materials.

3. Visit with people who see the problem from a different perspective

What does the swine farmer say he wants in the farrowing barn? What do the salesmen tell you are needed and will sell in he farrowing barn line? Who produces a similar product (e.g., poultry housing) for different applications? What do your engineering colleagues working in other areas think about the problem?

All these people can help you. They each have different ideas and perspectives on the problem. People are the most important element in the creative process. You need all the ideas and views you can find. Don't ever forget to talk to the end-users; they are the people who must be satisfied since they will ultimately pay for the new design.

4. Attend professional meetings and trade shows

You will never be a state-of-the-art expert on all facets of agricultural engineering. You will never even be a state-of-the-art expert on the "Structures and Environment" area within agricultural engineering. If you work hard, you may be an expert on confinement hog buildings for a North Central United States climate. You, a design engineer, have to be a generalist; you cannot know all there is to know about the various facets of your design problem, and *you need to know people who can help you.* Professional meetings and trade shows provide many opportunities; they are worth singling out from method 3 above.

5. Competiton between two or more groups.

Competition is an important factor in economic and social systems throughout the world. People thrive on the challenge of competition. No one should be surprised to learn that many creative design solutions evolve from this competition. The groups are often from competing firms but sometimes the same company will have two separate design teams working to solve the same problem. In the latter case, the competition may be light-hearted and add to the fun of engineering while leading to increased creativity!

Creativity demands that you seek additional sources

Creative information-finding is among the most important abilities needed by a design engineer. In this age of specialization and information overload, you need to know people who can give you answers or aim you in the right direction. Your professional colleagues are your most valuable resource. Professional and trade organizations are the best ways to meet, develop and maintain these needed contacts. Anyone serious about design engineering should expect to belong and participate actively in at least one professional or trade organization. Examples of such organizations are the American Society of Agricultural Engineers (ASAE), the National Society of Professional Engineers (NSPE) and the Farm Industrial and Equipment Institute (FIEI).

An important activity undertaken by many professional societies is the development of standards. Participation in technical standards committees on the subject areas of interest is also an important way of staying current and on the "cutting edge" of the technological developments in a selected field. The "experts" you meet can provide an invaluable resource for your creative activities.

Do not attend a technical meeting only to listen to the technical papers. That is a small part of the activity—you can nearly always learn the same information at home by reading the technical papers. Do attend the technical meeting to ask questions of the authors and speakers. Do attempt to read the paper ahead of time and then listen to the speakers to pick up on subtle points. Do attempt to corner the speaker(s) after their presentations and discuss their work and how it might relate to your work.

Attend professional meetings to socialize with your colleagues. Have coffee, a drink or go out to dinner with them. Some of the best, most creative ideas are born in such an environment. You have the stimulation of technical presentations and displays, the freedom of a new environment away from the familiarity and pressures of school or work, and the fantastic opportunity to meet people from around the world with similar interests but different approaches and philosophies. Make use of these for creative discussions!

Creative individuals share common characteristics

Creativity can be developed. Study the following list of characteristics that most creative people exhibit. You can cultivate your creative abilities by consciously trying to think and act in these ways.

1. **Sensitive** — the ability to be in touch with the people-related aspects of problems. This implies being aware of social values,

aesthetics and moral issues.

2. **Flexible** — the presence of mind to view each mental frame of reference as acceptable until a better one can be developed or recognized. To assume that an absolute position or frame of reference exists for any given design problem is absolute folly.

3. **Curious** — each situation or event must be viewed in the light of the question why? Anyone who knows "how" can find a job working for the person who knows "why!"

4. **Confident** — an inherent belief in your abilities to be successful. An important element is to recognize your limitations, seek additional sources of help and information, and to accept failure as a new starting point.

5. **Patient** — a willingness to set a problem aside while encouraging the subconcious to continue to struggle with the problem. Don't permit the lack of proper scheduling to rob you of the opportunity to reflect on problems without the pressures of deadlines. (This is not to be confused with procrastination).

6. **Motivated** — an excitement about solving the problem or putting in place a design process which will produce a solution. Remember, problems are solved by systematically and methodically bringing together a set of basic "elements" which are assembled into a "solution."

7. **Analytical** — a process of breaking problems into parts and determining all pertinent relationships among them. Ask the questions "Does my problem exist in any other frame of reference?" and "How is it related?"

8. **Synthetical** — a process of combining solution "elements" into a potential solution. Basically the reverse of analysis, the iterative combination of synthesis and analysis is crucial to the design process and extremely productive.

Match and complement your talent

It is nearly impossible to find a designer who exhibits in equal measure all the characteristics of a creative person listed above. Even if they did, the magnitude of real-world design problems would restrict their activities to only a few design functions. For example, a person strong in computer stress analysis using finite elements may not be good at testing, costing, or synthesizing. Design teams should match people's emotional traits and technical talents in a complementary fashion.

Without question your early development, childhood experiences, fear of failure, fear of success and degree of perfectionism will affect your success as a design engineer. Be aware of your talents and of certain subconcious attitudes and beliefs which have an important impact on your ability to function as a design engineer.

The engineer with an analytical mind needs an intuitive mind to guide and develop a sense of direction. The intuitive person needs a counterpart who can empathize or feel the emotional content of the design project. The feeling person often experiences widely different emotional high or low states and needs an analytic thinker to even out these swings in emotional responses. The important observation to make is that whatever subconcious states you possess, you must view them as assets to be blended with others. Contribute your strengths!

Provide a creative environment

You are a manager. You manage yourself, and you manage others, if only through informal methods. Help provide a stimulating and productive environment for your design group. Obviously, the engineering manager has the responsibility and self-interest to provide a creative environment. Not so obviously, you too have the responsibility and self-interest to provide a creative environment. Providing this environment involves a myriad of policies including the following (Harriott and Jarrett, 1978):

1. Freedom to question and power (even small) to change the status quo.

2. Freedom to investigate peripheral research.

3. Freedom to pursue an unconventional approach.

4. Freedom to fail.

5. Stimulating work assignments.

6. Motivation for excellence.

7. Recognition for creative effort.

8. Reward for originality.

9. Support for external association activities and personal contact development.

10. Flexibility to accommodate individual characteristics and personal goals.

11. Enthusiasm and support.

References

1. Buhl, H.R. 1960. Creative engineering design. Iowa State University Press, Ames, 195 pp.

2. Harriott, B.L. and F.L. Jarrett. 1978. Boundless creativity. ASAE Paper 78-5505. ASAE, St. Joseph, 49085.

3. Jones, J.C. 1980. Design methods: — Seeds of human futures, 2nd ed. Wiley & Sons, New York, 407 pp.

4. Raudsepp, E. 1983. What makes an engineer creative? *Graduating Engineer*, Sept., McGraw Hill.

5. Von Oech, Roger. 1983. A wack on the side of the head: How to unlock your mind for innovation. Warner Books, New York, 141 pp.

Discussion problems

1. Divide into teams and brainstorm about ideas for a better lawn mower (i.e., a means for maintaining an even, lush, low profile, thick, etc. lawn).

2. Have a class contest to identify the machine that "should never have been built" and to suggest a better alternative.

3. Invite an industry engineer to come to class. Based upon the description of the company and its production capabilities, use class teams to brainstorm new product ideas for that company.

4. Tour an implement dealership or a trade show as a class and discuss design problems and possible solutions for the equipment present.

Project problems

1. Set aside all possible solutions that you have considered up until now to your present design problem or to a specific subproblem. Now develop one more new solution!

2. Repeat project problem 1.

3. Combine the best features of the two new solutions from project problems 1 and 2 above to form a third solution.

Chapter 9
Help from Others

*"Your problem is **sorting**,
not **finding**, information."*

*"Opinions should be formed with great caution
and changed with greater." Josh Billings*

Who knows?
Who is right?
How do you find the important stuff?

Detective or engineer, the questions are the same. So, lean back and think about these questions. Who knows something about your problem? Think about who has a financial stake in understanding the problem — they probably know a lot. Are they willing to talk about it? Have they likely written about it somewhere? Who can give you leads to someone who knows even more? This chapter lists some common (but unknown to many people) sources of information which you can use as a checklist in your search for relevant information.

Who is right? Half of what you read and hear is probably *wrong*. Sometimes this may be deliberate, but more often it results from the writer or speaker simply not realizing he has misinformation. Science is a continual process of discovery, which often disproves theories previously accepted as fact by the best minds in the field.

Samuel Clemmens (Mark Twain) once stated that the most important trait needed to be a good writer is a "built-in, foolproof crap detector." This is true for engineers as well. You need to develop a healthy skepticism about even the most reliable and trusted sources of information. How do you sift through the maze of available information to find what is relevant? How do you even know what is relevant? Those are tough but important questions in design engineering. The task is becoming more difficult exponentially because the volume of information published and the number of people working on research and development are increasing exponentially. Computers make it possible to develop, record and retrieve voluminous information *and* misinformation. Ironically, this makes the personal, professional contacts more important as a means of finding and sorting information.

The ultimate reliability of the information you gather is difficult to evaluate. The process of sifting, organizing, and fitting together your design project information should be so constructed as to facilitate this reliability evaluation. First of all, you must recognize a degree of hierarchical reliability. Standards are considered the most authoritative and reliable since they reflect the combined knowledge and experience of a wide variety of engineers practicing within the specific discipline or problem area. Testing and certification organizations that operate in the public interest also generally produce highly reliable information. Scientific literature which is published only after a critical review by selected peers should be considered the next most reliable information. Information from trade journals constitutes the next lower general class of reliability while manufacturers' sales literature probably contains less information of engineering importance as well as being less reliable. The popular press is often the least reliable information source, but at other times is both reliable and unbiased. The reputation and thoroughness of the popular press source is critical in assessing its reliability.

However, there is a timeliness factor which operates in the reverse direction of this hierarchy of reliability. New ideas and discoveries often surface in trade magazines and sales literature only to be incorporated into standards or technical journals years later. These new ideas and discoveries are often mingled with a preponderance of misinformation and false starts; so, new ideas are easily overlooked.

Finally, your information gathering should be organized and planned to provide double or multiple checks in the form of two or more independent source confirmations for crucial design information. If material strength is vital to the design from a human safety point of view, don't simply use the ultimate strength listed in the sales literature without other independent verification.

The best library information is in the reference section

The first thing you do when you need information is to look in the subject index in the book section of the library or in the periodicals index, right? These are important and will provide some leads, but there is much more information in the library. The reference section provides lists of manufacturers, standards on products, handbooks of engineering data and details on the financial conditions of organizations you may wish to contact. The reference librarian can direct you to patent abstracts, specialized directories and computerized search techniques that you probably have never used. Following is a list of information sources often available in libraries.

1. Books and periodicals which are identified by subject matter and author catalogs (be skeptical of books and magazine articles because simply publishing something does not make it true). These can also be checked using special computer search routines.

2. Business reference section

(a) Standard and Poors (Standard and Poors is a business rating service which publishes "Industry Surveys," "Credit Overview," "The Outlook," "Daily Dividend Record," "Statistical Service," "Register of Directors and Executives," "Register of Corporations " and "Corporate Records". These list corporate addresses, phone numbers, key personnel, stock data and significant business data.

(b) Moody's is a financial rating and stock investor reference similar to Standard and Poors.

(c) Value Line is another financial rating and stock investor reference.

(d) Dunn and Bradstreet is a fourth financial rating and stock investor reference.

(e) Wall Street Journal Index is a publication in which articles are indexed by firm name and by article subject.

3. Manufacturer lists

(a) Thomas Register categorizes a wide range of products alphabetically and lists business names and phone numbers by state from whom the products can be purchased. The most widely used and comprehensive manufacturer list, these also include information on the size of the company using ratings of A, AA, AAA, AAAA and X.

(b) Sweets Catalog of architectural products and manufacturers are organized by products.

(c) Farmer/Contractor/Dealer Indices list products which

I'VE JUST BEEN LOOKING FOR
SOMETHING TO TURN WATER
INTO FUEL.

appeal to an industry segment (e.g., Pork Producers Index, Farm Builders Index, Implement and Tractor's Red Book).

(d) Yellow Pages (from telephone directories) for several cities are often in libraries. Also Electronic Yellow Pages (on microfiche or in computer data banks) are available in some libraries.

(e) State directories of manufacturers by the SIC (Standard Industrial Classification) Codes are available in some states. The SIC major classifications are: (1) agriculture, forestry and fishing, (2) mining, (3) construction, (4) manufacturing, (5) transportation and public utilities, (6) wholesale trade, (7) retail trade, (8) finance, insurance and real estate, (9) services and (10) public administration. Within manufacturing there are over 600 classifications such as "3519 — internal combustion engines" and "3535 -conveyors and conveying equipment".

4. Professional society materials are available from organizations of individuals with interest and expertise on particular subjects.

(a) ASAE (The American Society of Agricultural Engineers)

publishes: (a) a book of standard and engineering practices annually, (b) a membership roster with addresses and phone numbers annually, (c) a yearbook with committee membership, comprehensive list of ASAE publications indexed by subject and author and general information annually, (d) two bi-monthly magazines (one in newspaper form) with general interest material (e) *Transactions of the ASAE* bi-monthly and (f) specialized materials (e.g., "Ventilation of agricultural structures" monograph, "Agricultural energy" conference proceedings). The *Transactions of the ASAE* prints technical articles that *have been reviewed by experts for accuracy*. ASAE Papers may be available on microfiche; these include papers presented at national meetings, but these *have not* been reviewed by experts.

(b) ASHRAE (The American Society of Heating, Refrigerating and Air Conditioning Engineers) publishes handbooks, develops standards, lists equipment manufacturers , publishes a Transactions similar to the *Transactions of the ASAE*, reprints technical papers, and publishes a monthly magazine.

(c) There are several others. SAE (Society of Automotive Engineers), ASME (American Society of Mechanical Engineers) and NSPE (National Society of Professional Engineers) are a few of the many other professional societies which may have information relative to your design problem (Appendix II). Professional societies are particularly valuable because they are likely to be one of the most accurate information sources and because they can also direct you to legitimate experts.

5. Trade societies are organizations of companies manufacturing or selling similar types of products.

(a) FIEI (The Farm Industrial and Equipment Institute) is an organization of companies which produce agricultural equipment. It develops standards proposals, sponsors research on topics of concern to member companies and supports agricultural engineering student/industry activities.

(b) Numerous other trade societies relate to agricultural engineering. Some publish directories, standards or recommended practices. Trade societies often draft proposals or ideas for submission to professional societies or government agencies, and these often form the basis for standards or laws.

6. Standards groups are organizations which exist solely to develop standards. These may be voluntary, meaning supported by financial contributions from affected companies and through sales of the standards publications or they may be governmental with compliance mandated by law.

(a) ASTM (The American Society for Testing of Materials) is a voluntary standard organization which has a 66 volume set of standards specifying rating and testing procedures for building and machine components. This is a highly-respected umbrella standards organization. General subjects include (a) iron and steel products, (b) nonferrous metal products, (c) metal test methods and analytical procedures, (d) construction, (e) petroleum products, lubricants and fossil fuels, (f) paints, related coating and aromatics, (g) textiles, (h) plastics, (i) rubber, (j) electrical insulation and electronics, (k) water and environmental technology, (l) nuclear, solar and geothermal energy, (m) medical devices, (n) general methods and instrumentation and (o) general products, chemical specialties and end-use products.

(b) ANSI (The American National Standards Institute) is a voluntary standards organization which has a $25,000 plus multi-volume set of standards pertaining to equipment, building and environmental safety and reliability. ANSI is The United States coordinator of all U.S. voluntary standards under the auspices of The International Organization For Standardization. It crosslists many ASAE, SAE, ASTM and other engineering society standards, encompassing nearly all professional, technical societies.

(c) Federal Government Standards such as The National Bureau of Standards (NBS), the Occupational Safety and Health Act (OSHA), the Environmental Protection Agency (EPA), the Housing and Urban Development Department (HUD), and the Farmers Home Administration (FHA), all establish mandatory standards. Some government standards apply only if you are working with or receiving financial assistance from the government entity. Some standards are for the public benefit and are mandatory regardless of government participation in your work.

(d) State and local government standards, building codes, planning codes, engineering certification codes and safety codes are law for many state and local government groups. These most commonly apply to building and land development projects, but there are exceptions.

7. Insurance company codes and data. Insurance companies have a major financial concern for human safety, building longevity and equipment reliability. They develop the *National Electric Code*, which is almost universally accepted as *the* source on electric wiring. They develop the *National Fire Codes* which are incorporated into many government codes. They are the source of financial support for many codes and standards which ultimately appear as laws or as voluntary standards approved by professional societies.

8. Testing agencies

(a) Nebraska Tractor Test Center, mandated by state law, requires that all tractors sold in Nebraska be tested for performance and efficiency at the Nebraska Tractor Test Center. Virtually all farm tractors sold in the U.S. are tested there. Abbreviated or condensed Nebraska Tractor Test reports are in the ASAE Yearbook, more detailed reports are probably in your library.

(b) AMCA (The Air Movement and Control Association) is the accepted standard testing and rating agency for air moving equipment. They publish information on air movement in buildings on fan design and on fan testing. They guarantee that all fans certified deliver air within 2.5% of the manufacturer's claims.

(c) PAMI (The Prairie Agricultural Machinery Institute) tests farm implements and rates their performance and power requirements.

9. University affiliated groups

(a) MWPS (The Midwest Plan Service) is a group of 12 North Central United States agricultural engineering departments. Building plans and building design information are published and updated on a regular basis. Some materials are directed toward engineers and some toward builders or farmers.

(b) NRAES (The Northeast Regional Agricultural Engineering Service) is patterned after the MWPS and operates in the Northeast United States. It publishes similar material but is more directed to specialty crops, greenhouses, small-farm agriculture and the part-time farmer.

(c) CAST (Council on Agriculture Science and Technology) is a group of agriculturalists and engineers. They study national, agriculturally-related problems and publish policy recommendations.

10. Patent abstracts

To obtain a patent, one must describe clearly the process or machine patented, and one must compare this potential product with competing technologies. Consequently, patents are an excellent source of information on products or processes which may relate to your design. Besides, you need to know which ideas are patented to minimize your chances of infringement (Chapter 22).

11. Company literature

Companies prepare detailed catalogs describing their products, and many include practical information on the correct uses of their products and on related scientific and engineering theory and practice. For example, Omega Corporation, maker of a variety of temperature, pressure and flow measuring devices, distributes one of the most complete handbook sets on temperature, pressure and flow measurement.

12. Company product line microfiche

Compilations of company product literature catalogs, arranged in a style similar to the Thomas Register, but with actual product specifications included, are available in large libraries and from some manufacturers. For example, the makers of axles are listed on microfiche and you can then see excerpts from the pages of each axle-manufacturers' catalog the axle product members which you need. All information is on microfiche, but a hard-copier is available to copy the microfiche on pages.

13. Business, scientific and engineering consultant directories

Market research companies and consultants specialize in selected industries and provide market trend reports for a fee. Scientific and engineering consultants specialize in technical subjects and can provide help for a fee.

Personal contacts are as important as literature for information

Personal contacts are perhaps the most important. The right people can help you sort through the volumes of information to find the important facts. Personal contacts can relay personal experience with new and emerging technologies as the result of recent personal experience. Anything you find in a book is usually *at least* 2 years old. That is out of date if you are working on a new design incorporating state-of-the-art techniques.

So, who are these personal contacts and how do you develop them? They include engineers, manufacturers, salesmen and users. Here is a helpful list:

1. Professional contacts

(a) Colleagues you have met at ASAE (or from other professional and trade organization) technical meetings.

(b) Former classmates whose names you can now look up in the ASAE Directory.

(c) Colleagues you meet while working on design problems.

(d) Personal friends met through a wide variety of means, and who have relevant expertise.

2. Manufacturers

(a) Who makes products competitive with the type you are developing? Pick up their product literature and talk to them if possible.

(b) Who makes products with some similar features with the product you are developing? Find something unrelated but with some similar components. Ask them how the components work.

(c) Particularly look for mass-produced components or products that could possibly be used in your design. Mass-produced components can be orders of magnitude less expensive, plus they tend to be highly reliable. Often it is worthwhile to select a component with less than ideal features because it is mass-produced.

3. Salesmen/distributors/dealers

Salesmen are "user-friendly". These people can point out problems and strong points that the manufacturer may not know about or be willing to discuss. They can guide you to unique situations (e.g., product failures and peculiar applications). You will make a serious mistake if you do not check with these people.

For the typical product engineer, vendor sales representatives are a very important resource. Many of these people are engineers and are in constant dialog with other (competitor) engineers working on similar problems. They can offer some valuable suggestions and offer insight on potential problems.

4. Users

These people can point out problems without that salesman's facade. They know their needs better than anyone else. They may be misusing the product and you need to know about that. Obviously a good salesman and the manufacturer know how to care for the product. Does the user? If not, is it because instructions are poorly written, because he does not have time, or because it is too complicated? This information can help you improve on that design.

Don't be afraid to write letters or call

Appendix II contains a variety of sources of additional information. Do not hestitate to write or call any of these organizations. The primary reason many of these organizations exist is to act as clearinghouses for information. Remember to be as specific as possible in your request because a general request will usually result in a non-specific response. Appendix II has been arranged by general subjects to help you in locating an appropriate information source.

References

1. Todd, Alden, 1972. Finding facts fast. William Morrow and Company, New York. 109 pp.

Discussion problems

1. Determine which major agricultural machinery and manufacturers earned profits of 10% or more last year.

2. Identify the professional societies which have standards related to grain augers and summarize the contents.

3. Identify the Butler Manufacturing Company (Kansas City) subsidiaries and discuss. What products do they manufacture?

4. Find 10 manufacturers of gears in the Chicago metropolis.

5. Who makes farm loaders world-wide?

6. Refer to Chapter 22 and select one patent to be reviewed in as much detail as practical. Prepare a 2 minute oral class summary.

Project problems

1. Find three or more references from the scientific literature that relate substantively to your current design project. List the reference in proper form; write a paragraph about how each reference is related to your current project.

2. Find three or more standards that relate substantively to your current design project. List the reference in proper form; write a paragraph about how each reference is related to your current project.

3. Find three or more patents that relate substantively to your current design project. List the reference in proper form; write a paragraph about how each reference is related to your current project.

4. Identify three or more standard parts that might be involved in your current design project and obtain by telephone or writing the current specifications, pricing and availability.

5. Call or visit two or more engineers and explain your current design project to them. Beforehand, prepare a specific list of questions about your problem that they can answer for you. Report your results to the class.

Chapter 10
Project Scheduling

*"There are two kinds of failures;
the man who will do nothing he is told,
and the man who will do nothing else."*

*"The world stands aside for someone who
knows where he is going."*

Millions of dollars and people's careers are at stake

Taking an idea from concept to product is expensive. New Holland estimates a minimum of $1 million to develop a new model implement if they already manufacture a similar implement (Crane, 1985). Even seemingly simple projects , such as a new machine component, involve considerable expense in terms of time and equipment usage. Design and production scheduling is a means for planning this development and estimating the cost.

Virtually all companies and organizations use formal methods for scheduling. Everyone from the beginning design engineer to the president accepts responsibility for this process and literally gambles their career on being successful. Computer methods are frequently used because progress can be programmed in and the project re-evaluated and updated daily.

Design and production scheduling involve projecting the financial, facilities, equipment, labor and expertise requirements to solve a problem. Scheduling is an estimation of "what, how much and when." Most organizations have several projects underway simultaneously, each in different stages of development. Scheduling involves weighing the demands of each and planning for efficient use of all resources.

Overall scheduling responsibility lies with management, but the engineers provide important inputs. Engineering design, market analysis, testing, manufacturing, product promotion and sometimes additional items are scheduled as parts of the product development process. Management can meet their scheduling responsibilities only with the help of the people involved with the project. Part of your design job is helping management plan and monitor the design project.

This planning is a give-and-take process. Your boss needs to know "what, how much, and when" you think you will need to solve the problem. Your group's requirements and estimates need to be coordinated with other groups' schedules and requirements. Your boss has to commit to solve the problem with X dollars in Y amount of time. The careers of both you and your boss are dependent on meeting such schedules.

Planning is never perfect and unforseen problems arise; so, don't expect that every project will stay on schedule. Your group needs to check progress relative to the plan on a frequent basis. If you discover a problem or anticipate a schedule change, inform your boss. You are in the game together and management is as concerned as you that things progress well. The last thing your superior needs is a surprise too late to act upon.

Scheduling can be viewed two ways. It can be viewed as an ogre hanging over you and causing stress. You can avoid developing and using the schedule. A more positive approach is to view the schedule as an incentive or goal. It can be a course of direction in the exciting game of engineering design and business. It can be a challenge and a means for unifying the design group to achieve a team goal. Those who view and use scheduling in the latter way fare the best and have the most fun!

Corporations first define activities which must be scheduled

It is instructive to review some of the methods and activities used by industry for project planning and scheduling. The scheduling process begins by identifying the tasks which must be completed. New Holland identifies the 21 activities that are required to complete an engineering design project from problem identification through the introduction to sales (Fig 10.1). Steps 1 through 6 explain how an idea is started, step 7 is the design development, steps 8 through 20 describe the testing, evaluation

New Holland Inc.

ENGINEERING DIVISION OPERATIONS

1. Ideas come from many sources, but are generally based on a need expressed by customers through Marketing, Service, Service Parts, Engineering or Management. These ideas end up in Engineering for initial evaluation and an attempt to turn them into a workable product.

2. Patentable ideas have an inception date established and an attempt is made to obtain a patent.

3. New concepts are sent to Engineering Development to take them from a concept to a workable idea. 30% to 50% may eventually get into production.

4. Design groups are: Combines; Balers; Harvesters; Hay Tools; Industrial Products; Spreaders and International.

5. Project proposal is written by the Product Committee consisting of Engineering, Manufacturing and Marketing members. Engineering member consults with Product Test, Drafting, Engineering Shop etc. and comes up with a budget request for the project. Marketing prepares forecasts and Manufacturing evaluates production and shipping.

6. Proposal includes other supporting data and is then presented to Management for approval. Reviews are held twice a year, but new projects may be approved at any time.

7. The design now starts and draftsmen are assigned as needed to produce layouts, sketches and a shop work order. A set of experimental prints are also sent to Manufacturing.

8. The Standardization Group evaluates the work orders for compliance with Engineering standards and parts standardization. Special approval is required for deviations from standards.

9. The first unit or units are made by hand in six to eight weeks. An assembly and servicing report is written by Product Test.

10. Product Test consists of a stress lab, mechanical lab and field testing operations. These are used to meet the pre-determined test objectives. Function can often be achieved in the first test season, but reliability and durability require an additional two years of a normal three year project. During this time an attempt is made to test in all possible field and crop conditions.

11. First units are up-dated in the shop or in the field and additional units are built for additional testing. A preliminary product test report is written stating how the project is progressing and pointing out possible problem areas, safety aspects, etc. Daily reports are received from all field units and monthly summary reports are written by all Product Test groups.

12. After objectives have been met, product design and drafting prepare drawings for preliminary release.

13. These drawings are checked for accuracy and given a last check for standards compliance.

14. The specifications section prepares microfilm cards, parts listed and cross references and issues approved information to Manufacturing.

15. Engineering changes are used to correct errors or improve items in line with late test results.

16. Product Test approval reports gives OK for final release.

17. Final release tells Manufacturing they may start tooling for manufacture.

18. Features, Operations and Performance Specifications are issued by Product Design to Marketing (Service included) listing what the unit will and will not do.

19. Machine for use by Advertising and Service is generally built by Engineering.

20. Final Product Test report gives approval for sale.

21. Unit is then introduced to the Sales Organization.

FIG 10.1 Product development activities list (Courtesy of New Holland Inc.).

and improvement of the design, and at step 21 the design is ready for marketing. Some companies use a grid and sign-off product scheduling system which has activities similar to those of New Holland. Approval of the plan by the entire corporate management which is affected by the plan may be required. This ensures communication and minimizes conflicts later over responsibilities and deadlines.

Corporate scheduling for a project varies in breadth and detail according to responsibility level.

Top-level corporate management coordinates major product development and marketing plans, manufacturing expansion or contraction, borrowing and investing of money, long-term corporate direction and similar issues involving major resource commitments. They want a broad picture, not the intimate detail of what you, in design engineering, will do this Tuesday.

The most critical project scheduling role of higher-level management is to continue support at each major development stage. Each project can be thought of as consisting of the following four stages: (a) product definition, (b) design and engineering tests, (c) reliability testing and (d) manufacturing. Through each of these four project stages the investment of capital grows exponentially. Likewise the level of confidence must increase significantly as the project progresses through the stages or the project will be halted. Most new product ideas do *not* emerge as products. Top level management usually reviews at or near the end of each major stage *before* a commitment of money is made for the next stage.

Middle-management (e.g., Director of Engineering or Product X Manager) tracks engineering design more closely. This person will probably meet with the design team during the problem definition stage so that cooperatively they can schedule each individual's time and specific equipment needs. The proposal, design development and testing steps from New Holland (Fig 10.1) are defined in more detail to ensure that all necessary steps are scheduled, using something like FMC Corporation's Project Identification List (Fig 10.2).

The manager responsible for the design will condense these details into major development phases and present the plan with budget estimates to higher level management. The higher level management will likely use a team approach with design, marketing, manufacturing, financial, and other affected middle-managers agreeing on the schedule and how they will work together.

You, the design engineer, schedule your detailed daily activities. Your boss, the design manager, will aid with the definition of project steps and the estimating of complexity. You must then decide how to achieve each step in the time available.

Corporate project scheduling crosses departmental boundaries

It is inefficient for the design engineer to have to work through one or more management levels, across to another department (e.g., sales, marketing, manufacturing) and back down one or more levels to learn the projections for sales or how a piece part will be manufactured. This may not be a serious problem for small companies or autonomous divisions, but it can be serious for large companies. A simple sign-off system works well for companies that are small enough to coordinate formally on the management level and informally across departmental boundaries.

Most large companies use some sort of formal or informal matrix scheduling system to bring together the most critical people from multiple departments at the early stages of the project. Deere and Company's (Skromme, 1983) matrix management scheme (Fig 10.3) is an excellent way to minimize bureaucratic time wastage without losing management control. Deere and Co. appoints a team of people with representation from departments which must be involved to study the problem, evaluate its feasibility and develop a schedule. The project manager for that team has management responsibilities similar to middle-management but perpendicularly in terms of organizational structure (i.e., the responsibilities cross departmental boundaries and are horizontal on the "tree-type" management structure chart). Chapter 21 discusses organizational structures in more detail.

CPM and PERT aid systematic scheduling of complex projects

Critical Path Method (CPM) and Program Evaluation and Review Technique (PERT) are similar methods of estimating and managing time requirements for projects which have interdependent (parallel and series) steps (Fig 10.4). Their advantages over the previously-discussed corporate scheduling methods are: (a) they show how steps interact (i.e., which steps are dependent on which others and in what sequence), (b) they allow a range of time estimates for each step (pessimistic, optimistic and most likely) so that the possibility of adjustments is more readily apparent and (c) they provide a method for identifying your most critical tasks for timely completion of the project and the necessary sequencing. A limitation of the method is that it requires event structures that are independent and can be completed without the interactive process (Fig III.1) which actually occurs.

Central Engineering Laboratories   **PROJECT STEP DEVELOPMENT**

Step 1—Engineering Analysis

1. Evaluation of requirements
   1.1 Consultation with Marketing and Industrial Design.
   1.2 Consultation with potential customers.
2. Prior technical art.
   2.1 Patents.
   2.2 Competition.
3. Conception & evaluation of alternative approaches.
4. Estimate of time and cost for all steps and special tooling.

5. Estimate of manufacturing cost.
6. Possible financial return.
7. Preliminary safety considerations.
8. Preparation of report to include:
   8.1 Analysis of critical technical elements.
   8.2 Performance requirements.
   8.3 Preliminary design specifications.
   8.4 Detailed recommendations including appropriation request for subsequent steps if necessary.

Step 2—Development Exploration & Research

1. Thorough study of alternatives.
   1.1 Calculations.
   1.2 Study layouts & schematics.
   1.3 Preliminary safety considerations.
   1.4 Conclusions.
2. Jury rig tests of untried principles.
3. Further check of patents.
4. Consultations with unbiased technical sources.
5. Consultation with Manufacturing, Marketing and Industrial Design.

6. Preparation of report to include:
   6.1 Summary of test results.
   6.2 Evaluation of potential technical success.
   6.3 Manufacturing feasibility of approach chosen.
   6.4 Review of Marketing Department comments.
   6.5 Revised estimate of total steps cost.
   6.6 Revised estimate of manufacturing cost.
   6.7 Recommendations & appropriation request for further work, if necessary.

Step 3—Development Model Design

1. Preparation of layouts.
   1.1 Initiate safety analyses (Hazard Analysis, FMECA, Operating Safety Analysis)
   1.2 Design/safety review
2. Re-check with Manufacturing, Marketing and Industrial Design.
3. Consultation with outside specialists.
4. Preparation of detail drawings.
5. Patent infringement investigation.
6. Issue drawings for development model

construction.
7. Preparation of report to include:
   7.1 Evaluation of progress to date.
   7.2 Re-evaluation of all costs.
   7.3 Discussion of necessary compromises.
   7.4 Recommendations for changes to specifications.
   7.5 Recommendations for future action and new appropriation request, if necessary.

Step 4—Development Model Construction

1. Update safety analyses.
2. Purchase materials.
3. Methodize.
4. Manufacture & shop tests.
5. Product Safety Committee Review.
6. Modifications.
7. Engineering liaison with Shop.

8. Preparation of report to include:
   8.1 Manufacturing feasibility.
   8.2 Recommendations for modifications to ease manufacturing problems.
   8.3 Review of manufacturing costs and projects costs to date versus estimate.
   8.4 Recommendations for future action and new appropriation request, if necessary.

Step 5—Development Model Test

1. Establish test specifications compatible with performance requirements.
   1.1 Update safety analysis.
   1.2 Design/safety review.
2. Installation and operation of model.
3. Installation of instrumentation.
4. Evaluation of test data.
5. Sales Department opinion.
6. Preparation of report to include:
   6.1 Comparison of test data with specifications.
   6.2 Recommended design changes.

   6.3 Revised specifications (if necessary) for production models.
   6.4 Re-evaluation of all costs, comparing with estimates.
   6.5 Re-evaluation of competition.
   6.6 Re-evaluation of success
       (a) Commerically (economics)
       (b) Technically
   6.7 Recommendations for future action and new appropriation request, if necessary.

Step 6—Production Model Design

1. Consultation with development engineers.
2. Consultation with outside specialists.
3. Re-affirmation that device which has been developed to date will meet specifications.
   3.1 Update safety analysis
   3.2 Design/safety review.
4. Preparation of layouts, details, assemblies.
5. Bills of Material.
6. Set up liaison with development engineer for his confirmation that final drawings will meet performance specifications.
7. Re-check patents.

8. Cost reduction studies.
9. Manufacturing and tooling cost estimates.
10. Re-check with Marketing and Sales.
11. Preparation of report to include:
    11.1 Discussion of how well design will meet specifications.
    11.2 Prediction of manufacturing difficulties.
    11.3 Recommendation for areas of future cost reduction effort and/or changes to improve saleability.
    11.4 Other recommendations for future action including appropriation request, if necessary.

Step 7—Production Model Construction

1. Update safety analysis.
2. Temporary tool design and manufacture (if production type required, apply to Step 10).
3. Purchase materials.
4. Methodize.
5. Manufacture and shop test.
6. Product Safety Committee review.
7. Modifications.
8. Engineering liaison.
9. Preparation of report to include:
   9.1 Actual manufacturing and tooling costs compared to estimates.
   9.2 Evaluation of manufacturing problems.
   9.3 Recommendations for improvement.

Step 8—Production Model Test

1. Establish test plan compatible with performance requirements.
2. Check with development engineer who tested previous model for common problems.
3. Update safety analysis.
4. Safety review.
5. Installation and operation.
6. Evaluation of test data.
7. Impartial evaluation preferably by competent technical man not connected with organization.
8. Customer reaction—Sales Department?
9. Preparation of report to include:
   9.1 Comparison of test results with performance specifications.
   9.2 Recommended modifications for first production lot.
   9.3 Recommended final inspection.
   9.4 Review of competition.
   9.5 Review and re-evaluation of success.
       (a) Commercially (economics)
       (b) Technically.
   9.6 Recommendations for future action and appropriation request, if necessary.

Step 9—Final Engineering Drawing

1. Finalize drawings and bills of material.
2. Update safety analyses.
3. Special engineering-manufacturing instructions.
4. Preparation of data for installing operating and servicing.
5. Product Safety Committee Review.
6. Training service personnel.
7. Release of drawings.
8. Preparation of final report to include:
   8.1 Review of all costs compared to estimates.
   8.2 Final review of economics with current prediction for sales obtained from Sales Department.
   8.3 Review of engineering performance noting areas which should be improved.
   8.4 Further recommendations.
9. Disposition of equipment, material, etc.

Step 10—Special Tooling

CEL 502 (8/82)

FIG 10.2 Detailed project development task identification list (Courtesy of FMC Corp.).

Before considering an example, let us develop a basic understanding of the terminology and the scheduling process. The CPM/PERT schedule is a flow diagram (Fig 10.4) which consists of arrows (activities) connecting numbered circles (events). The activities are often synonymous with the event, (e.g., conduct market survey is an activity while market survey completed is an event). In some cases several activities combine to form one completed event, (e.g., prototype complete is the event which results from the activities of fabricating sub-assemblies A, B, C and D). Clearly if any of the four sub-assembly fabrications are delayed or incomplete, then the final event, prototype complete, will not occur. Arrowheads indicate the sequence (direction) in which the activities and events must occur. Sometimes it is necessary to show the interdependence or precedence of one event over another by a dashed-line arrow called a dummy activity. No more than one activity (arrow) may ever be used between any two path nodes (events). The critical path is defined to be the sequence

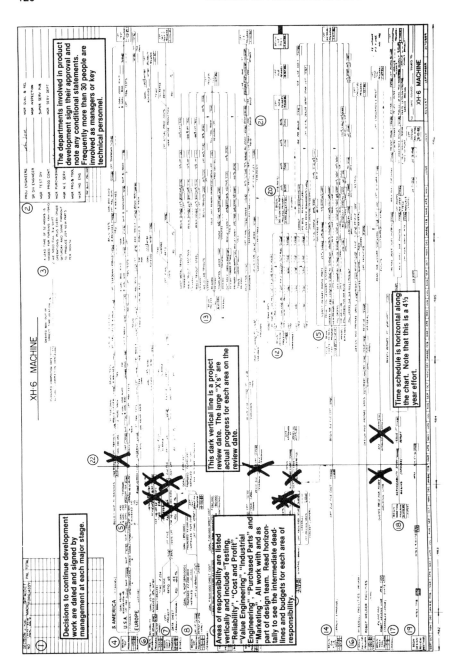

FIG 10.3 Matrix style project schedule adapted from Skromme, (1983) (Courtesy of Deere and Co.).

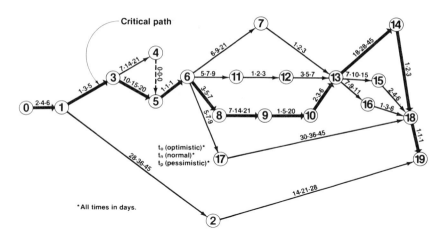

FIG 10.4 CPM/PERT flow diagram for insulation tester.

Table 10.1 Task list for the CPM/PERT insulation tester example

Node	Event
0.	Begin (time equals zero)
1.	Problem definition complete
2.	Market survey complete
3.	Specifications (objectives) developed
4.	Concept A (temperature profile method) study complete
5.	Concept B (heat loss supplied and measured) study complete
6.	Concept A or B selected
7.	DVM and circuitry constructed
8.	Thermal resistivity decided upon for sensor
9.	Device built to measure thermal resistivity of sensor accurately
10.	Thermal resistivity of sensor calibrated
11.	Case constructed
12.	Diodes calibrated
13.	Prototype complete
14.	Theoretical analysis of heat transfer complete
15.	Theoretical analysis of propagation of error complete
16.	Experimental operation conducted
17.	Patent disclosure filed
18.	Patent application filed
19.	Marketing arrangements signed

of events which requires the longest time to complete and hence controls the earliest project completion date. Activities on the critical path are shown as heavy arrows.

For example, consider the list of events given in Table 10.1 which must be completed during the engineering design of an insulation tester. Each event is included in the diagram (Fig 10.4). Illustrated in this figure is the use of a dummy variable between events 5 and 4. This dummy activity says that both events 4 and 5 must be completed before activity (arrow) leading up to event 6 can begin.

Each activity (arrow) in Fig 10.4 has three completion time estimates: the optimistic (shortest), t_o, the normal (expected), t_n, and the pessimistic (longest), t_p. These time estimates are based upon past company activities or experience. The inexperienced practitioner or student will find it difficult to make meaningful time estimates. These time estimates can be made in any convenient but consistent set of units, (i.e., hours, days, weeks, etc.).

The details of the CPM/PERT calculations are not considered here since there are many software packages available on micro to mainframe computers, or you can refer to Hill (1970) or Hillier and Lieberman (1974). More important are the results of these calculations and their utility to the project manager. Computer techniques are especially well-suited because the project manager can program in actual progress and the computer can then re-evaluate critical paths quickly and revise the schedule if necessary.

CPM uses one set of time estimates

The critical path method (CPM) works with a single set of completion time estimates for each activity; usually, the normal time estimates are used. For each activity leading between two nodes in the network, the earliest starting time (EST) and the latest completion time (LCT) are calculated based upon the completion times required for all preceeding activities in the network. Both the EST and the LCT are accumulative, starting at zero initially, and ending at the critical path length. If the difference between the LCT and EST is *greater* than the time estimate for any activity, then the surplus time is called the slack time (ST). The slack time for events on the critical path is zero.

Let us return to the example of Table 10.1 and Fig 10.4. Thus, if the normal time estimates for each activity prove to be true, the entire project can be completed in no fewer than 77 days. Slack times indicate the maximum delay for beginning each step with no expected delay in project completion (see Table 10.2).

A Gantt chart usually accompanies a CPM diagram (Fig 10.5). Each activity is represented by an open horizontal bar over a

Table 10.2 CPM analysis of the normal time estimates shown in the network in Fig 10.4.

Nodes		Activity Times		
From	To	EST	LCT	ST
0	1	0	4	0
1	2	4	56	16
1	3	4	7	0
2	19	40	77	16
3	4	7	22	1
3	5	7	22	0
4	5	21	22	1
5	6	22	23	0
6	7	23	44	12
6	8	23	28	0
6	11	23	39	9
6	17	23	40	10
7	13	32	46	12
8	9	28	38	0
9	10	38	43	0
10	13	43	46	0
11	12	30	41	9
12	13	32	46	9
13	14	46	74	0
13	15	46	72	16
13	16	46	73	18
14	18	74	76	0
15	18	56	76	16
16	18	55	76	18
17	18	30	76	10
18	19	76	77	0

The Critical Path Length is: 77

corresponding sequential time and date scale. The left end of each bar is the EST for that activity while the right end is at the LCT. In non-critical events the slack time is shown as the left-most cross-hatched section of the bar graph.

Interactive project scheduling occurs when the project manager shades in each bar on the Gantt Chart as the individual tasks are completed. The necessary sequencing of each task is clearly visible in the Gantt Chart and total project timeliness is easily viewed.

PERT uses a range of times for each task

A PERT analysis, on the other hand, takes into account the uncertainty of completing each activity in the exact time estimated as the normal time. For each activity the pessimistic, normal and

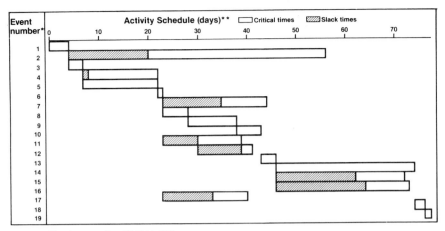

*Events are numbered in Table 10.1.
**The activity schedule is created from Table 10.2 using normal times.

FIG 10.5 Gantt chart for the insulation tester example (Tables 10.1, 10.2, and Fig. 10.4).

optimistic times are combined to produce a normally-distributed random time variable for each activity. Based upon many repeated samplings of each activity's distribution, a number of different critical path lengths are estimated. Indeed the critical path goes through different events based upon the random event completion times produced. After several hundred random critical paths are analyzed, it is possible to produce the probability distribution of the critical path lengths (Fig 10.6). Thus, we see that there is a 50%

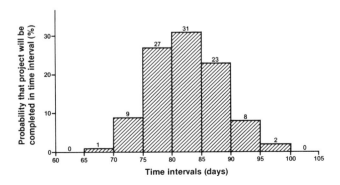

FIG 10.6 The probability that the insulation tester will be finished during a specified time interval using both mean and variabilities of time estimates (Fig 10.4) in a probabilistic analysis.

chance that the project completion will take longer than 83 days compared with the normal time estimates from the CPM analysis of only 77 days.

Advice to students from Ken Finden, University of Arizona and retired Toro engineering manager.

"Estimating project time schedules and costs are rather imprecise tasks. Most are based on experience, and engineers typically underestimate both costs and time. One of the best estimating tools is a detailed PERT or CPM project plan. Just the act of working out the details forces consideration of each step.

"I've used the bar-chart schedule (Fig 10.7) to guide co-op students working on a one-semester design project. Notice that actual project activities overlap considerably. Also, notice that project analysis and experimental activities can extend over

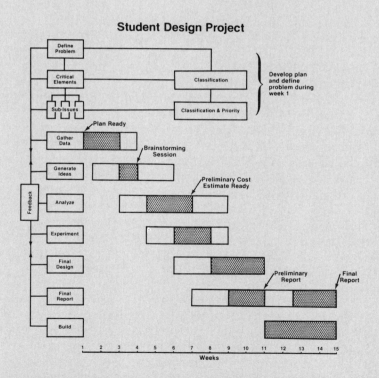

FIG 10.7 A one-semester student design project activity organizing and scheduling chart.

virtually the entire process; however, their missions change as the project progresses from broad concepts, to refining details, to finalization and validation.

"First, identify the project with faculty assistance (see chapter 7 advice). After identifying the project, it's equally important to back away and, with faculty assistance, classify the project in broader terms. Is this a human engineering, heat transfer, fluid mechanics or a power transmission design? Classification will help the literature search and priority assignments; particularly if there is new technology available in the projects design field, the students need to brush up on the fundamentals involved or a specific issue needs resolution before the project can proceed. With this information established, the student with faculty assistance should then be able to establish the project plan by the end of *week 1*.

"*Weeks 2 and 3* should be directed toward intensive literature searching and data collection including field data such as soil samples, surveys, etc. Another week or two will be needed for turn-around time on inquiries, and there will also be added information needed all during the project, but making this concentrated effort early in the project is important. *Week 4* should be set aside for a little blue-sky day dreaming about all the possible alternative design options no matter how ridiculous or unlikely they might be. An excellent milestone event would be a formal brainstorming session in *week 4*.

"Analysis of all the design options can then begin in *week 5*. Many alternatives can obviously be quickly rejected with a few calculations, others will require more detailed calculations, layouts and cost analysis. A preliminary cost estimate could be a second milestone event for *week 6 or 7*. There will always be a few design options with both advantages and disadvantages with no clear best design where the student will need to learn to accept trade-offs and make a few arbitrary design decisions. Then there will always be one or two tantalizing ideas that can't really be qualified without testing and experimentation to determine feasibility.

"The experimental phase can begin shortly after analysis begins and the two activities progress simultaneously. A student project may not have time for extensive experimentation but bread-board prototypes, scale models and individual components can be tested. Mathematical or computer models can also be used.

"If the design is relatively small and intended to be built within the semester schedule, the final design phase involving producing the working drawings and specifications to build the design should start by about *week 8* and be due by *week 11*. The report activity starting about *week 9* could be a preliminary report due *week 11;* then the final report and drawing package due *week 15*.

In summary, it's important to fit the plan to the project, and as the feed back arrows show in Fig 10.7, continually refine and review the initial parameters in the view of new information. Creative engineering is the recognition of unanticipated opportunities."

Timely decision-making is an important part of scheduling

Indecision is an important source of delays. This is particularly true for the young or inexperienced design engineer. As we have seen in Chapter 7, problems of interest to engineers fall into three types: factual, judicial and creative. Since answers to factual problems are often difficult to find with a sufficient level of accuracy, the real decision to be made is how much effort should be expended in the search. For example, it may be important in your problem analysis to know the coefficient of dynamic friction of steel on green oak, or the specific volume of air dried-chicken manure, or the static pressure drop through rough rice, etc. You, the design engineer, must decide how much time to spend searching the literature until you find the answer, or, conclude that this type of information is not available. If it is unavailable, then decide how much time you can spend experimentally measuring the information or calculating it based on data from similar materials. How important is accurate information relative to the costs of obtaining it and the cost of delays to the overall project schedule?

Decisions for judicial and creative problems can be an order of magnitude more difficult than for factual problems. Usually, facts are involved as subparts of the problem, plus the decision must be made with the effects of different choices somewhat unknown and without ever knowing whether you are aware of all the options.

The Kepnor-Traegner decision matrix is a tool for systematic decision making

Decision matrices can be applied to a variety of engineering and non-engineering judicial problems (e.g., choosing among several

Factors	Weighting factor	Alternatives					
		Iowa State	N. C. State	S. D. State	Texas A&M	University Florida	University Texas
Fees and tuition costs	35%	6 / 2.1	9 / 3.2	7 / 2.4	9 / 3.2	5 / 1.8	5 / 1.8
Distance from home	25%	4 / 1.0	9 / 2.1	3 / .8	4 / 1.0	7 / 1.8	10 / 2.5
Climate	20%	5 / 1.0	8 / 1.6	5 / 1.0	8 / 1.6	10 / 2.0	8 / 1.6
Distance from grandparents	15%	8 / 1.2	5 / .8	10 / 1.5	5 / .8	4 / .6	6 / .9
Family nostalgia	5%	10 / .5	7 / .4	8 / .4	4 / .2	4 / .2	4 / .2
Total	100%	5.8	8.2	6.1	6.8	6.4	7.0

Note that Student x's first choice is North Carolina State (8.2) with University of Tennesee as the second choice (7.0).

FIG 10.8 Decision matrix applied to selecting a college or university.

design concept options, selecting test and computer equipment, deciding where you want to live or even choosing among job possibilities). The Kepnor-Traegner type of decision matrix (Fig 10.8) allows you to weigh the relative importance of each factor affecting the decision and to scale each alternative relative to the others for each factor.

Consider, as an example, a hypothetical student's (Student X) decision to enroll in Agricultural Engineering at North Carolina State University (Fig 10.8). Student X knew that he wanted to be an agricultural engineer (probably from a previous decision matrix used to select a major) and wants to choose from among six alternatives (specifically: Iowa State University, North Carolina State University, South Dakota State University, Texas A&M University, The University of Florida and the University of Tennessee). Home is just west of Asheville, North Carolina and the University of Tennessee is closer than North Carolina State University, but Student X would have to pay out-of-state tuition at Tennessee. Grandma and Grandpa live on a farm in South Dakota, and Student X would like to spend more time there. Mom and Dad are Iowa State grads, and it sure would be nice to go there. Student X has a rodeo scholarship at Texas A&M University and he has always loved the semi-tropical climate in Florida. Where should he go?

Student X can now construct a decision matrix by first listing the factors he wishes to base his decision on. Five factors are selected: (a) fees and tuition costs, (b) distance from home, (c) climate, (d) distance from grandparents and (e) family nostalgia.

Student X then weights each factor according to importance to him and decides that fees and tuition costs are 35%, distance from home 25%, climate 20%, distance from grandparents 15% and family nostalgia 5% (cumulatively totalling 100%). Now Student X rates each alternative on a scale from 1 to 10 for each factor and writes these ratings in the upper left-hand corners of the alternatives-versus-factors grid (Fig 10.8). Each ranking is then multiplied by the weighting factor and written in the lower right-hand corners of the grid. Finally, all the weighted rankings are totaled for each alternative and the best one is chosen. Student X attends North Carolina State University.

Characteristics of a good decision

Good decisions for judicial problems using a decision matrix have several important characteristics. As we have seen the decision maker must have a "stake" in the outcome. Often this is a personal desire simply to "be right." Sometimes it means jobs or careers are on the line. All valid alternatives must be included in the decision matrix. If any alternatives are omitted, the resulting decision will not be valid. Finally the decision matrix forces the decision maker to appraise all alternatives realistically, subject to all factors. Thus, decisions obtained represent the "best" decision possible based upon available information. Notice that many factors may be simply factual problems (e.g., fees, tuition and distance) while others are judgemental (e.g., climate, nostalgia, and weighting scale).

References

1. Crane, J. 1985. Personal communications. Director of research and development. New Holland Co. New Holland, PA

2. Hill, P. 1970. The science of engineering design. Holt, Rinehart and Winston, New York. 372 pp.

2. Hillier, Fredrick S. and Gerald J. Lieberman. 1974. Operations research, Holden-Day, San Francisco. 800 pp.

Discussion problems

1. Develop a decision matrix for selection of your career path upon completion of your present BS degree. Be prepared to discuss in class.

2. Discuss, from a realistic point of view, the relative maximum number of factors and alternatives that could enter into a typical decision.

Project problems

1. Develop a detailed schedule of specific design activities for your project along with a proposed completion time table.

2. Develop a decision matrix for a judgmental project problem.

3. Develop a CPM/PERT table of events and a network diagram for your design project. Identify the critical path for the normal completion time. What is the estimated normal completion time? What is the probability that your project will be completed by the normal time critical path length?

Part IV
How Shall I Develop This Design?

"When the going gets tough, the tough get going."

"Consider the turtle who only moves forward by sticking out its neck!"

CHAPTER CONTENTS

$$F = ma$$

11. Analysis

The ability to combine scientific theory, mathematics and empirically derived equations to solve practical design problems is the major difference between the engineering approach and the "blacksmith" approach. Real design problems are complex and require engineering judgments in the selection and use of analytical techniques.

12. Synthesis

Dissect the problem into parts, analyze each part; then, recombine the now better-understood parts to conceive alternative solutions. This creative and powerful capacity of the human brain to synthesize solutions is not possible in the largest electronic computers!

13. User Considerations

The physical and psychological needs and capabilities of humans, encompassed within the disciplines of ergonomics, human factors, safety engineering, environmental engineering, physiology and psychology, are important considerations in nearly all engineering designs. Engineers design for people.

14. Materials Selection

Composite materials, plastics, ceramics and alloys combined represent more than 80,000 materials already used by manufacturers. Materials selection today cannot be limited to steel, concrete and forest products if the design is expected to compete in quality and price.

15. Product Safety and Liability

There are systematic methods for engineering safe products. Engineering ethics should guide the design process. Product safety and the accompanying liability are important topics to the design engineer.

16. Cost Estimating

Money is a factor in all engineering activity. Value to the consumer dictates the allowable price, and the engineer must design so that the combined costs of materials, labor, overhead, sales and investment are less than this allowable price.

17. Component and Supplier Selection

"Value-added," the combination of manufactured, processed and raw materials to create products is the essence of engineering design and manufacturing. Even the largest companies routinely use components from other manufacturers in their products; so, it is essential that a design engineer be able to identify and draw upon the expertise of appropriate component suppliers.

18. Manufacturing Considerations

Each firm's manufacturing capabilities are different. Only by carefully matching the problem solution with manufacturing methods can optimally designed products be produced in a cost-effective manner.

19. Standardization and Simplication

Considerable effort is spent to produce the "best" design. Often significant cost reductions can be obtained by using standard parts and simplifying the design usually enhances customer acceptance.

20. Testing and Evaluation

Measuring and evaluating performance is essential for determining if the design performs as intended. Whether engineering tests to validate an important analysis or field tests by the end-user to determine mean time between in-service failures, the design process is heavily dependent upon this feedback.

You have a good start! You have defined your problem and design objectives. Your design specifications have been developed to measure your progress in meeting the overall objectives. By now you have researched your problem in the literature and perhaps even looked at related design problems. You may have created some preliminary designs. Now you need to "hammer-out" the final design, the complete specification of each and every last detail important to the success of your design project. How *exactly* will this thing be built or accomplished?

Perhaps the most interesting and rewarding phase of design now awaits you — the interlocking roles of analysis and synthesis. Undergraduate curricula are full of analyses courses in which *all* or nearly all the assumptions are given — just find the equation, fill in the values for the variables and out comes the answer. Not so in design work. Real-world problems do not lend themselves to assumptions of mass-less members, infinitely long flow-fields, rigid-end connections, perfectly elastic materials, homogeneous conditions, etc. Analytic and synthetic efforts must be combined with the practical considerations of materials, costs, safety and manufacturability to develop a good design. An exciting but complex task awaits you!

Complications in the design process will arise. Cost constraints are universally present. How do manufacturing methods impact costs? What about materials selection? Should parts be welded, bolted or fastened by other means? What about standard parts? Can you easily incorporate into the final design some standard parts without sacrificing functional design principles? And who will use your design — and what about their safety? It is the design engineer who bears the ultimate responsibility for addressing these questions as the final design is "hammered-out."

And lastly, it is not too soon to think about testing. Plan to redesign, rebuild and retest. Expect and don't be afraid to make mistakes, but learn from them. Design is a trial and error process. Remember, it is the final design that ultimately counts. (Design costs are important, too!) Don't be afraid to try some things that you believe have analytical bases for success; if they don't work, learn from what you observe; you are in the iterative design process of analysis and synthesis.

F = ma

Chapter 11
Analysis

"The obscure we see eventually, the completely obvious, it seems, takes longer."
Edward R. Murrow

"If you inadvertently stumble over the truth, don't get up and run off as if nothing happened."

This chapter is not intended to develop any specific, technical analysis but to show the role of technical analysis in the design process. As a student you have taken (or will take) strength of materials, thermodynamics, dynamics, fluids and a variety of more specialized courses to develop technical expertise in each area. Those courses are important. You can continue to develop technical expertise through graduate school, self learning, company training programs and continuing education.

This text is a general design methodology text oriented toward all specialties of agricultural engineering. There are general suggestions regarding technical analysis which are discussed here. It is expected that you, like your industry counterpart, will undertake the responsibility for learning the needed specialized technical subject matter required to solve your respective design problems.

Determine the relative novelty of your design problem

Most design efforts are directed toward improving existing products. The projects may be new and novel to the design engineer, but if the product is in production and in use by the customer, then much can and should be learned from those who service the product. Furthermore, analytic design methodologies were probably applied in the original and subsequent designs and these have continued to be refined. Often enough previous product history is known within a real service environment that the design process can rely heavily upon the analytic engineering tools available, with current field testing needed for only the critical design variables.

Also, note that nature has often produced deceptively simple solutions to complex problems. The flight of birds, oxygen intake by fish, photosynthesis and manual dexterity begin a nearly endless list. Consider whether your problem can be simplified by study of some such natural phenomena.

Approach technical analysis from a "bracketing" view

Real problems are complex. Rarely can you predict the loads and stresses on a machine part prior to building and testing. Seldom is the soil infiltration rate and the surface elevation uniform throughout an irrigated field. Try bracketing the problem.

For example, if you are designing the poles for a machine-storage pole building you can assume as a worst case that the pole is a cantilevered beam withstanding the wind load. You can assume a best case that the end walls absorb much of the wind loading through an action called the diaphragm effect. Experienced building designers know that the actual loads are somewhere in between. The end walls cannot support all of the horizontal wind loading, especially for poles located on the side walls several meters from the end wall. However, it is also known that the poles do not act as true cantilever beams to support all of the load. The experienced designer will calculate the pole stresses for both instances and effectively bracket the true stress. Once this range is calculated, engineering judgment is used to select a reasonable design load from the range.

Bracketing the desired design value can be approached from another point of view. Suppose you are designing a head-gate restraining device to be used for marking, vaccination, and other related animal health operations on hogs. What are the expected maximum design loads? Or to re-phrase the question, how quickly does a large hog decelerate when it runs head-long, at full speed, into the closed head gate at the end of the restraining chute?

You can estimate the maximum hog mass, the "terminal" velocity of an "upset hog" and the total deceleration time to yield an analytic estimate of the maximum deceleration force of the hog crashing into the head gate. But don't forget that you are not the first design engineer to face this question — what is the competition doing? How big is their head gate and what deceleration force will their head gate stand before the yield strength of the material is exceeded? Analysis is the process whereby the design engineer takes the problem apart into the related engineering variables.

Bracketing the desired value can take on still another meaning. Often the critical design conditions do not represent the intended purpose at all. When designing a flail knife forage plot harvester, the knife cutting forces for the harvested material, such as grass, are insignificant when compared with the cutter forces which result from the accidental intake of a stone!

Sensitivity analysis is a form of bracketing

Economists, business managers, and systems modelers routinely use a form of bracketing termed a "sensitivity analysis." This is because much of their work involves predicting the future, using equations which combine independent variables like inflation, interest rates, potential pork sales, and U.S. corn production. At best, these independent variables can be predicted only within a range of likely values.

A sensitivity analysis involves varying each independent variable from minimum to maximum expected values, while other independent variables are constant at their most likely values, to determine the effect of each independent variable on the dependent variable. For example, Van Zweden et. al. (1985) conducted a sensitivity analysis on the return on investment for an agricultural solar collector. Ten independent variables determine whether the solar system is a good investment (return on investment is the dependent variable) (Fig 11.1). Most importantly, this sensitivity analysis shows that the energy inflation rate is by far the most critical variable affecting return on investment; so, a potential investor would particularly scrutinize the likely trends on energy inflation before reaching a decision.

Sensitivity analyses can be more sophisticated and involve simultaneous varying of independent variables. Also, a probabilistic approach can be used for each independent variable to calculate the dependent variable range and the probability of the dependent variable being within increments of that range.

Be careful with equations

Most engineering equations are developed empirically. They

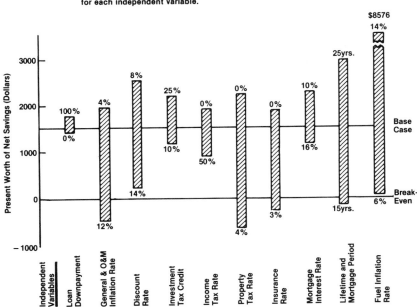

FIG 11.1 Sensitivity analyses on the effects of economic variables on the return on investment for an agricultural solar system.

are based on experimentation. There are usually simplifying assumptions necessary just to develop the equations. These equations are published often without clearly stating the assumptions and restrictions which apply. Now you come along with a new problem and a unique application. Chances are the equation has never been tried for applications similar to yours.

The problems encountered using solar and heat transfer equations to design agricultural solar collectors are an excellent example of this problem. Equations for sizing solar systems and selecting air flow rates were based on residential and commercial applications. These equations were not accurate for most agricultural applications, but many designers used the equations for lack of better equations. Furthermore, the Darcy-Weisbach equation for predicting static pressure losses through collectors is quite inaccurate using the same friction factors used in duct-work design. These equations were developed to predict friction loss through ducts, and they overpredict the friction losses through most collectors. Yet reading the literature suggests that the Darcy-Weisbach equation can be used in solar collector design.

Use simplifying assumptions or experimental approaches

The design of a self-feeding sorghum molasses mill is a good example of both simplifying assumptions and the use of experimentation. Basically, the design concept called for counter-rotating cylinders which would crush the sorghum stalks at the pinch-point of the rollers. The important design question was, "How big in diameter should the rollers be to insure that the sorghum material would be self-feeding?" Try to find the coefficient of friction between sorghum stalks and steel — it's not available! Yet, clearly there is some radius of the matched rollers large enough that self-feeding occurs even for the lowest imaginable coefficient of friction (as long as it is not zero).

The simplifying assumption is that at the region of contact, a curved surface, of radius r, can be approximated by a straight surface. The experiment consists of using a hinge arrangement made from the steel from which the rollers will be made (Fig 11.2). A maximum-diameter sorghum stalk is placed inside the hinge to approximate nearly exactly the conditions of self-feeding. As the hinge is closed slowly, the sorghum material slides to the right until the horizontal component of force exerted upon the sorghum is not sufficient to sustain horizontal motion by overcoming friction forces, and crushing begins. Noting the precise angular relationship between the hinged plates at the time of initial crushing permits the design engineer to answer a very difficult question satisfactorily.

Beware of computer models

Computer models are an excellent tool for evaluating alternatives for certain types of applications. For example, computer models for truss design, finite element analysis applied to certain machine parts, building heat transfer calculations,

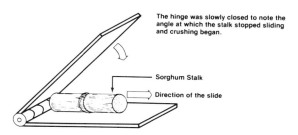

The hinge was slowly closed to note the angle at which the stalk stopped sliding and crushing began.

Sorghum Stalk

Direction of the slide

FIG 11.2 Experimental set up to evaluate geometry-friction effects on self-feeding for a sorghum juice mill.

statistical representation of random processes, systems modeling, differential equation solving and optimization algorithms have been proven over years of combining theory and experience (empirical data). The challenge is to determine how *your* design problem will benefit from these computer analyses.

But, do not accept computer outputs as fact any more than you would an empirical equation or a text. Many assumptions are necessary to develop even simple computer models. Consequently, models should be viewed as a method for obtaining "ball-park" solutions and as a check on ideas. Computers are no substitute for thinking, testing and critical analysis.

Try using some fundamental laws of science

This is another method for checking whether you are in the "ball-park." We know conservation of energy applies, except in nuclear reactions. If you are designing a solar collector, you cannot collect more energy than is available. You can look-up how much solar radiation strikes the earth by location and time of year. If you are designing a grain-drying solar system, you know that you can expect an efficiency in the range of 40%. Consequently, you can calculate approximately how much solar energy you can reasonably expect to collect during a typical drying season.

Don't be afraid to use equations in any way that assists your design efforts and is, of course, mathematically correct. Analysis combined with sound reasoning can be a powerful tool for a subset of the problems you will need to solve in each project. Suppose, for example, that you are designing a machine or process that requires a continuous rate of deformation of the process material. Perhaps you are deforming small diameter steel stock to make reinforcing type material. The question is how much power is required to provide this continuous deformation process? After a little thought, you should realize that the power required to deform steel (P) is approximated closely by:

$$P = q * E$$

where q is the time rate of volumetric deformation in l^3/t and E is the modulus of elasticity in f/l^2 resulting in the fundamental power units of f-l/t.

List engineering variables

Unless you can list *all* the engineering variables *with units* that define your design problem, you will stand little chance of developing a successful analysis. Once you have developed this comprehensive list of variables you should divide the list into those variables which are *independent* and those which are *dependent* (upon the independent variables). If you have "n" dependent variables and you can write "n" independent equations you have reduced your design project to one of mathematics!

However, more often than not, your design problem will result in more independent engineering parameters than equations. Analysis only provides a formalized basis for understanding the design project. As the design project progresses, continue to review the lists of independent and dependent variables which affect the design.

Look to professional or trade handbooks and some advanced textbooks

These have three major advantages compared to traditional undergraduate texts. First, they are critically reviewed for accuracy and have in many cases taken years to evolve through several editions. Second, they are accepted by most practicing engineers as valid approaches. Third, they are closest to the problems and usually address the assumptions that are required to solve the problem. "Fudge factors" are often included which allow you to apply ideal scientific laws to the realities of practical problems.

References

1. Bolz, Ray E. and George L. Tuve, eds. 1973. Handbook of tables for applied engineering science, 2nd Edition. CRC Press, Boca Raton, FL. 1166 pp.

2. Faupel, Joseph H. and Franklin E. Fisher. 1981. Engineering design. John Wiley and Sons, New York. 1056 pp.

3. Richey, C.B., Paul Jacobson and Carl W. Hall, eds. 1961. Agricultural engineers' handbook. McGraw-Hill Book Co., Inc., New York. 880 pp.

4. VanZweden, J., L. Christianson and T. Dobbs. 1984. Economic analysis of a multipurpose, on-farm, solar energy intensifier system. ASAE Paper 84-4563. ASAE, St. Joseph, 49085.

Discussion problems

1. Why do you believe it is often difficult to find an equation which exactly fits your design problem?

2. What is the most critical design variable and its approximate value for the following designs in your locale?

    (a) Roof load on a farm building.

    (b) Channel flow on a grass waterway.

    (c) Cooling load for animals during the summer.

    (d) Drying of an agricultural commodity produced locally.

    (e) Firewood harvester.

Project problems

1. List, by name with appropriate symbols and units, all

engineering variables that are associated with your present project.

2. Using references and your analytic skills developed in other courses, list all possible equations that relate the variables involved in your problem. Explain why you nearly always finish with fewer equations than variables.

3. Identify one or more independent engineering variables in your present project and estimate the maximum and minimum values that are expected to occur.

4. Based upon your understanding of the maximum and minimum values of the independent variables in your present project, estimate the maximum and minimum value of selected dependent variables that you expect to occur.

Chapter 12
Synthesis

*"Imagination is more important than knowledge,
for knowledge is limited, whereas imagination
embraces the entire world..."*
Albert Einstein

*"The responsibility of the design engineer is to
use the maximum powers of creativity, judgment,
technical perception, economic awareness, and
analytic logic to devise uniquely useful systems,
devices or processes."*
R.J. McCrory

Synthesis is the antithesis of analysis. Synthesis is the combination of the parts or the design project problem subsets; Design synthesis implies a *uniquely* desirable combination of these parts. Synthesis is a creative activity in which the problem parts, dissected and understood through analysis, are re-combined in a special way to achieve a design result that meets all of the design specifications.

Identify the "bottom line"

The successful conclusion of almost every design rests with the solution of one important and central issue within the design.

One often says, "If only I could get this one thing figured out, everything else would fall into place." Experienced design engineers identify and focus on this central issue. But, two problems immediately confront the inexperienced design engineer. First is the inability to "cut through" the situation to identify the "real" or central design issue, and the second is to recognize that all progress on the project is likely to stop until this issue is resolved! One way to help identify this important design issue is to ask the question, "What design specification will be the most difficult to achieve and why?" Whatever the answer, your analysis activities should be structured such that their results can be re-synthesized (or re-combined) to answer or meet the design criteria.

Synthesis is the development of alternative analysis scenarios

Remember, your design problem is determined by that unique collection of design specifications that you have developed. In an effort to meet, simultaneously, the design project requirements, we *propose* (synthesize) a solution which we believe meets your design specifications. Often this proposed solution is in the form of a conspectus sketch, diagram or drawing, (Fig I.10 illustrates a conspectus sketch). The conspectus sketch represents *all* the solution elements necessary to meet the design specifications. Detailed analysis and testing will confirm the completeness of this synthesized solution later.

Now put aside the first conspectus drawing of your project solution, and generate a second conspectus solution. Set this second aside and generate a third, and continue as many times as you can to create new potential solutions to your design specifications. Your success in generating multiple solutions will be heavily dependent upon your past experience and your ability to draw upon the help of others. The following example should illustrate the central role of synthesis in design. Considerable detail is included to illustrate how synthesis is followed by analysis and vice versa over and over again as the design evolves.

An example: harvesting and handling wet blueberries — define the problem

The problem is that mechanized harvesting and handling of naturally wetted fruit, washing, specific gravity sorting, and anti-decay treatments of blueberries is advantageous to the industry, especially for the fresh market. The free surface moisture remaining on the fruit after one or more of these processes is considered unsightly and contributes to mold growth, particularly if the fruit is not refrigerated.

The design objectives can be given as follows: Design a drying system for fresh-market blueberries which:

1. Removes all (and only) surface moisture (i.e., does not remove internal moisture from the berries).

2. Handles commercial capacities.

3. Does not damage the berries.

4. Uses minimum amounts of process-energy.

Based upon these objectives, it is clear that specific design specifications must be developed such that judgments may be rendered by the success of the final design. It should be evident to even the inexperienced design engineer that strict compliance with design objective no. 1 is not possible. Fresh blueberries are a biological material and internal water is a major component. Furthermore, experience showed that removal of liquid moisture from the stem scar depression and the calyx (bud scar depression) is extremely difficult. Thus emerges the first design specification:

1. Dry 99% of all stem scars and calyxes such that no visible liquid moisture remains. The initial dry weight and the final dry weight of the berries should be within 1%, (i.e., not more than 1% internal moisture should be removed).

Most commercial growers of fresh market blueberries agree that the second objective translates into a 1360 kg/hr capacity or about 250 individual berries per second. Thus, objective two translates into the following specification:

2. Dry berries at the rate of 1360 kg/hr or 250 berries per second.

Damage to fresh berries as noted by objective no. 3 cannot be zero! If the berries are handled then a certain amount of softening and reduction in shelf-life will result. Specification no. 3 emerges as:

3. Shelf-life after drying must be at least 95% of the shelf-life of control berries not subjected to the wetting and drying process.

And finally, whatever drying method is used, the method should use the minimum process energy. Notice that objective no. 4 does not specify the drying process to use. Objective no. 4 is not a suitable statement of a design criterion because it is not quantified. A better, though less quantified than desired, design criterion would be:

4. Minimize drying process energy for the selected drying process.

Analyzing the blueberry drying problem

Theoretically, surface moisture can be removed in the liquid phase, the vapor phase or a combination of both phases. The only other phase of water (ice) can be rejected because we are dealing with fresh blueberries.

Shelf-life as expressed in criterion no. 3 must be analyzed and defined. In this example shelf-life has come to mean the average percentage of fresh berries that are judged to be fit for consumption by a group of untrained observers. Statistical analysis of past results must be used to determine the number of untrained observers needed to generate statistically significant results at any selected level of significance. Since blueberries have a relatively high internal moisture content, care must be taken so that the process designed to remove surface moisture does not remove internal moisture. If the moisture to be removed were uniformly distributed over the surface then evaporative drying could be used and terminated such that no internal produce moisture would be lost and complete surface drying could be achieved. Unfortunately the surface moisture is not uniformly distributed but tends to be concentrated in droplet form on the berry surface, in the calyx and in the stem scar. It, therefore, appeared desirable to remove as much moisture as possible in the liquid phase and the last remaining film by evaporation. Drying with a towel is a good conceptual example of a moisture removal system which utilizes, primarily, liquid phase removal.

Synthesis of a blueberry drier

Now the design engineer begins one of the more creative phases of engineering design. This phase of design has traditionally resisted quantification or standardization within textbooks. Cartoonists represent the instant at which an unusual connection is established between seemingly unconnected or unrelated events as the symbolic light bulb suddenly "turning-on". Some believe that systematic and comprehensive lists of all possible combinations of functions, forms and materials will trigger insight and create new solutions.

Whatever the case, in this example, it was observed that an air jet could control a sphere and might be capable of stripping liquid moisture from that sphere (Fig 12.1). The essentials of the final synthesized solution (Fig 12.2) in this example are the downwardly directed air jet which "centers" the berry directly underneath the air jet and a single-knit stainless steel wire mesh conveyor which supports the berry. The supply tube absolute pressure, P_s, is greater than the absolute atmosphere pressure P_a. Fig 12.2 is an example of a conspectus drawing showing each of the important elements of the proposed solution. Since blueberries are nearly spherical, any horizontal *relative* motion between the centerline of the *air jet* and the center of the berry will be resisted as a consequence of the fluid forces generated.

But will it work ?

Often, the fundamental or underlying concept can be verified

FIG 12.1 A beach ball being supported by an air jet from a household vacuum cleaner.

with some relatively inexpensive tests. In this case a short length of iron pipe with some small drilled holes was coupled to a shop air supply to demonstrate that air jet velocities in practice are high enough to provide liquid-phase moisture removal. Relative motion between the air jet and the support conveyor induced berry rolling which exposed all sides for nearly total liquid-phase moisture removal. Evaporative drying of the remaining surface moisture film proceeded rapidly due to the high air velocity, when the proper drying potential of the air was present.

The importance of concept testing or verification cannot be overstated. In this example there was no question after concept testing that the fundamentals were correct. A no. 70 drilled hole with 90 psi air pressure was effective for testing even though impractical as a production capacity drying system.

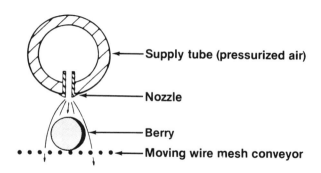

FIG 12.2 The air jet drier concept.

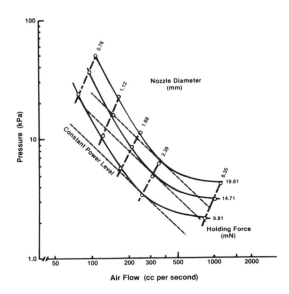

FIG 12.3 Experimentally determined horizontal force generation by a downwardly directed air jet upon a 15.5 mm plastic sphere resting on a wire mesh conveyor.

Air jet pressure and flow requirements

An important feature of the air jet drying system is its ability to provide a very gentle rolling action of the berries as the moisture is being removed. It was experimentally determined that, if an air jet developed a 19.6 mN force on a 16 mm diameter plastic sphere, the air jet would have ample horizontal force generation capacity to roll blueberries on a horizontal wire mesh conveyor since many berries require a 9.8 mN force or less.

The relationship between the horizontal rolling force developed on the 16 mm diameter plastic sphere as a function of air jet pressure, flow and diameter (Fig 12.3) was determined experimentally. By plotting pressure as a function of air flow for various nozzle diameters, the minimum power required to generate a given level of rolling force is clearly noted since constant power levels are straight lines. Therefore, the required 19.6 mN rolling force can be generated with a minimum power input if a 2.4 mm diameter nozzle is supplied with a 6.5 kPa pressure resulting in 375 cc/s air flow per nozzle. The power required per nozzle would be about 2.4 W (3.3 x 10⁻³ hp).

In addition to power considerations, the final selection of the air jet nozzle was based on availability and ease of fabrication. Increasing the length of the nozzle was observed to influence the performance favorably. The final selection of a nozzle was a hollow "pop" type aluminum rivet (9 mm long by 3.2 mm ID) which was press-fitted into the air supply tube. Careful calibration at the final design conditions of a single "pop" rivet type nozzle revealed a flow rate of 550 cc/s at 6.9 kPa pressure which produced ample horizontal forces on a wide range of sizes and varieties of blueberries.

What controls the synthesis process

In the example we have just seen there are two factors which control the synthesis process. Firstly, and most importantly, the exact definition and statement of project design specifications provides the design engineer with a word picture of what must be achieved. Real-world problems are difficult to solve; double check your design specifications so you are certain that they define your design problem. Secondly, the evolution or synthesis of the solution itself raises new questions and new problem solution options which must be explored further. Don't limit your thinking or view of your problem. Be open to alterations of design objectives, specifications, function and form.

References

1. Rohrbach, R.P. 1977. Air jet drying and dewatering of blueberries. *Transactions of the ASAE* 20(5):992-995.

2. Siddall, James N. 1982. Optimal engineering design. Marcel Dekker, Inc., New York. 523 pp.

Discussion problems

1. Discuss the difference between synthesis and creativity. What is the role of the conspectus sketch?

2. Synthesize a new conceptual design along with conspectus sketches for:

(a) A plateless corn planter.

(b) An evaporative cooling system for a poultry house in your area.

(c) An automatically recording rainfall gauge.

(d) A device for measuring the firmness of peaches.

(e) A waste management system for a riding horse farm in a predominately residential urban area.

Project problems

1. Redefine carefully and completely the design specifications that must be achieved to complete your present project.

2. Develop a proposal for an *analysis* which, when completed, will provide additional insight into your present project design criteria.

Chapter 13
User Considerations

*"And who will buy, use and service
this creation of the design engineer?"*

"Design engineers serve customer needs."

Engineers design for people. We know people want an economical product which is safe and reliable. We often forget that products should be aesthetically pleasing. We often forget that products should meet the needs and improve the efficiency of the product user in an interesting and pleasing way.

Automotive manufacturers pay large salaries to stylists to develop a pleasing exterior and pleasant passenger areas in cars. Builders pay millions to architects to design interesting and efficient buildings. Manufacturing and service firms have discovered that money invested in providing the right kind of work places can be repaid many times over in increased productivity! "Human factors engineering," "anthropometry" and "ergonomics" are all terms which refer to the people-aspects of engineering design which we have called user considerations.

Most firms do not expect their product engineers to be proficient in human factors. Consultants from within the company or outside consultants are used to augment the design engineer's knowledge and understanding of the customer needs and wants. Firms do expect that product engineers be aware of the

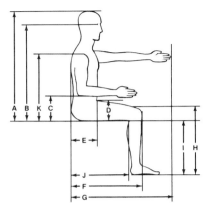

Body Size Data (unclothed)

	Body dimension	U.S. Adult Males- 95% are smaller cm	U.S. Adult Females- 95% are larger cm
A	Body height sitting	99.75	80.00
B	Eye height sitting	85.75	69.25
C	Elbow height sitting	28.00	21.00
D	Thigh height sitting	17.25	12.75
E	Abdominal depth sitting	31.75	20.25
F	Buttock-knee length	64.75	52.75
G	Anterior arm reach	95.25	72.50
H	Knee height sitting	59.75	45.75
I	Popliteal height sitting	45.75	35.50
J	Buttock-popliteal length	52.75	42.50
K	Shoulder height sitting	64.25	49.00

FIG 13.1 Representative human body size data.

scope of the human factors field and able to judge when outside help is needed.

Anthropometry is the study of human physical dimensions

There are tables of data based on the probability distribution of arm length for male caucasians between 20 and 40 years old. You can design a lever that all but the shortest, 5%, of the adult caucasian males can reach from a chair without leaning forward (Fig 13.1). You can design a tractor cab door height to accommodate 90%, 95% or 99.5% of the adult population with less than a 0.3 m stoop at entry. Engineers, psychologists and other efficiency experts have tabulated information on the average eye-to-hand reaction time for different population segments. There are tables showing the probability distribution of heights, weights, hearing abilities, sight characteristics, reaction times and numerous other human characteristics which are important for designers. The references listed at the end of this chapter are

FIG 13.2 Example form used for time and motion studies.

Time and Motion Data Form	Date: _____		
Study Type: _____		Recorder: _____	
Time	Activity	Operator No.	Machine No.
00:00			
	Lift Plate to Punch	3	Punch Press 1
00:35			
	Operate Punch	3	" "
00:46			
	Take Plate to Rack	3	Rack 6
01:03			
	Lift Plate to Punch	4	Press + Die 2
01:18			
	Form Plate	4	" "

examples of the many sources of this type of information for humans. The ASAE Standards, in *D321.1*, has similar body size data for animals.

Time and motion studies are a commonly used means for improving productivity

Time and motion studies are a means for evaluating the efficiency of people, machines or people-machines combinations. Such studies are conducted using a stop watch and log sheet (Fig 13.2). Times required for each movement or operation are recorded in the order of performance. There are even standard tables which tell the average time required for each movement based on the material and the machine. Some manufacturers base pay and rate workers by comparing their performance with these Predetermined Motion Time Systems (PMTS).

Time and motion studies are important to you as an agricultural engineer in three ways. First, you are responsible for designing machines which can be economically produced. Efficient use of people's time in manufacturing, stocking, and handling parts is important in minimizing manufactured costs. Many design engineers are not experts on the production methods for manufacturing. Consequently, it is important that they work closely with the manufacturing engineers to develop a product which can be manufactured economically.

Second, the design engineer should design equipment which can be used efficiently. You can design a tractor with a non-synchronized manual transmission which requires stopping to shift gears. Such a tractor may cost less than a tractor with a power shift transmission. But, with a power shaft transmission, operator convenience and tractor productivity are substantially improved. These attributes are important as evidenced by the fact that non-

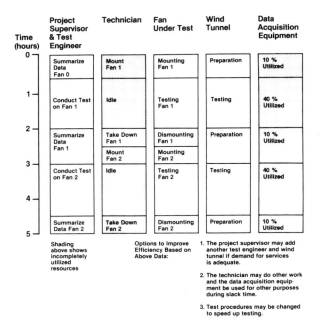

FIG 13.3 Results of a time and motion study displayed for interpretation.

synchronized manual transmissions have all but disappeared on farm tractors.

Third, the design engineer must consider how quickly people can be trained to use and maintain the equipment. Usually, you try to design equipment for simplicity of operation and for minimization of training time. Today much agricultural equipment is operated by unskilled labor and non-owners. Unnecessary complications (e.g., on-board computers) will, in general, meet market resistance unless there is a strong benefit/cost advantage. Also, systems should be designed to minimize service and maintenance time.

Performance is affected by environment

There are specialists who work on optimizing work environment just as there are specialists on anthropometry and time and motion. Optimal and tolerable environments for different types of work are studied and tabulated. Temperature, humidity, ventilation, air quality, noise, acceleration, "stray" electric voltage, shock waves, light intensity, light spectrum and odor are examples of environmental factors which affect human productivity. The environments that the machine operator and machine repairman will be exposed to are important human factors concerns. Environment is important to the designer because it affects productivity (which is an economic issue) and because it affects health (which is a moral, legal and economic issue). The American Society of Heating, Refrigerating and Air Conditioning Engineers (ASHRAE) provides temperature, humidity, ventilation and air quality recommendations for optimal productivity. The Illuminating Engineers Society, in their Lighting Handbook, suggests ranges of light levels depending on tasks performed and the age of the workers.

The Occupational Safety and Health Act established legal standards pertaining to air quality, noise levels and other factors which affect operator health and safety. There are a variety of other medical, physiological, psychological and engineering groups which study the effects of environment on people's health, safety and performance.

An example particularly relevant to agricultural engineers is cab design for tractors. Older model tractors (pre-1960's) produced noise levels above the safe threshold level recognized as producing no hearing loss over long-term operation. Tractor seat vibrations in some models were near the resonant frequency of human body parts. The result of the noise is hearing loss among a large group of older farmers. The result of the vibration was reduced comfort, operator fatigue and limited productivity (speed) in the field. Tractor cabs were developed to solve these problems and to provide a more pleasant, air conditioned, dust-free environment for operator comfort.

Psychological factors are important to designers

People perform best when they are alert, happy and comfortable. It is the engineer's responsibility to think carefully about how to make a product-use environment better and safer. That is why engineers have developed sophisticated machinery for tracking eye motion. Pilots sit at a mock-up flight-control panel and their eye movements are tracked as different flight scenarios are modeled. Using simulators the engineer can test the location and types of controls and warning features to maximize safety.

Put yourself in the place of the user. Can you make this machine easier to use or this building a more pleasant place in which to work? Can you help a tractor operator be more efficient by displaying certain data (e.g., forward speed, engine efficiency or drawbar draft)? If you provide amenities such as a radio or automatic coffee maker, will they serve as distractions or will they improve productivity? Can you help operators make better use of

PUTTING ZERKS HERE FOR THIS
BEARING SAVED US $1.50!!

their time by asking them to do two things at once? Should
provisions for telephone service at the operator's work station be
provided?

These are all important considerations for the design engineer.
To optimize safety and satisfaction, you want to avoid an overload
of information and responsibility, but you also want to avoid
boredom!

User considerations may be subtle

Sometimes user considerations may not involve on-site
individuals. A good example might be the drying of corn. In this
case the "user" is the "end-user" of the dried corn. If your dried
corn will be used on-site to feed hogs then drying rates and drying
temperatures are of little concern except when considering their
effect on drying economics. However, if you are drying seed corn
or corn that will be subsequently transported and milled for
human consumption, the drying rates and temperatures are
important user design considerations. Excessively high drying
temperatures reduce seed corn germination percentages and high
drying rates induce stress cracks in corn that increase fines
generation and adversely affect milling characteristics.

In summary, understanding customers, their needs, their

motivations, their preferences and their expectations for a product are imperative. Also, being aware of advantages and disadvantages of competitive products from the *customer's perspective* can provide invaluable design direction. The designer or product engineer does not function in a vacuum but must rely upon inputs from marketing (market research), sales, manufacturing, service and management to make certain the product will be manufacturable, servicable, salable, safe, usable and profitable.

References

1. ASAE. 1986. Dimensions of livestock and poultry, D321.1 Standard. American Society of Agricultural Engineers, St. Joseph 49085.

2. ASHRAE. 1985. ASHRAE handbook of fundamentals. American Society of Heating, Refrigerating and Air Conditioning Engineers, Atlanta, GA.

3. Bennett, E., J. Degan and J. Spiegel (ed.). 1963. Human factors in technology. McGraw Hill. 685 pp.

4. IES. 1981, 1984. Lighting handbooks — applications (1981) and references (1984). Illuminating Engineering Society, New York, 505 and 482 pp. (respectively)

5. Purcell, William. 1981. Human factors, ASAE Distinguished Lecture Series. ASAE, St. Joseph 49085.

6. Roebuck, J.A., Jr., K.E. Kroemer and W. Thomson. 1975. Engineering anthropometry methods. John Wiley and Sons, New York, 459 pp.

7. Tichauer, E.R. 1978. The biomechanical basis of ergonomics. John Wiley and Sons, New York. 99 pp.

8. Woodson, Wesley E. 1981. Human factors design handbook: Information and guidelines for the design of systems, facilities, equipment, and products for human use. McGraw-Hill, New York, 1047 pp.

Discussion problems

1. Backhoe control motions are based upon ASAE Standards. Do you believe the control motions are logically consistent with your experience and understanding?

2. Conceptualize a tractor control system for an operator with no leg function and only use of one arm. List all the required control functions and how they would be performed.

3. Discuss the relative merits of an am/fm stereo radio in a tractor cab. Repeat for a television.

4. Measure the seat and operator station geometric characteristics for a tractor and obtain anthropometric data to determine, if possible, whether the seat was designed for a male or female operator. Be prepared to discuss results in class.

Project problems

1. Develop a list of specific human factors that directly affect your present project.

2. Assess the social impact of your present project. Will society benefit from your design and, if so, by how much?

3. Define and defend the educational grade level of the operator of your present project design.

4. If your present project requires a human operator, plan and

conduct a time and motion study using data collection forms similar to those shown in Fig 13.2.

5. Define the maintenance problems and the maintenance program necessary for your present design project.

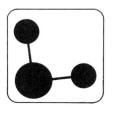

Chapter 14
Materials Selection

*"Seldom will the design result in having
to select only one material."*

*"An understanding of materials, their strengths,
weaknesses and characteristics, is essential for
all design enginers."*

There are too many materials to consider them all

There are over 40,000 useful metallic materials and another 40,000 plus useful non-metallic materials (useful defined as currently used in some engineering design as opposed to biologically or environmentally useful). The numbers are growing. Obviously, material selection is a difficult and complex task. There are engineers and firms that specialize in materials science — often in just one aspect of materials science such as high-quality stainless steel, ceramics, plastics, alloys, etc.

You do not have time to research all 80,000 plus materials, and you do not have the millions of dollars required to hire a team of experts to do this. Therefore, you need a simplified approach which might start by asking questions. Which materials are being used in applications similar to yours? Why? What advantages and disadvantages do the more common materials have for your type of application? Also, consider that there are at least 3 million

SCIENTIFIC APPROACH TO MATERIAL SELECTION

standard fasteners produced in various materials, sizes, styles and types. Obviously, material selection is a complex problem, and you have to make decisions after considering only a few of the possible alternatives.

Criteria for selection of materials

Comparing the properties of the proposed material with the requirements in the design is obviously important. One helpful technique is to list all the material properties needed or desired for the design. Needed properties, such as the ability to withstand temperatures in excess of 500°C for an engine cylinder wall, will automatically preclude certain materials from consideration. Desired properties, such as the low roughness or surface finishing characteristics for the cylinder wall material, are also important means of evaluating materials. Desirable properties do not automatically preclude materials from further consideration. You can construct two grids. One, listing material requirements, serves as a screening mechanism for rejecting alternatives. The second, listing desirable material features, serves as a means for rating the remaining alternatives relative to each other.

Manufacturing cost is a less obvious, but equally important, consideration for materials selection. First, what are the relative costs of the material alternatives? Second, what are the relative costs of manufacturing (e.g., labor and machinery costs)? Third, do the manufacturing processes alter the material properties in an unacceptable manner? Fourth, what types of materials does the company you are working with normally stock and use? Frequently, one design alternative will have a lower raw material cost but a higher manufactured cost than the best alternative.

User acceptability is the final important materials consideration. If you are designing farm machinery, design something that the farmer can operate and maintain. Product acceptability will hinge on the ability of the farmer to use it properly and maintain it. A manufacturing firm that plans to remain in business must plan to educate salesman and product users on product care. If the product incorporates new materials requiring specialized education efforts, that is an additional material expense.

Time and money often dictate conventional materials

Failure to explore alternative materials is a frequent mistake causing the product to be less profitable to the manufacturer and the user. This failure may result in a competitor underselling you with a better product. Yet, you are always limited in time and money to explore materials.

Materials can be reduced to some common alternatives: (a) steel, (b) cast iron, (c) powdered metals, (d) wood products, (e) aluminum, (f) copper, (g) plastics, (h) ceramics and (i) concrete. Within each of these categories there are a few *commonly* stocked and used types (e.g., dimensions and ratings of construction grade lumber, plywood and particle board). Generally the commonly used materials are the most economical alternatives. Justification of more exotic materials usually depends on large scale production and/or unusual material requirements which cannot be met with conventional materials.

Company design philosophies also influence the relative time and expense entailed in using different materials. Some companies may employ expertise in many exotic materials and already use such materials in numerous applications. They can use certain unusual materials more quickly and with much less expense. Many issues associated with changing to different materials require extensive testing and justification by the designer since these decisions may have a major influence on product success. Changing to a new material can be risky, and hence the advantages which may seem to be offered can quickly be overshadowed by such concerns as:

1. Long term fatigue life under all possible product applications.

2. Wear resistance throughout the product life.

3. Material behavior in the temperature extremes expected for the product.

4. Strategic or commercial availability of the material.

5. Effects of specific environmental factors like ozone, sunlight, etc.

6. Non-selected but important material properties like coefficient of friction, thermal conductivity, mass density, etc.

Other companies, especially many smaller companies, have expertise in only one or a few materials. They may only have steel fabrication equipment. When a specialty material component is required, they may prefer to buy the component elsewhere and simply assemble it into the finished product. Standardized purchased parts are almost always preferred to specialized components that must be manufactured in-house or by contract.

Do not be ashamed of using another manufacturer's parts

Few companies produce a product in its entirety. DuAl Manufacturing buys steel, tires, bearings, belts, pulleys, chains, electronics and other components from firms which specialize in such items. Even the largest companies, such as Deere and Company, buy many components and sub-assemblies from other manufacturers. As a farm equipment designer, you will not be an expert on how to produce the optimal tire. Instead you will compare manufacturer specifications and prices for the alternative tires and select the one best suited to your equipment. For components using specialty materials, you will of necessity use the purchased parts approach.

Where do you find detailed material data

One of the best, concise sources is the Materials Reference edition of Machine Design Magazine which is updated annually. A second excellent general source is *Engineering design: A materials and processing approach* (Dieter, 1983). A general, but more detailed source is the CRC Press *Handbook of materials science* (Lynch, 1975).

Detailed materials data are best found in specialty publications pertaining to a specific material type (Table 14.1). Usually these are compiled by professional or trade groups who work with these particular materials. Supplier literature and data are essential for many specialized materials and alloys.

Table 14.1 Sources of Material Properties.

A. Metals

   1. American Society for Metals. Metal Handbook Series: "Vol I -Properties and Selection: Iron and Steel", "Vol II — Properties and Selection: Nonferrous Alloys and Pure Metals", and "Vol III -Properties and Selection: Stainless Steels, Tool Materials and Special Purpose Metals".

   2. Battelle Memorial Institute. Structural Alloys Handbook, Vol I and II.

   3. Society of Automotive Engineers, SAE Handbook, Part I, Materials, Parts and Components.

B. Wood Products

   1. American Plywood Association, Applied Research Department Technical Services Division, Tacoma, Washington.

   2. Midwest Plan Service, 122 Davidson Hall, Iowa State University, Ames, Iowa 50011.

   3. National Design Specification, National Forest Products Association, 1619 Massachusetts Avenue, N.W., Washington, D.C. 20036.

   4. National Forest Products Lab, U.S. Department of Agriculture, Forest Service, Forest Products Laboratory, P.O. Box 5130, Madison, Wisconsin 53705.

C. Plastics

   1. Association of Rotational Molders, Rotational Molded Plastics, 221 N LaSalle Street, Chicago, IL 60601

   2. Modern Plastics Magazine's annual Modern Plastics Encyclopedia.

   3. Roff, Scott. *Handbook of Common Polymers* CRC Press, Bocu Raton, FL.

   4. Wallace, B. (ed.) "Handbook of Thermoplastic Elastomers" Van Nostrand-Resnhold.

D. Ceramics and Inorganic Materials

   1. American Ceramic Society. 1966. "Engineering Properties of Selected Ceramic Materials"

E. Electronic Materials

   1. Plenum Publishing Corp. 1971 and 1974. "Handbook of Electronic Materials, Vol. 1-9".

F. Concrete

   1. Portland Cement Association. 5420 Old Orchard Road, Skokie, IL 60077

References

(Material-specific references are incorporated in Table 14.1).

1. Dieter, G. 1983. Engineering design—A materials processing approach. McGraw Hill, NY. 592 pp.

2. Faupel, J.H. and F.E. Fisher. 1981. Engineering design—A synthesis of stress analysis and materials engineering, 2nd ed. Wiley and Sons, New York. 1056 pp.

3. Lynch, Charles T 1975. Handbook of materials science. Four volume set. CRC Press, Cleveland 44128.

4. Machine Design. 1986. Materials reference edition, Machine Design Magazine, Penton Press, Cleveland.

5. Yankee, H.W. 1979. Manufacturing processes. Prentice-Hall, Englewood Cliffs. 765 pp.

Discussion problems

1. List at least five important material properties which have significant consequences to a design. Suggest ways to quantify the relative importance of each property listed.

Project problems

1. Select at least three alternative materials for a principal component in your present project. List the pros and cons for each material.

2. Select a material for an important application to your project and list all engineering properties (and values) of the material that significantly affect your present project.

Chapter 15
Product Safety
and Liability

*"A disaster can be accomplished subconciously,
but a cure cannot. A cure requires
conscious knowledge."*
Ayn Rand

"Product safety is no accident."

Product safety is a moral and legal responsibility

Engineers have a moral and legal responsibility to design safe products. The design engineer is expected to anticipate external factors such as severe weather, product misuses and poor judgment that may result in injuries. Ideally, the engineer should design to eliminate hazards wherever possible. When hazards cannot be designed-out (eliminated), warnings and protective devices must be part of the design to maximize operator control and safety.

An engineer's design philosophy should be: (a) if making a product safer does not interfere with function or increase the cost unreasonably you have an obligation to do so and (b) if making a product safer adversely affects the function (reduces utility) of a product, you must shield to the extent possible and warn if the danger is not open and obvious. Safety is not simply a concern of professional ethics, it is a direct legal and financial responsibility. Failure to produce a safe design and resulting product can lead to expensive product liability lawsuits involving many end-users of the product and needless human suffering and loss.

Identifying situations where injuries may occur and minimizing the chances of such injuries is the subject of safety and engineering. Safety engineering is common sense and caution combined with scientifically-based methodology and is described in Section I of this chapter. Section II of this chapter discusses the legal issues and terminology associated with product safety which have evolved into major public policy concerns and must be considered during the design process.

SECTION I—SAFETY ENGINEERING
Apply safety engineering techniques while developing the design

Safety engineering includes three major topics: (a) avoiding system or component failures that may result in injuries to operators or bystanders, (b) minimizing the likelihood of injuries due to misuse, abuse or accidents and (c) evaluating the likelihood and seriousness of dangers. The concepts of safety factors, reliability, redundancy of critical parts, planned inspection and maintenance, quality control and quality assurance apply to the avoidance of failure category and are important measures of product value as well. Methods used to minimize injuries from unintended product use, abuse and accidential product contact include designing-out where possible, safety shut-off devices, interlocks and permenantly attached shields. Hazard analysis, failure modes effects analysis (FMEA) and fault tree analysis are popular methods for identifying and assessing the seriousness of dangers which are often based on statistical probabilities and quantitative measures of seriousness.

Factors of safety

One of the universal constraints of materials and component selection is the effect of the component on the over-all products factor of safety. Factors of safety should be carefully selected with due regard to human life, animal welfare and economics. Attention should be given to the prospects of catastrophic failure. Whenever possible, the design should include fail-safe provisions within the limit of personal safety, animal welfare and economics. Remember that, regardless of the factor of safety selected, if enough products are produced and operated over a long enough time,at least one will fail.

Factor safety (f_s) is often defined as:

$$f_s = \frac{\text{expected minimum component capacity}}{\text{rated component capacity}}$$

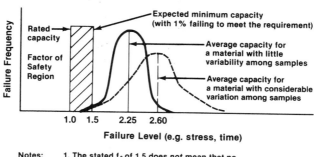

FIG 15.1 Typical relationships among expected minimum capacity and rated capacity for a material type or component.

Expected minimum capacity may be allowable design stress, expected component life or expected tolerance to an environmental extreme (e.g., temperature effects on electrical insulation). The confusion with the concept of expected minimum capacity results because this usually means that fewer than x% of the material specimen or components do not meet the expected minimum capacity during testing, and x can be from zero to several percent. Materials or components typically have some average failure point with sample failure normally distributed about this average (Fig 15.1). The average failure point can be quite near the expected minimum capacity or considerably more conservative, depending on the allowable percent failures and the material variability. Obviously a design comprised of several components and materials has a difficult-to-define expected minimum capacity.

Rated capacity must be a similar kind of measure to expected minimum capacity (e.g., required design stress, required component life or required tolerance for an enviromental extreme). Rated capacity is the minimum design value calculated or selected by the engineer. It is usually related directly to an expected worst case condition (e.g., a 50-year flood, 50-year peak snow-load or maximum dynamic force on a hydraulic cylinder). Additional factors of safety may be included in the rated capacity, especially when this rated capacity is obtained from building codes of engineering standards. While design loads are usually conservative (i.e., it is not expected that such a severe condition will occur during the use of that product), there are instances in which design loads are liberal, providing, in effect, a negative factor of safety in the rated capacity. Design temperature data are examples of the latter and are usually figured on a 99 or 97.5% probability, meaning the designer expects conditions to be worse than the rated capacity 1 or 2.5% of the time.

It is clear that the engineer must first understand the meaning of f_s as applied to the specific application. Often this requires testing and statistical analysis. If costs of designing conservatively are less than the expense of testing to measure f_s, the engineer may prefer to use the conservative design approach. More likely, there is considerable expense associated with over-design; so, the engineer wants to select an appropriate factor of safety which balances economics with the consequences of failure.

If the consequences of failure are minor, perhaps the inconvenience of replacing a light bulb, f_s, may be very nearly 1.0. If failure will likely result in deaths or severe injuries, f_s may be 1.5, 2, 3 or even larger. How much larger depends on the certainty with which the engineer can rely on the true capacity of the material and the true maximum capacity to which that material will be exposed. Considerable testing is usually justified for mass-produced designs, because the cost of testing can be recovered through minimizing over-design without sacrificing needed capacity.

Reliability is closely related to factor of safety

Statistical data are available on failure rates for many standard components and materials from both industry sources (the manufacturers) and from government sources (e.g., Government-Industry Data Exchange Program, Corona, CA, 91720). Reliability is expressed as a fraction between 0 and 1, with 1 being absolutely reliable and 0 being completely unreliable for any given point. Reliability as a function of time (or other variable) usually resembles an S shaped curve (Fig 15.2). No failures are expected up to a minimum level (reliability = 1.0); then, failures begin and continue in a normally distributed fashion to a maximum level (at which point the reliability = equals 0.0).

Component data can be mathematically combined to calculate system reliability. Reliability of a design comprised of a series of interdependent components is the product of the reliability of the individual components. When the component reliabilities are statistical probabilities, the system reliability may be expressed as "mean time between failures" or some similar concept which allows for the combination of probabilities. Factors of safety can even be applied to reliability data.

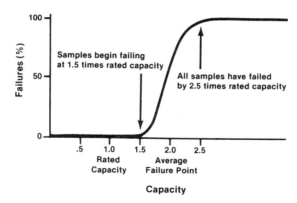

FIG 15.2 Reliability curve for a typical component.

Redundancy is a method for enhancing reliability

The adage that "nothing is certain except death and taxes" applies to the reliability and safety of engineering design. Because it is impossible to design a practical machine or system which will not fail under some circumstance, engineers often resort to redundancy as a means for minimizing the adverse consequences of a failure.

"Dual" or "back-up" components are one type of redundancy. Two drive-lines may be connected by a multi-belt drive so if one belt fails there is an excellent chance that the remaining belt or belts will maintain the connection between the drivelines. An integrated circuit chip sometimes has alternate pathways to protect against the shorting or failure of one of the pathways.

Layered safety-protection devices are another example of redundancy. Most electrical appliances have internal fuses to shut down the device in the event of certain kinds of failure; plus, the wiring systems in the facility where the appliances are used have fuse systems. Even the building wiring system has some redundancy in protection through equipment grounds, ground-fault-interrupts, individual circuit fusing and main-breaker fusing. Systems where failure may be especially catastrophic often contain layers of redundant safety devices (e.g., nuclear power plants and civilian air craft).

Inspection and planned maintenance improve safety

Engineers know that brakes will fail, sometimes without warning. The ideal solution is to design brakes that will slightly outlast the vehicle. However, even the best braking system will fail in some instances. Routine inspection and maintenance is a way of detecting failures before they occur and preventing the failure through component replacement, adjustment, lubrication or some similar procedure. User inspection and maintenance should not be relied upon as a substitute for designing a product which is safe unless the designer can be absolutely sure that planned inspection and maintenance will occur.

Laws mandate elevator inspection, certain types of vehicle inspections, building inspections, manufacturing facilities inspections and in some instances even on-farm work conditions inspections. Even where not mandated, the engineer designing a product should define inspection and maintenance procedures to maximize safety associated with that product. The recommended practice may go so far as to require scrapping of the product prior to the earliest expected failure if a failure would have particularly disastrous consequences.

Quality control ensures that the product is manufactured as designed

Quality control actually extends into the design process and involves specifying components and manufacturing practices within narrow enough tolerances so that the end-product fits together and works properly. Periodic testing and statistical analysis of part variabilities are ways of monitoring the quality of the product inputs. If a component is critical to safety or performance, all components may be manually or electronically inspected for dimensional tolerances, cracks or faults, load-carrying capacity or similar types of parameters.

Quality control applies to the manufacturing process as well, and may involve sampling at several stages of production to make sure that all the steps of the process are being performed correctly. Finished products are almost always identified so that, if a defect is found in a finished product, that defect can be identified with a specific lot and other items produced at that time checked. Certain types of quality assurance testing may be conducted on all finished products.

Quality control maximizes the likelihood that the product will be produced as designed and without defective materials. A second important aspect of quality control is that manufacturing and design personnel may be brought together as part of a "quality control" team which leads to better, safer designs through improved communication and idea exchange.

Anticipate product misuse and accidents

The design engineer may prefer that people only use walk-behind lawn and garden equipment on reasonably level ground and during mild weather conditions so that there is little chance of the operator slipping or falling. The engineer may explain this carefully in an operator's manual, and place a warning on the machine that the user should read the operator's manual before operating the machine. These are unrealistic expectations! Many users won't ever read the manual, several of those who do will forget many of the important points, and even some of the most careful (most of the time) users will operate the equipment when conditions are slippery if the job requirements seem to demand immediate attention (e.g., operating the snow blower when the surfaces are icy).

You, the engineer, have an ethical and legal responsibility to anticipate misuses and to minimize the chances of injury from misuses. If you are the snow blower designer, you would want to make handle-area protrusions blunt to minimize eye and cutting or poking injuries. A "kill-switch" which shuts off power if the operator releases the handles lessens the chance of a slipping injury. More importantly, the kill-switch lessens the chance that the operator will walk around to the front of the machine while it is operating and accidently come into contact with the cutting blades.

There is no substitute for a careful evaluation of a proposed design. It is preferable to include input from a group of people comprised of users, salesmen, experienced designers and safety specialists to identify possible misuses and accidents. This is the first step in a "hazard analysis." These people should use a checklist procedure carefully considering each item on the list (Table 15.1).

After developing the list of possible misuses and accidents, the safety team should evaluate the likelihood and the seriousness of impact for each identified hazard. Initially these may be grouped into general categories so that the designers can concentrate on the most serious and highest probability hazards, and yet not ignore the lower probability and less serious hazards.

Design, remove, guard, warn or train

The design engineer has the responsibility to design-out those foreseeable dangers associated with the design, providing that doing so does not interfere with intended function. Clearly, it is not good design to string non-insulated 110 V electrical lines within the normal reach of people because the danger is foreseeable (electrical shock and possibly death) and because there is a solution which does not interfere with the function (insulating the wires and perhaps placing them in conduit). Conversely, the

**Table 15.1. Checklist for anticipating product misuse
and accidents.**

---

1. What are the conditions under which the design will be used, when used for its intended purpose, in terms of:
    (a) locations?
    (b) environmental conditions at location?
    (c) knowledge and training levels of users?
    (d) health and physical conditions of users?
    (e) mental fatigue and concentration status of users?
    (f) proximity and characteristics of bystanders?

2. How might a user try to use this design for something other than the intended purposes?

3. What will happen if children play on the machine or system?

4. How might an unskilled user try to repair the machine when it malfunctions and:
    (a) is that person likely to be injured while identifying and trying to correct the problem, or,
    (b) is that person likely to get the machine running but in an unsafe manner?

5. Which parts (and under what conditions) are dangerous to someone who comes into accidental or intentional contact with them?

6. How will someone unfamiliar with the machine try to operate the machine?

7. Are there foreseeable accidents which are not due to operator error or machine failure (e.g., being struck by an automobile or being a target of lightning)?

---

tractor-loader design engineer in the 1960's could not be expected to foresee the danger of people using those loaders to haul large round bales (because the large round balers were not invented) and having the bale roll down the loader onto the operator. Also conversely, the windrower designer cannot eliminate the cutting mechanism from the design, or the windrower would not be capable of swathing hay or grain.

Dangers which cannot be designed out of a product should be removed from proximity of the user. High voltage electrical lines suspended 8 m in the air are dangerous, but they are removed from the proximity of people. The drive shaft in a tractor spins at speeds in excess of 2000 r/min and is clearly dangerous, but it is confined within the tractor chasis, and therefore, removed from people.

When the design engineer cannot design-out the danger or remove it from proximity to people, the danger should be shielded if possible. Drive lines, gears, electrical wiring, high temperature conduits and similarly dangerous components may need to be in locations where people could come into contact with them through misuse or accidents. Such components should be shielded effectively so that injuries are impossible or much less likely to occur.

Choosing and wording warnings are important in engineering design

Some dangers cannot be designed-out, removed from proximity of people or shielded because they are integral to the function of the equipment (e.g., blades on saws, knives and gatherers on crop harvesting machinery, tips of welding rods). If the danger is "open and obvious" to all users capable of reading and comprehending, it is not necessarily good practice to warn because doing so may detract from reader attention to other less obvious dangers. Dangers that are not obvious to a significant population group require carefully phrased and selected warnings.

ASAE has four standards dealing principally with the use of colors, symbols and wording within warnings (ASAE EP 415 — Safety color code for the training and educational workshop, ASAE S 304.5 — Symbols for operator controls on agricultural equipment, ASAE S 350 — Safety-alert symbol for agricultural equipment and ASAE S 441 — Safety signs). Numerous other ASAE standards specify content of warnings for specific types of applications. The ASAE warning standards are in concert with warning standards developed by other professional societies that are within the ANSI standards umbrella. This is important because people use or are around wide varieties of products and equipment. Choice of wording, graphic symbols and the location of warnings are critical because users become familiar with the general appearance of warnings and act without carefully reading the content (Fig 15.3).

Again, it is important that the engineer realize that warnings are not a substitute for designing safe products. People will overlook, ignore, not understand or not heed warnings in some instances. Poor judgment by a product user does not absolve the designer if the designer had an alternative way of making the product safe for that type of accident or misuse.

Training is like warnings — a method of encouraging safe use of products and not a substitute for designing the products as safe as possible. Well-handled training can be quite effective, and the

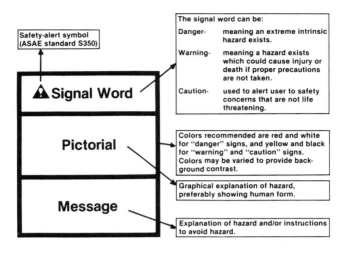

FIG 15.3 Safety-sign format for agricultural equipment as specified by ASAE
Standard 441 "Safety Signs".

proper use of warnings may reinforce the training. It is not
realistic to rely on the user being trained, in most instances,
because owners can sell equipment to untrained buyers and
because untrained users may operate the equipment with or
without owner permission.

Safety shut-off devices are important for many products

The public expects fuses for electrical circuits, pressure or light
sensitive door opening devices for people entering elevators and a
variety of other manual and automatic shut-offs on equipment.
Manual safety shut-off devices may be provided near potential
injury locations, particularly if : (a) a user or on-looker might be
tempted to get close without shutting off the equipment because
shutting off is inconvenient or (b) someone could become
trapped or caught in the equipment but still have time to shut off
the equipment before more serious injury occurs.

Automatic shut-offs protect the user or bystander from both
foolish actions and unknown hazards. A light beam switch can
shut off equipment if someone approaches too closely. Seat
switches and hand grip switches shut off all or portions of
equipment when the operator leaves the seat or releases a grip on
the controls. Shields and protective doors may be included in the
control circuitry so that when the shield is opened or the access
door opened, the device stops.

The engineer should use judgment when specifying the level at which automatic shut-off switches are activated because nuisance triggering will almost certainly cause the user to disconnect the safety switch. Similarly, judgment is important in the use and location of manual shut-off switches. The availability of the manual switch may increase the likelihood that a user will approach the machine at a dangerous location while the machine is still operating and actually increase rather than decrease the numbers of injuries.

Permanently-attached shields are superior to removable shields

A shield which hinges out of the way for repairs and routine service is much more likely to remain with equipment than is a shield which is totally removed for access to the shielded parts. If the operator forgets or feels rushed it is faster and easier to leave the shield off if it already is completely off the equipment, and it soon becomes lost or discarded. The shield should also be durable; if it is damaged through frequent openings or normal equipment use, the shield is apt to be discarded and not replaced.

For the most critical shields the engineer may design a shut-off system that prevents operation when the shield is open. This might be electronically or mechanically an integral link in the system (e.g., an electrical switch in a drier door or on the shield over a combine grain separator). The engineer may deliberately complicate some aspect of the shielding or protective device so that an untrained person without proper tools will have difficulty even opening the shield without destroying the equipment. Use caution with this approach though and consider the adage "it is impossible to make anything fool proof because fools are so ingenius."

"Hazard analysis" describes techniques to assess the seriousness of hazards

The first step in a hazard analysis is to identify hazards that may result from failure, product misuse or accident by using an approach like that in Table 15.1. These hazards can then be categorized according to two schemes: (a) the seriousness of the hazard in terms of safety and property loss and (b) the likelihood of occurrence.

"Failure modes and effects analysis" (FMEA) is simply a methodical analysis of the components in an assembly to determine under what circumstances each component will fail. The consequences of component failure on other components of the assembly are examined. Probability data on components, combined with the economic consequences of each type of failure (partly due to its system effect), can be used to calculate the costs of failures and hence which types of failures are most critical. FMEA is principally a method to improve the design of a product which uses components that are well-understood by engineers. Totally new designs or major departures in designs from traditional products do not lend themselves to FMEA.

"**Fault hazard analysis**" (FHA) is similar to FMEA. FHA emphasizes hazards associated with human error or use under adverse conditions not just component failures and the effects on the system.

"**Fault tree analysis**" (FTA) is a method of flow-charting possible failures and leading the reader through a logical procedure of diagnosing and correcting the problem. Repair manuals and expert systems often use similar techniques. However, the fault tree analysis procedure has unique symbols and logic which convey specific meanings to those skilled in the use of FTA.

SECTION II—LEGAL ASPECTS OF SAFETY

The case where the Fortune 500 Johns Mansville Corporation acted legally, but perhaps not morally, when they declared bankruptcy, despite financial strength, exemplifies the serious economic consequences of product liability. Mansville was not in immediate danger of financial failure, but the corporation anticipated asbestos-related lawsuits involving billions of dollars, dragging on for years and sapping the company's strength. Several companies have failed financially as a result of liability suits. Product-related lawsuits over the past 20 years have increased twenty-fold.

Liability laws are always changing

Seldom is liability defined as a right or wrong issue. Many factors are weighed in rendering decisions, and often the decision reached is a compromise between the two sides. Liability laws vary from state to state. Often, what is legal may not be viewed as moral and vice versa.

New laws, passed at local, state and national levels, change the interpretations of liability. Every court case is an opportunity for a new interpretation, and if the new interpretation is upheld, a new method of defining liability is created. Consequently, the definitions and discussion of liability in this chapter should be viewed as general guidelines and not as precise legal explanations.

Engineers must be concerned with product and professional liability

Product liability can result in a suit against the product manufacturer or some other party which sold the product. Professional liability results from an engineering malpractice suit directed to the engineer who actually designed the product. Most suits involving a product and an injured party are the product liability type. This is because the manufacturing company is usually more able to pay than the design engineer; so, it is not worthwhile to pursue the design engineer under professional liability.

Product liability can be negligence or strict liability

Negligence accounts for about one fourth of the product liability cases. The seller (whether a retailer, distributor or manufacturer) is liable for negligence if the seller fails to do something that a reasonable person, with an understanding of the problem, would do. Design negligence is usually based on: (a) the design created a concealed danger, (b) the design failed to include the needed safety devices as part of the product or (c) the design was inadequate, based on accepted standards. "Failure to warn" is another common area of negligence cases involving products. Warnings affixed to the product should clearly show dangers from foreseeable misuse. Quantity and content of warnings must be limited in order for those warnings present to be seen and read. Additionally, the designer should warn against foreseeable misuse in the owners manual.

Strict liability does not require that the plaintiff (injured party) prove negligence (i.e., the injured party does not need to prove fault by the manufacturer). The plaintiff must show that the product: (a) failed to perform as safely as an ordinary consumer would expect in its intended or reasonably foreseeable use or (b) proximally caused the injury. In the second case the defendant then has the burden of proving that the benefits of the design outweigh the risks inherent in the design. Carelessness by the user is not a reliable defense by the manufacturer against strict liability. Courts have held that a designer should anticipate carelessness and misuse.

There are three principal ways by which a product can be considered defective. First, it may have a manufacturing defect that was not intended in the design but occurred during manufacture (e.g., a cracked fan blade). Second, it may have a design defect which is unreasonably dangerous to the user. Third, it may have a marketing defect (i.e., it was sold with insufficient warning or instruction).

A "design defect" is the least clear of the above strict liability criteria. Successful evidence for the plaintiff may include: (a) the availability of a safer means of meeting the same need, (b) the ability to eliminate the danger without seriously impairing usefulness or making the product unduly expensive, (c) common knowledge of the danger, yet it was not properly handled by the design or (d) the existence of a professional or governmental standard recommending that such a design is unsafe. Successful defense evidence may include: (a) the danger which caused the injury was obvious and essential to proper operation of the product, (b) the danger could have been reduced, but doing so would have increased costs so excessively as to outweigh the benefits of reduced risk or (c) the product was misused in a manner which could not reasonably be expected.

Product liability is a civil case not a criminal case

A criminal case occurs when someone is accused of breaking the law, and if found guilty the defendant will pay a fine, serve time in jail or suffer some other form of punishment. "Guilt" is not an appropriate term for a civil case. In a civil case the judge or jury "rules in favor" of the defendant or plaintiff. The ruling stipulates the amount of money, if any, that shall be awarded by the defendant to the plaintiff. The ruling may also preclude one party from certain actions, such as building within a specified distance from a neighbor's property.

The plaintiff in a civil case is the party (individual or corporate) who alleges injury (physical or financial) for which the defendant should compensate the plaintiff. The defendant may also be an individual or a corporation. You, a design engineer, will probably become involved in a product liability case if your employer, the manufacturer, is sued. The suit usually results when someone is injured or when a product fails. The engineer who designed the allegedly faulty product cooperates with the employer's legal counsel to defend the manufacturer.

The case may be settled out of court before the trial if an agreement can be reached between both parties. Most product liability cases are settled this way to avoid the expense of a trial. Prior to the trial an engineer may "have his deposition taken." This testimony, under oath and before the trial is usually at the request of the plaintiff's lawyer. The plaintiff's lawyer may ask the defendant written questions which the engineer, through the employer, is legally required to answer. Written questions are called "interrogatories." Interrogatories and depositions are pre-trial information sought by the lawyers.

If the case does go to trial, you, the design engineer, will probably testify on the design and testing of the alleged faulty product. Any conflicts or apparent conflicts with your deposition or interrogatory statements will be highlighted by the opposition lawyer.

Justice is not perfect. A judge or jury makes a decision regarding who is most nearly right; they never know all the details and they seldom thoroughly understand the case. Judges, and especially juries, are influenced by the abilities of the lawyers. Consequently, firms often settle out of court for a compromise sum rather than risk a trial.

Engineers have common misconceptions about product liability defense

One misconception is that fault (bad intent or irresponsible behavior) is a requirement for liability. A firm may be held financially liable despite excellent intentions and professionalism by the firm's engineers. Sympathy may be a factor when a physically injured person sues a large corporation.

A second misconception is that misuse of the product absolves the manufacturer of liability. Misuse will strengthen the defendants case, but does not guarantee a successful defense. If the misuse was foreseeable (though stupid), and if warnings and shielding were inadequate, the chances are excellent that a jury will find for (agree with) the plaintiff.

The third common misconception is that designing according to state-of-the-art safety standards and practices protects the manufacturer from liability. Adherence to standards certainly strengthens the manufacturer's defense, but the court may rule that the standards are not rigorous enough. This is especially true when the standards are "voluntary" standards developed by organizations of manufacturers. Most standards fit that category. Failure to comply with standards, when an injury results from the product, results in near certain loss for the defendant.

A fourth frequent misconception is the belief that training and instruction in proper use are sufficient protection against misuse. Warnings are also necessary. Unfortunately, machines are often borrowed and sold outside the dealer network, and inexperienced people may operate the equipment; therefore, users often are not trained no matter how carefully the manufacturer attempts to train them.

Protect yourself in case of a lawsuit with records and careful design

If there is no record of a design activity, that activity may not have been done in the eyes of the court. Courts are skeptical of memories, particularly after several years have elapsed and personnel have changed. The product you design and test today may be in a lawsuit 10 years from now. The recorded results of your design efforts today may influence the outcome of a future lawsuit.

Use separate, carefully-defined safety checks and document those. Establish a committee to review and approve designs. Industry frequently uses outside groups (other than design) from within the firm to do this check. This can be viewed as a positive mechanism to develop better designs. It is part of your professional responsibility to seek checks and reviews. Reviews, from others' perspectives, can improve the design.

Document all steps in the design. Explain why and how decisions were made. Write these down, sign them and date them. Note alternatives considered and rejected; explain why they were rejected. Documentation is important in patent cases, in corporate planning, in corporate reviews and in protecting you against product liability.

Record and explain engineering change notices. An engineering change notice refers to a change in the product after it was first introduced. A common ploy among plaintiff lawyers is to reveal the product changes that took place since product introduction and imply that those were to correct safety defects. Therefore, you need records stating why and when the changes were made. Sample drawing forms with places for noting engineering changes are included in Appendix III.

Establish testing procedures and describe those in detail. How was the product tested? How did it perform? Who witnessed the tests? Why were certain tests not performed? All these should be answered.

However, some firms require that design records other than those essential to the manufacture and service of product be destroyed once the design is complete. Their reasons are that: (a) the increase in lawsuits, often frivolous, makes it easy for outsiders to obtain company records through interrogatories and thus gain access to confidential design information that may be unknown by some competitors and (b) details can be twisted and deliberately misinterpreted by plaintiff lawyers and, furthermore, serve to educate the plaintiffs at the defendant's expense. A third reason is when the defendant feels the need to hide a mistake, though that type of behavior is clearly unethical if not illegal, and is not common practice among the reputable firms. Even if the design engineer knows that company policy requires destruction of records shortly after product introduction, it is a good idea to keep detailed records for use by the design team up until such time as the company policy would normally discard those records.

Company product safety responsibilities

The product safety committee within a company has the overall responsibility of providing for and reviewing product safety activities along with facilitating internal communications. Remember, product safety includes engineering, sales, service, advertising, technical publications, manufacturing, quality assurance and legal departments within the company. The product safety committee may establish ad-hoc committees to develop answers to selected problems, recommend redesign or recall, analyze accident trends or evaluate warranty experience.

Engineering ethics extend beyond product safety

Professionalism for an engineer is more than technical competence or attention to product safety. As a professional engineer you must apply the highest standards of honesty and integrity in all of your activities. You are often providing your efforts knowing that neither your client, employer or the public is capable of evaluating your engineering effort. Avoid possible conflicts of interest or even the illusion of conflicts of interest.

The National Society of Professional Engineers has adopted a Code of Ethics for Engineers as a guide for practicing professional engineers. Many of the basic principles are based upon good judgment. You and your colleagues can make the difficult moral and ethical judgments by openly discussing the issues and carefully referencing the Code of Ethics (Appendix I).

References

1. ASAE Standards, Updated annually by the American Society of Agricultural Engineers, St. Joseph, MI 49085.

2. Barker vs Lull. 1978. Product liability reports, Commerce Clearing House Inc., 4025 W. Peterson Ave., Chicago, IL 60646, No. 382, Feb. 16.

3. Dieter, G. 1983. Engineering design — A materials and processing approach. McGraw Hill, New York. 592 pp.

4. Hammer, W. 1972. Handbook of product safety. Prentice Hall, Englewood Cliffs, NJ. 351 pp.

5. Woodson, Wesley E. 1981. Human factors design handbook: Information and guidelines for the design of systems, facilities, equipment, and products for human use. McGraw-Hill, New York, 1047 pp.

Discussion problems

1. Investigate the cost and coverage of professional liability insurance.

2. List advantages and disadvantages of removable safety shields.

3. Discuss a recent product liability case reported in the media and defend your verdict.

4. Consult the Code of Ethics for Engineers to answer the

following questions. Reference the appropriate sections and sub-sections of the Code.

(a) Under what conditions may an engineer accept a gift?

(b) What obligations does the engineer have regarding use of his employer's equipment, supplies and facilities?

(c) Under what conditions should engineers review and comment on work of other engineers?

(d) What notices must engineers give to their present employers before seeking other employment?

(e) What portion of an engineer's work belongs to the employer?

(f) Can an engineer advertise?

Project problems

1. Develop a list of possible ways that someone could be injured with your design. Do the benefits outweigh the potential risks? Conceptualize design alternatives which can reduce these risks.

2. What are the engineering ethical issues raised by your design project?

3. Determine where your project is likely to fail and define a suitable factor of safety. Is this factor of safety within the generally accepted practice of engineering?

Chapter 16
Cost Estimating

"Cost reduction is 50% of engineering design."
Dick Mott

"Engineering is doing well with $1.00,
that which any bungler can do,
after a fashion, with $2.00."

Profitability is the measure of engineering success

Profit is the goal of business. Your success as an engineer is measured by the profit your designs earn. Even if you work for government or a nonprofit organization, financial efficiency is a key measure of your success. All types of organizations operate on a budget. Consequently, the design engineer must be concerned with the relative costs of ideas even in the early phases of design. This is more difficult than it sounds because there is seldom a uniform means for comparison. You can walk into 10 different hardware stores, and you will likely receive 10 different prices for the same hammer.

When you, as an engineer, start collecting cost data, you will have a hodge-podge of retail, wholesale, and raw material costs. Firms from which you obtain cost information will have a different system for bidding components based on estimated volume and internal policies. How many units are you planning to buy? They may adjust preliminary estimates upward or downward almost at whim; yet, you need to make screening decisions early based on economics.

A design engineer needs to develop knowledge and techniques for estimating costs and assessing economic feasibility. Experience will help and developing reliable personal contacts in other organizations will help. This chapter discusses the following topics in order: (a) estimation of market size and allowable selling price, (b) approximation of the minimum retail price based on manufacturing costs, (c) understanding general cash flow and budgeting factors, (d) calculating the time value of money and (e) conducting cost-reduction engineering analysis.

Market size can probably be estimated using census and trade association data

How many prospective users of your product are there in your planned market region? Chances are that you can establish an upper limit on the potential market by determining how many people could possibly use the design. For example, you can look-up the number of farms raising hogs in Iowa and the average number of pigs sold from these farms to approximate the maximum number of farrowing crates that could be sold in Iowa. The United States Agricultural Census, available in most university libraries, has these types of data. Obviously, not every Iowa farmer needs new farrowing crates. Perhaps, assuming that you can sell farrowing crates to 1% or 2% of the Iowa farmers is more reasonable. Try talking to an extension economist at Iowa State University to check the validity of this assumption.

Consider another example. Suppose you want to approximate the upper limit of the market of 30 to 45 kW, 2-wheel-drive tractors. The Farm Industrial Equipment Institute compiles such data, and it is published annually in *Implement and Tractor* on a state by state basis. Chances are excellent that some trade association can tell you how many products similar to your design are sold and that Census Data can help you estimate the number of prospective buyers.

These are only a start. What is your competition today? Do you expect a competitive product will come out in the near future? Do you have reason to believe that the total market size will increase or decrease? Give some thought to each of these questions.

Now consider the user's financial situation. How valuable is your product to these users? If a competitive product which performs a similar function as yours is available, you cannot expect the user to pay more for your design unless it offers some important advantages compared to the competition. How much are those advantages (or disadvantages) worth? Perhaps your design represents a totally new approach. If this is the case, how much will your design save over the next most economical alternative?

It is likely that part of your design's value is qualitative, meaning it offers comfort, convenience, aesthetic or some other features that are difficult to quantify. Here, particularly, experience and advice from others will help you assess the value. Recognize that the buyer will quantify these into dollars (perhaps not systematically) to make a decision on which product to buy or at what price to buy.

Market surveys can help define the market size, needs, and selling price

Consider a survey of potential users as a means for determining what these users want and how much they would be willing to pay. Use caution, though, because surveys only provide an indication. Surveys may be most valuable as a tool for determining just who the prospective buyers are. Remember, if only one-tenth of one percent of the farmers in the United States buy a product, that still represents 10,000 farmers! Suppose that you estimate your market as being one tenth of one percent of United States farmers — there are probably characteristics and needs for these farmers different from the total United States farm population.

Go talk with the potential users as a follow-up to your survey. What would make them excited about your design? Try to learn what factors would influence their decision to buy or not buy. How much would they pay?

Establishing selling price is not always easy since one can seldom expect the buyer to answer the question directly. An important measure of selling price can be obtained by looking at the pricing of a competitive product or group of products which perform the same or similar functions of the proposed product. Remember also, products required in production agriculture will generally follow rational cost versus benefits analysis while luxury products or features usually do not.

Now, look back to your problem definition and design specifications. Have you specified a maximum selling price and estimated a market size? If not, or if these need re-examination at this stage, try some of the techniques discussed in this chapter.

Manufactured and retail prices can be estimated as multiples of the raw materials costs

One method for estimating manufactured and selling price is using the "1-3-9" rule for engineering cost estimation.

YOU DON'T EVEN NEED ELECTRICITY
IT RUNS DIRECTLY ON MONEY.

$P_S = 3C_g = 9C_m,$
where,

P_s = retail selling price of a product
C_g = manufactured cost of the product or components used
          in the product (cost of goods)
C_m = raw materials cost in product

Materials' costs can be estimated by multiplying the weight or purchase unit of each material type, times the per unit cost for that type of raw material, times a wastage factor and times a tooling factor. The wastage factor is normally about 1.1 and accounts for materials lost from holes punched or left over from cuts which have little value. On simple parts this may reduce to about 1.06. Tooling factor is for the tooling set-up for each production run of a part. Normally this is 1.1, but it can reduce to nearly 1.0 when production is continuous.

Manufacturing cost consists of materials, direct labor and overhead. Overhead refers to costs such as equipment costs, interest, heating, lighting, plant maintenance, accounting, legal, janitorial services and a variety of similar costs which are part of doing business but may not be directly traced to each product sold. Engineering costs are generally included as overhead. Direct labor cost refers to the wages plus fringe benefits paid to all employees directly involved in producing the product.

Selling price includes manufacturing costs, costs of sales, advertising and taxes plus profit. Competition usually keeps profit margins low, but highly innovative products can be very profitable. Reducing this three-fold markup compared with manufactured cost over an extended period usually leads to bankruptcy. For a company to stay healthy it must receive a long-term return on investment exceeding that available from money-market rates. This means a minimal profit of 10% to 15% in today's economy.

The 1-3-9 rule becomes 1-4-9 for components purchased from outside suppliers

Most manufacturers purchase some components from outside sources in a manufactured rather than raw form. Case International does not make tires; it buys them from Firestone or some other tire manufacturer. Conversely, Dana Corporation is a major United States Corporation that few people are aware of because it makes a business of selling axles and other components to manufacturers who assemble and sell finished products. Case International is an original equipment manufacturer (OEM) while Dana and Firestone are component suppliers.

Component suppliers need a profit, and they need to cover some advertising, legal and accounting costs to stay in business. Consequently, manufactured cost for a component they produce and sell to another firm includes these costs. This is in addition to the material, labor and overhead costs, and raises the manufactured cost to about 4 times the raw material cost. Since component suppliers often sell to several OEM's and major parts dealers, high product volumes result in lower manufacturing costs. In other words the contribution of components purchased from outside sources to the minimum needed retail price is 9/4 times the quoted price from the component suppliers.

Note that the mark-up for a component supplier selling to an OEM is considerably less than the traditional retail price mark-up by the OEM. This is because the component supplier does not need the extensive wholesale-retail distribution network and because the component supplier does not need to invest in advertising to the extent that an OEM does. There is also a tendency on the part of OEMs to be less vertically integrated. Thus, lower capital investments result in lower fixed costs with a greater flexibility to weather down-cycles in the market.

Use the 1-3-9 rule cautiously

There are several limitations to the 1-3-9 rule. First, it assumes volume production. The selling price for a one-of-a-kind product or for small volume production is much higher. Engineering for a low volume product may be several times more expensive than the product materials.

A second limitation is for unique products protected by patents or trade secrets. Businesses charge what the market will support. A new pesticide may be worth $40 per hectare to the producer yet cost only $.50 per hectare in raw materials. Development, testing and capital costs may be major cost considerations. The manufacturer may need to sell at nearly $40 per hectare to recover these costs plus investments in other unsuccessful products. View the 1-3-9 rule as a means for calculating the minimum needed selling price for a product to be profitable. The actual selling price will be higher if the buyers will accept higher prices.

Unusually complex components are the third limitation. The electronic logic circuit used to manage a ventilation system requires only pennies worth of raw materials. That circuit requires a lot of engineering design time and some sophisticated production equipment. Therefore, the manufacturer needs a higher mark-up on materials to recover expenses.

A fourth limitation might be products that have high liability potential (e.g., aerospace). Insurance costs are a significant percent of selling price.

Remember, the 1-3-9 rule is only a rule of thumb and a preliminary means for evaluating the relative cost of design alternatives. As the design progresses, more sophisticated cost estimation techniques are needed. Each manufacturer uses a different system for internal cost accounting and pricing.

Industry cost analysis methods vary

Businesses typically require a project plan and budget before approving work on any project. Forms, such as Fig 16.1, are filled-out by the engineering project leader in cooperation with management.

The design engineer often uses rules-of-thumb and experience in the early stages of screening design ideas. As the design progresses, more detailed cost analyses are needed. Production methods are analyzed step-by-step, and materials, labor and equipment costs for each step are calculated. Through experience, the firm generates tables or computer programs which predict the time required to perform each type of operation. Manufacturing engineers, shop personnel, accounting and others may work with the designer at this stage to estimate manufacturing costs and expected return-on-investment.

FIG 16.1 Project budget form used by FMC at the beginning of each research and development effort (Courtesy of FMC Corp.).

Understand the time value of money

If you own a house, chances are excellent that you paid more for the use of the money than for the original purchase price. That is called interest. If you paid cash for the house, you sacrificed the earnings you would have received had you invested the money in some alternative. You still, effectively, pay interest.

There are formulas for comparing present value (P), annual value (A) and future worth (F). In other words, you can compare $1000 now, $150 per year for 12 years at 8% interest, and $3000 received 12 years from now and determine which is the better deal.

Using Table 16.1, the present value of all three examples is calculated as follows:

Present value of $1000 now   = $1000

Present value of $150/year   = (P/A factor) (A)
for 12 years at 8%

$$= \frac{(1 + i)^n - 1}{i(1 + i)^n} \, (A)$$

$$= \frac{(1 + 0.08)^{12} - 1}{0.08 \, (1 + 0.08)^{12}} \times (\$150)$$

$$= \$1130$$

Present value of $3000   = (P/F factor) (F)

$$= \frac{1}{(1 + i)^n} \, (F)$$

$$= \frac{1}{(1 + 0.08)^{12}} (\$3000)$$

$$= \$1191$$

Therefore, $3000 in 12 years is the best deal *if* the interest rate is fixed at 8%.

Similarly, you could convert all of the three cases to annual worth or future worth equivalents. Case 3 would remain the best deal as long as i = 0.08. You multiply P by an A/P factor and F by an A/F factor to calculate annual worth equivalents. You multiply P by an F/P factor and A by an F/A factor to convert to future worth.

Inflation offsets interest; deflation adds to interest costs

There are major limitations to the above approach. This is obvious to the farmers who purchased land at low prices, lost money about as often as they made money, and emerged "wealthy" after 30 years. The interest they paid was less than the annual rate of land inflation. Effectively, the bank paid farmers for the privilege of loaning money.

On the other extreme, farmers, who purchased land at high prices anticipating higher land values-only to see land values decline, paid an effective annual interest rate greater than the

Table 16.1. Calculating the present, annual and future value of investments.

---

i = interest rate* — normally interest rate per year expressed as a decimal, but can be interest for any period length.

n = number of interest periods — normally design life or loan life in years, but can be for any period length corresponding to the interest rate.

P = present value — a present sum of money

F = future worth — a sum of money at the end of n periods from the present date that is equivalent to principal P with interest i.

A = annual cost — represents the end-of-period payment or receipt in a uniform series continued for the coming n periods, at interest i.

Single payment — compound amount factor
(F/P factor)

$$F/P = (1 + i)^n$$

Single payment — present worth factor
(P/F factor)

$$P/F = \frac{1}{(1 + i)^n}$$

Sinking fund factor
(A/F factor)

$$A/F = \frac{i}{(1 + i)^n - 1}$$

Capital recovery factor
(A/P factor)

$$A/P = \frac{i(1 + i)^n}{(1 + i)^n - 1}$$

Uniform series — compound amount factor
(F/A factor)

$$F/A = \frac{(1 + i)^n - 1}{i}$$

Uniform series — present worth factor
(P/A factor)

$$P/A = \frac{(1 + i)^n - 1}{i(1 + i)^n}$$

---

*This may be the interest paid on borrowed money or the interest which an investor would receive from the best alternative investment. It may also be "true interest" — meaning, interest minus inflation rate.

bank rate of interest. Many such farmers went from a strong financial position to bankruptcy under declining land prices.

Generally, the interest rates are slightly above the overall inflation rate. This true interest rate often ranges from 2 to 5%. However, some items inflate value with time. One of the basic factors which you, as an engineer, must consider is the estimated inflation rate for the investment required in your design. A way to approximate the effect of inflation is to call the "true interest" rate the actual interest minus the estimated inflation rate. Use this "true interest" for i in the formulas listed in Table 16.1.

Tax laws also influence a project's economic feasibility

Taxes are a governmental policy tool as well as a revenue source for government operations. Some investments can be deducted directly from due income taxes. The result is that a portion of the investment is essentially free to the purchaser if the purchaser pays income tax equal to or exceeding the value of the deduction. Recent law allowed a 30% direct deduction for certain alternative energy investments.

Certain investments may be treated as expenses and deducted from income (as opposed to being deducted from income tax due). The effect of this type of deduction is to reduce the price to the buyer by the percentage rate of the taxpayer's incremental bracket. A corporation or individual in the 50% bracket would receive an effective 50% price break.

Other investments can be depreciated over a period of years. Some income can be treated as capital gains and can be taxed at a lower rate. Some investments cannot be deducted in any fashion. Computer software programs are available to help an engineer understand and evaluate the tax effects of alternative decisions. Table 16.2 lists the terms which should be considered in a careful economic analysis.

Cash flow may be the critical factor

Don't forget that real-world problems are not solved overnight. Your employer is paying you with dollars today for the work you are doing today that *should* produce future revenue for your employer. Usually, your engineering manager or other administrator in your organization has evaluated the relative engineering costs versus the potential returns to the employer which will accrue upon the successful completion, production and sale of your design.

A negative cash flow is said to exist during the period of time your design efforts and project activities are costing your employer more than the net profitability of sales of your resulting design.

Table 16.2 Variables considered in a detailed economic analysis.

1. Loan down payment fraction, which is the fraction of the initial investment cost paid directly.

2. Investment tax credit fraction, which is the income tax credit available and usable by the business.

3. Fractional salvage value, which is the value of the facility at the end of its design life.

4. General inflation rate, which is the overall inflation rate.

5. Insurance rate, which is the insurance premium rate expressed a proportion of the initial facility cost.

6. Mortgage interest rate, which is the interest rate paid on the money borrowed to purchase or construct the facility.

7. Depreciation lifetime, which is the life of the facility for income tax depreciation purposes.

8. Mortgage period, which is the loan repayment period.

9. Period of economic analysis, which is usually the useful design life of the facility or 20 years, whichever is less, and is not necessarily the mortgage period or depreciation lifetime.

10. Property tax rate, which is the effective real estate and/or property tax levied against the facility as a percentage of the initial value.

11. Energy inflation rate, which is the rate of energy price inflation for the type(s) of energy required by the facility.

12. Maintenance inflation rate, which is the rate of maintenance costs inflation.

13. Operation cost inflation, which is the rate of operating costs inflation.

14. Incremental income tax rate, which is the incremental income tax rate appropriate to the facility owner.

15. Discount rate, which is the rate of return realizable by the owner if the initial investment were invested in the best alternative.

Obviously, a net positive cash flow over the life of the design is expected. It is anticipated that some new products will lose money for a couple of years. If the product is successful it will later recover this lost money plus interest plus profit. Businesses sometimes are forced to abandon projects which they believe will be economically profitable over the long-term because they do not have the financial resources to absorb the short-term losses.

Most businesses estimate a cash flow diagram (Fig 16.2) and

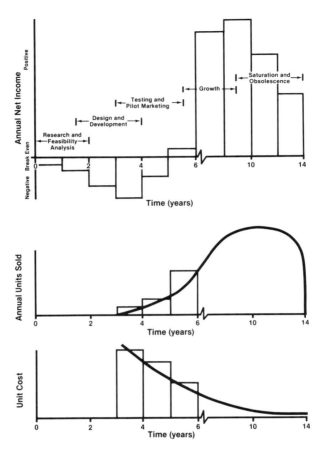

FIG 16.2 Cash flow, production volume and unit-cost history for a typical new
product.

analyze their economic position on a year-by-year basis to
determine whether they can afford an investment. Usually, the
business must choose among several possible, new projects to
select those which appear to have the greatest profit potential so
that the company does not assume an unhealthy debt level.

Cost limits assigned to project engineers

For most designs (tractors, farm equipment, etc.) you, the
product engineer, are given an upper-limit cost for which you
must design. It is based upon: (a) market competition from
similar products, (b) costs of present product lines and (c)
corporate profitability goals. However, any new products should
have improvements (e.g., performance, features, reliability) over

what is already in the market. Thus, you need to ask, "What is the customer willing to pay for these improvements?"

Cost-reduction engineering is a major part of design

When a design is developed conceptually and technically proven, a manufacturer will usually spend significant engineering time determining how to reduce the manufacturing cost without sacrificing quality. Bids on components and materials are solicited while alternative materials and modified part designs are evaluated Then, the entire manufacturing process is restudied to determine whether the manufactured cost can be further reduced.

Cost-reduction is often the motivation for redesigning an existing product that is already performing well mechanically. Competition may have a product similar to yours selling at a cost lower than your company can afford to sell. Therefore, your choices are to develop a less expensive design or abandon the product.

Cost-reduction engineering is also part of the continuing profitability plans for companies. On low volume products this may be limited to the enginer being alert to possibilities to reduce manufactured costs while placing primary efforts on other projects. However, for high-volume products several engineers may work full time to try to lower the cost of an existing product. They continually test alternative materials and components and watch for technological and economic developments which offer lower-cost design alternatives.

Understand the "bottom line"

Cost is so *important* in determining the success of a product that it should *always* be defined initially in the product definition phase as a product goal. Conceptual designs that will not meet these cost goals are as unacceptable as ones that will not function properly and should be eliminated.

References

1. Dieter, G. 1983. Engineering design: A materials and processing approach. McGraw Hill, New York. 592 pp.

2. Rondeau, H. 1975. The 1-3-9 rule for product cost estimation Machine Design Magazine, Penton Press, Cleveland, OH.

Discussion problems

1. For your state determine the three agricultural commodities produced with largest dollar volume of producer sales.

2. Determine the production and consumption of high fructose corn syrup in the three largest consuming nations in the world in the most recent year available. Repeat for 10 years ago.

3. Determine the number of 30 to 45 kW tractors sold in the United States last year.

4. Estimate the market for 3-point-hitch, category-1 rotary mowers in your state.

5. For a labor intensive United States crop, estimate the potential market of a labor saving harvest machine. (Consider the effects of import and export charges.)

6. Estimate the wholesale and retail price of an item that you might purchase from a local agribusiness enterprise.

7. Estimate the 20-year return-on-investment for installing a tile drainage or irrigation system in your state.

8. What effects do tile drainage have on machinery costs?

9. Assess the feasibility of installing a solar system for preheating live-stock ventilation air in your area (consider energy, inflation, and interest costs).

Project problems

1. Estimate the potential market size for your design.

2. Approximate a maximum retail price for your design based on economic value to the user.

3. Estimate the minimum retail price for your design based on the raw material and component costs.

Chapter 17
Component and
Supplier Selection

*"Component manufacturers can let you focus
your design efforts on other projects."*

"A $0.20 'O' ring can cost your design months."

One of your responsibilities as a design engineer is to consider as many alternatives and sources as possible prior to specifying a final design or component. All manufacturers are dependent on outside sources for materials, components, and/or production equipment. You cannot do that by checking only retail and wholesale outlets. You need a systematic approach.

Find suppliers through product directories, trade journals and professional contacts

The Thomas Register, Sweets Catalog, specialty product guides and the yellow pages are important sources (Chapter 9). Trade journals and specialty magazines such as the *ASHRAE Journal, Machine Design, Measurements and Control* and *Heating, Piping and Air Conditioning*, have advertising and articles which can help you locate potential component suppliers. There are thousands of similar sources, and probably several are closely related to your needs. Check with peers and colleagues who may know good sources. If you are looking for tires, you have a list of six farm tractor tire manufacturers. If you are looking for electric motors, the list is almost endless!

Check your contacts again and determine their experiences with, for example, the different tire manufacturers. Call engineers at each company and discuss your needs with them. The tire engineer who works only on tire design will know more about tires than you, the tractor designer. Ascertain how much and the nature of the design help they can provide. Will they develop a special tire for your needs and help with testing? Check the business references in the library to make sure your prospective supplier is financially sound.

Suppose you are looking for electric motors and not tires. You can locate a list of 5247 electric motor manufacturers. You cannot spend the next three years researching each one. Consequently, you will need to rely heavily on contacts and past experience. Often, reputation and a good working relationship with a component supplier are worth more than the lowest price. If you need the lowest price, the purchasing department can advertise for the lowest bidder once the production scale is established.

What if no one produces the component you need?

This is a common problem. You need a specialty component, and you do not have the time, money or inclination to develop the component in your firm. Most component suppliers will work

with an OEM to develop a component if assured some return for their effort. Obviously, the unit price is less if the supplier anticipates a large quantity of sales.

There are also consulting firms and engineering job-shops which specialize in developing new components. Perhaps you should hire an outside firm to design something which you can manufacture. Perhaps you want a consultant to design the component and then you will contract the production out to a specialty engineering job-shop. Many OEM's function also as an engineering job-shop. DuAl, for example, is a loader, manure spreader, silage wagon and deep tillage equipment manufacturer. DuAl is also a hydraulic cylinder component supplier for other OEM's.

Be careful of product claims

Just because the product literature claims that a battery will provide over 1000 cycles does not make it true. Just because the sales representatives believe they can provide a battery for use in a prototype in 4 weeks does not mean they will, in fact, be able to do so. Product claims are usually based on a specific set of test conditions which may not apply to your design problem. Similarly, delivery dates quoted usually assume that everything will go right. Frequently, that does not happen.

Sometimes suppliers quote excessively conservative product claims because they do not want to risk being wrong. After all, you are designing something new. The component supplier probably does not have test data and experience for their product in applications exactly like yours.

Know your component suppliers

The consistent ability of your component suppliers to provide high quality purchased parts is very important. The design engineer has a two-fold responsibility : to design *quality* parts and to provide relevant specifications for those parts. For example, don't design injection-molded parts that have large, thin web areas or close-tolerance, welded parts that cannot be ground after heat treating. Any component supplier will have a difficult time meeting these types of specifications. Don't make the part specifications overly restrictive. If C-1020 steel is not specifically needed, don't specify it. If steel with a minimum ultimate strength is required, specify this requirement because it is relevant to the design. Remember, you must work with your component suppliers to insure that the parts you need are produced to your specifications on a consistently reliable basis. Your problems with their parts are *their* problems and vice versa!

Both the supplier and the manufacturer must take steps to insure that components produced and components accepted, respectively, are of the appropriate quality. Most companies are moving from inspection programs which looked at many or all the parts to statistically-based methods in which a lot of parts are accepted or rejected based upon the failure rate of a statistical sample of parts from the lot.

Look for suppliers who mass produce components similar to those you need

You can buy a calculator for less than $20 that once cost millions. Part of the reason is technological changes, but part of the reason is volume production. A one-of-a-kind chip which is quite similar to the calculator chip would cost thousands of dollars. The lesson is simple. Do not design special chips if you can use mass-produced calculator chips without impairing your product function. Later, if your design becomes a product with a high volume sales, your company may decide to design a chip specifically for your product.

Do not overlook the need for global suppliers. This is especially relevant if you plan to assemble and market your product world-wide.

Do not stop looking when you find one source

Many of your sources will prove unacceptable. The claims may be wrong, the delivery may not be soon enough or you may modify your design in a way which makes that component ill-suited. One of the most common mistakes by an inexperienced designer is to find one source which looks good for each component, order the components and then wait for arrival. Find at least three suppliers for each component and maintain a good working rapport with each of them. You may be going back to a lower choice in order to meet needs.

Learn how to talk with a sales rep on the telephone

Sales reps may or may not be engineers, but chances are sales reps know more about their product and their competition's product than you can learn in a long time. Don't be afraid to approach a sales rep with questions. Non-technical questions will often be answered easily; the technical questions will often be answered indirectly by referring you to other specialists and engineers. These additional contacts are invaluable.

Don't approach a sales rep with the attitude that you know all the answers and the rep only writes up the orders. If they don't know the answer to your question or they don't handle a product line that meets your needs, ask them for a lead through one of their competitors. Sales reps know they aren't going to make a sale from every call, but they do know that if they help you this time, you'll remember and call them the next time. Remember to add their name to your file of professional contacts.

Supplier selection should be a planned process

Initially in the design process, attempt to survey all potential component suppliers. The information generated from this survey may also prove useful in developing design specifications and project directions. Screen the suppliers to two or three at the early stages of design concepting. As the design moves toward production, you may select one supplier (with perhaps an alternate) and obtain a long-term commitment. Remember that the component supplier becomes an integral part of the production of your product.

References

1. ASAE Technology Issue, Published annually by ASAE, St. Joseph, MI 49085.
2. Industrial pages, Telephone directory published annually for selected regions of the US.
3. Information Handling Services. Product data microfilm file. Published annually, Englewood, CO 80150.
4. Thomas Register and Thomas Register Catalog, 16 volumes published annually, Thomas Publishing Co., New York 10119.
5. Yellow pages, Telephone directory published annually for local areas.

Discussion problems

1. Obtain three price quotes for a specific purchased part or raw-material item and explain why you think the quotes differ.

2. List all factors which should be considered in selecting a component manufacturer or supplier. Which factors are most important and why?

Project problem

1. List all purchased parts and raw materials for your present project along with suppliers, prices and delivery dates.

2. List three suppliers, along with prices and delivery dates, for what you believe will be the most expensive purchased part required in your present project.

Chapter 18
Manufacturing
Considerations

"If you can't make it — you can't sell it."

"Thousands of engineers can design bridges, calculate stresses and strains, and draw up specifications for machines, but the great engineer is the one who can tell whether the bridge or the machine should be built at all ... "
Eugene G. Grace

Design and manufacturing work together

One of the myths about engineering practice is that the design engineer will develop a product design, turn it over to an independent department called manufacturing, and it is then manufacturing's problem as to how to make each part and assemble the product. It is true that most firms have design engineers and manufacturing engineers, each with distinct areas of expertise and responsibility; however, these people usually work closely to develop good-quality designs which can be manufactured affordably.

Product development schedules have become shorter in consideration of the time value of money (i.e., the investment in development) and in response to the increasing rate of techno-

BUT I DIDN'T KNOW THIS WOULD
CAUSE A PROBLEM!

logical advancement. There isn't time for the design to pass back
and forth between departments in an effort to compromise on an
acceptable design which manufacturing can produce efficiently.
Industries' response is to emphasize team design, beginning in the
early stages of the design process. This closer cooperation between
design and manufacturing results in better quality designs, lower
manufacturing costs and less time needed to develop the design.

Design decisions should be joint decisions involving both the
design and the manufacturing engineers. Manufacturing's ability,
willingness and desire to aid new product introduction is
proportional to their involvement.

Know your firm's capabilities

Design and manufacturing engineers must work together as a
team. Start this cooperation early in the design process. The most
important consideration related to a designs manufacturability is
the firm's manufacturing capabilities. Optimal production
techniques vary depending on the equipment and expertise of
each company. Consequently, the most economical design varies
from firm to firm.

Most manufacturing companies produce several products. They have production runs for different product lines and components that may last from a few hours to several days. Changes from one production run to another are expensive because labor and equipment time are lost during the change-over. This change-over problem is more common than you may realize. It is estimated that 75% of the metal parts manufactured in the United States are produced in lots of 50 or less. Studies on equipment usage in such instances show an average 5% use-time for machine tools.

By cooperating, design and manufacturing engineers can develop designs which minimize the time and frequency of change-overs, increasing the profitably to the firm. The best ways to do this depend on that particular firm's product mix, management style, equipment and a variety of factors unique to the firm.

Companies develop standard costs for each manufacturing operation that they normally use. By knowing these, the designer can select the least-cost manufacturing process that will produce the level of quality needed in each part or assembly step. For example, drilled holes cost more than punched holes; so, drilled holes are specified if the value in terms of improved product quality justifies the added cost. Consider a loader bucket which has bolt-on teeth. Should the mounting holes in the bucket be punched or drilled? Generally, they are punched because as long as the bolt can be inserted and match the teeth, there is little value in a more perfectly formed hole.

The general implications for the design engineer are:

1. Design parts that can be made with the available manufacturing machines rather than require new machines.

2. Strive for parts standardization among the products a firm produces to lessen manufacturing and inventory costs.

3. Select tolerances and specifications that optimize product value relative to production costs for your firm.

Computer-routing controls material flow

Gravely Manufacturing uses a computer-scheduled routing system in which each part has a specification packet that includes the drawing, the material requirements and the exact flow sequence through the manufacturing process (Fig 18.1). The manufacturing process is defined in detail *during the design stage* and includes which production machines and attachments are to be used, how to set and operate the production machines for that part, how and when to assemble parts, what quality checks and procedures are required, where on the manufacturing floor each

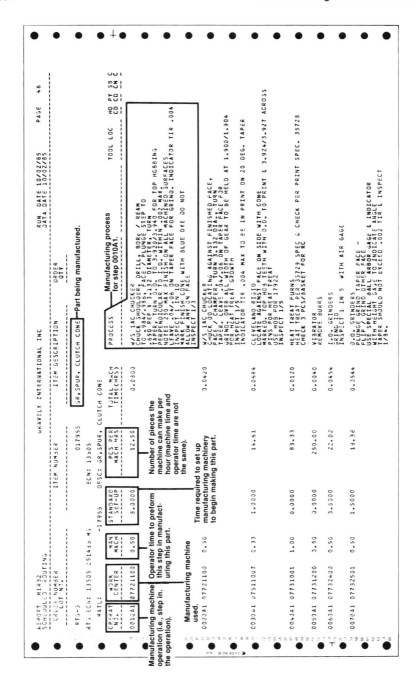

FIG 18.1 Computer routing sheet for describing the manufacturing steps, time and equipment needs for each part in an assembly (Courtesy of Gravely International).

part begins and is combined with other parts, etc. A manufacturing engineer will likely prepare the routing sheet for each part, but the design engineer works with the manufacturing engineer to think the design step-by-step through manufacture.

This kind of approach is especially critical for companies that use production line or low-inventory methods. For example, on a production line the production rate is determined by the slowest step on that line. It is preferred that the time requirements for each step be as closely matched as possible to minimize wasting of employee and equipment time. Therefore, the design engineer and manufacturing engineer will work together during design to determine which are the limiting steps in production associated with that design. Time requirements for the limiting steps may be reduced by using extra production equipment and personnel on that step, but often this is impractical because the company uses that same production line for numerous types and models of equipment and cannot afford to rearrange the line dramatically nor to add equipment that is needed for only one model. Instead, the design engineer will try to find ways to change the design which reduce the time requirements for the most limiting steps. These changes may add to materials costs, (or in other ways seem illogical when the design process is viewed as independent of manufacturing), but the manufacturing cost savings can more than offset the added materials cost.

Minimizing production line change-over time requirements is another reason why the manufacturing engineer and design engineer should prepare a "computer routing" for each part while still in the design phase. Manufacturers prefer not to maintain large quantities of finished products stored in warehouses until needed, but the consequence of minimizing inventory is that production lines are changed-over frequently. Therefore, it is important that the manufacturing machinery settings and tooling for each part not require unusually long change-over times. This, too, may mean that a design change which appears illogical can substantially lower the cost to produce that product.

Automated manufacturing is the third industrial revolution

Manufacturing methods and philosophies are changing dramatically in response to computers and electronic advances. Water and steam power for manufacturing caused the first industrial revolution, and fractional horsepower motors were the impetus of the second industrial revolution. Both meant better and more abundant products at lower costs, and both caused upheaval in business structures and economic geography. Automated manufacturing technologies encompass computerized routing, numerically-controlled machine tools, robotics, computer-aided design (CAD), computer-aided manufacturing (CAM) and more.

Philosophy and procedure changes accompany and are possible because of new computer and electronic technologies. Manufacturers have long wanted to minimize their stocks of raw material and finished product, the frequency and time required for product change-over, their investment in production machinery, manufacturing floor space and variations in personnel needs. These goals often conflict (e.g., making more model "x" grain elevators while the manufacturing machinery is set for that product means less cost/unit for the product changeover, but more inventory cost because it will take longer to sell the extra elevators); so, the firm makes demand forecasts and calculates the overall least-cost strategy. Historically, production line change-over has taken hours or days to accomplish and results in major costs; so, firms would often make one or two production runs per year and store inventory until sold. Numerically-controlled manufacturing machinery and computerized production and inventory data make possible "single-minute" die changes and rapid, low-cost changeovers. Consequently, concepts of "manufactured-to-customer-order" and "zero-inventory" have become popular.

The ability to changeover rapidly means also that there are more possibilities in product variation without substantially higher costs. In a completely computerized manufacturing environment, products can be customized from a computer keyboard by the customer and salesman, and this information can be relayed directly to the manufacturing line so that the finished product is exactly what the customer wanted.

Higher precision and more easily operated and controlled manufacturing machinery mean better product quality as well as more diverse options. The physical procedures of punching and drilling holes have not changed much, but the capabilities of numerically-controlled machines to locate the holes and produce the wanted pattern are greatly improved. Uniformity of same-design parts and conformity of manufactured parts to the designed parts are better.

CAD-CAM makes automated low-volume production possible

Computer aided design—computer aided manufacture means using the computer as a tool to visualize and analyze the design while under development, to specify (draft) the design more quickly and then to control the manufacturing process to produce that design. It is the control and rapid adjustment of the manufacturing process from the designer's computer terminal that makes automated low-volume production possible. Considerable cost savings are possible, especially when these low-volume products are quite similar to other low-volume products made by the same company.

Duct layout for air-type heating and cooling systems is an excellent example because duct work varies from building to building. Once the sheet-metal ducts were hand-drawn and specified by a design engineer; then, the sheet metal contractor studied the plans to bid the project; later, the contractor and employees hand-measured and cut the pieces and installed the duct. Today the design engineer can more quickly draw and specify the duct work with the aid of computer software specially developed for duct layout. A bid is easily prepared using the computer plan-reading software and standard cost data plus judgment on unusual characteristics of the design. Finally, computer-controlled sheet metal cutting and forming machinery can cut, form and assemble the duct work with no hand measurement and with much better precision and quality. This automated duct design and manufacture process (CAD-CAM) means lower-cost manufacture and more competitive, customized and low-volume products.

Costs are proportional to tolerances

The higher the tolerance required, the more expensive it is, in general, to manufacture (Fig 18.2). Similarly, the more exacting

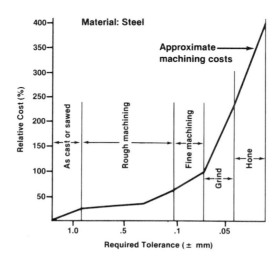

FIG 18.2 Guide for selecting machining finish requirements used by Deere & Co. (Courtesy Deere & Co.).

the surface requirements of the part, the more expensive it is to produce. Manufacturing machinery is more costly, more manufacturing steps are required and the skill level required of the production employee increases as the tolerances become more refined.

One of your responsibilities as a design engineer is to decide the minimum acceptable tolerance and refinement. This does not mean designing for low quality. Loader bucket design is a good illustration of this situation. Bucket width on a farm loader could vary two centimeters or more with no loss of quality. Yet, this is a large tolerance by manufacturing standards (3 millimeters is a common tolerance for steel parts where tolerance is not critical). Conversely, tolerances of only a few tenths of a millimeter are required for the pin diameter which connects the loader bucket to the loader frame.

Tolerances are seldom uniform on a given part. The example above illustrates that large tolerances may be acceptable in most loader bucket dimensions but are unacceptable at the attachment points between the brackets and frame. Determine which dimensions are critical and specify those with sufficiently close tolerances so as to reflect the level of quality necessary. Reference the less critical dimensions from the critical dimensioned parts (Fig 3.3).

There are statistical techniques which can predict the combined effects of individual part tolerances on the system as a means for defining the needed tolerance. You can use such techniques to determine tolerance levels which will keep the probability of part rejection at a value near zero yet not require excessively close tolerances.

Optimize product value relative to cost

Manufactured product quality is a function of closeness to the design specifications. There will likely be a part rejection range, based on geometric tolerances and material quality, which, if exceeded, means the part has zero value and, if not exceeded, means that the part is used and of value. In its most simplistic scheme, the product value may be a constant if not rejected and zero if rejected (Fig 18.3).

Taguchi and Phadke (1984) and other quality control/ manufacturing optimization experts recommend a more sophisticated measure of product quality. They state that the more closely the product conforms to design specifications, the better the performance (i.e., smoother operation, longer life, better appearance, fewer breakdowns, etc.); therefore, the product value is higher (Fig 18.3).

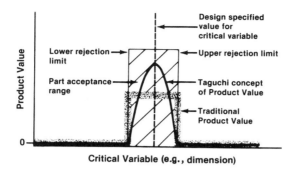

FIG 18.3 Product value functions related to design specifications and the part acceptance versus rejection regions for manufacturing variables.

Cost to produce is also a function of the closeness to the design specifications which must be achieved. Historically the cost of achieving narrow or fine tolerances has been relatively expensive; so, most manufacturers would specify tolerances only as closely as necessary to ensure that the product did not exceed the rejection tolerance limits. However, advances in computer-controlled manufacturing equipment make it possible to achieve finer tolerances without substantially higher costs in some instances (Figure 18.4). You, the designer, need to understand how your specifications are related to both product value and product cost functions.

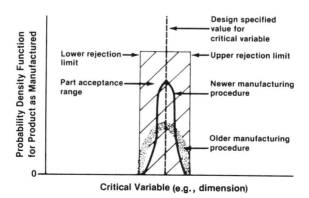

FIG 18.4 Using the Taquchi concept of product value to cost optimization, the newer manufacturing procedure may be justified while using the traditional product value concept (FIG 18.3); there is no incentive to change.

Manufacturing processes classified

This section classifies manufacturing processes in seven categories. Detailed information on these processes can be obtained from the references listed at the end of the chapter.

1. **Casting** — Molten metal, plastic or glass is placed in a mold and solidified. Investment castings can be held to tolerances of ± 0.03 mm while sand castings are ± 1.0 mm.

2. **Deformation** — Material is formed using pressure, heat or a combination.

(a) **Cold forming** — Punching, bending, shearing and rolling processes are the most common. Most sheet metal and light gauge steel forming are of this type. Punching tolerances are of the order of ± 1 mm.

(b) **Hot forming** — Forging, extrusion and drawing processes are most common. Thick steel (over 6 mm) and plastics are most commonly hot formed.

3. **Cutting and machining** — Material is drilled or cut using drilling, turning, milling, grinding, shaving or polishing equipment. It is important to note that drilling tolerances are ± 0.25 mm, reaming ± 0.025 mm and lapping are ± 0.0025 mm.

4. **Particulate techniques** — This is material processing on a molecular scale. Composite materials are formed by spattering on a few-molecule thick coating or by changing the crystalline structure of material by diffusing alternate materials into the base material. It is the most rapidly developing processing technique and used extensively in micro-electronics.

5. **Heat or surface treatment** — Material properties of the surface are improved by heat treatments, quenching techniques, carburizing, mechanical peening, spray coatings, dip coatings, electroplating and painting.

6. **Joining** — Materials are permanently joined with adhesives by welding, brazing, nailing, stapling, soldering or glueing.

7. **Assembly** — Components are assembled by welding, glueing, bolting, riveting and other means to produce subassemblies or the finished part.

There are generalizations that can help a designer

1. Cold forming is faster and less expensive than cutting or machining techniques. Punching, bending and shearing are generally preferable to drilling or sawing.

2. Automatic gas and plasma arc cutting are alternatives to cold punching and can also be relatively inexpensive, especially where a variety of types and sizes of holes need to be cut into a specific piece of steel.

3. Bending to form a shape is less expensive than welding

together components. If you can lay out an odd-shaped piece on straight stock, punch holes, then bend to shape, that is much preferable to punching holes and welding flat pieces together.

4. Welding deforms material by causing heat distortion. Manufacturing engineers can minimize this with properly-designed jigs and by welding alternately at different locations on a part to distribute weld-induced residual stresses. Also, machine parts after, rather than before, welding if possible to prevent distortion of critical surfaces.

5. Cold forming processes require minimum lips. The thicker the material, the wider the support required. For example, you cannot punch a 20 mm diameter hole in 10 mm plate steel located 15 mm from the edge of the plate. The 5 mm thick edge will tear away. Also, the higher the plate strength, the larger the minimum bend radius will be.

6. Formed stock manufactured on site is often less expensive than the purchased equivalent stock for a firm which has the forming capabilities. In other words, it may be less expensive to make a steel angle in a press using flat steel than to buy a steel angle pre-formed by the steel manufacturer. Similarly, it may cost less to form and use a steel channel and tubing from plate steel than to buy rectangular tubing or channel.

References

1. Pollack, H. W. 1968. Manufacturing and machine tool operations. Prentice Hall, Englewood Cliffs, NJ. 593 pp.

2. Schey, John A. 1977. Introduction to manufacturing processes. McGraw-Hill, New York. 392 pp.

3. Taguchi, G. and M.S. Phadke. 1984. Quality engineering through design optimization. Conference Record IEEE Globecom Conference, Atlanta, GA, Vol. 3:1106-1113.

4. Yankee, H.W. 1979. Manufacturing processes. Prentice-Hall, Englewood Cliffs, NJ. 765 pp.

Discussion Problems

1. List specific examples on farm machinery design where punching, drilling, reaming and lapping are used.

2. Compare manufacturing technologies for a pole barn machine shed with prefab roof trusses to a farm tractor loader.

Project Problems

1. Prepare a routing sheet for one of the manufactured parts in your present project.

2. Prepare parts drawings for one or more of the special parts required for your present project.

Chapter 19
Standardization
and Simplification

*"Standards are the primary means by which
the fruits of technology are accommodated
to our society." ASTM*

*"Simplification is not always obvious;
some things must be **seen** to be believed."*

Standardization has three meanings

Minimizing the number of specially manufactured parts required as components for a manufacturer's product line is referred to as parts standardization. Equipment interchangeability standards, a second meaning of standards, often occurs when industries form trade associations to promote interchangeability of equipment such as common thread series and pipe sizes, common lumber dimensions and a limited range of farm tractor drawbar configurations. Safety and consumer protection standards developed by trade associations, professional societies or government are the third type of standardization.

Standardize and simplify

Historians argue that the ingenuity and success of United States business during the 19th century resulted from a simple axiom: "standardize and simplify." Gun production was changed from a

...AND THE SATELLITE HOOKUP
GOES HERE...

craft where each part was handmade and handfitted by a skilled craftsman to interchangable parts which were mass produced and assembled. Guns were cheaper and produced much faster. Eli Whitney has been credited with being the father of standardized parts, but it is interesting to note how this happened. After Eli Whitney invented and patented the cotton gin there were numerous infringers. Whitney spent a good deal of money defending his patent against these infringers and, out of necessity, secured a gun manufacturing contract from the U.S. Government. In order to reduce his manufacturing costs he sought to standardize the parts.

The brilliance of Henry Ford was efficient production, not mechanized excellence, in the design of cars. Strong manufacturing firms in the 20th century owe their success to efficient production and controlled quality. It has been said that Henry Ford required all of the suppliers of fasteners (bolts, washers, nuts, clips etc.) to ship them in standardized wooden shipping containers. The reason, the shipping container boards became the seat boards of the Model-T!

Standardization and simplification have direct benefits to the manufacturer. Standardization means fewer tooling changeovers to manufacture batches of components because there are fewer components. Standardization means less inventory is needed by the manufacturer because there are fewer types of components in stock and because it takes less time to cycle through the entire product line. Parts standardization simplifies record-keeping because there are fewer components to track. Standardization in types of raw materials used in manufacture, allows better volume discounts. It also means less money and space committed to raw materials.

Standardization can mean fewer mistakes! For example, while 7/16 in. bolts are standard in the fastener industry, manufacturers often have a standard policy *not* to use them because a 1/2 in. nut can mistakenly be used with a 7/16 in. bolt at a considerable reduction in strength and hence safety. The proliferation of metric and English-sized fasteners can create further problems with mismatched fasteners and may lead to future standards.

Standardization has indirect benefits for the manufacturer. Standardization means wholesalers and retailers do not need to stock such an extensive array of repair parts. Consequently, they are more likely to have the repair parts on hand when needed. This promotes customer satisfaction. Standardization usually makes products easier to repair and maintain. This, too, promotes customer and dealer satisfaction. Remember your own experiences repairing equipment and finding parts when you design equipment.

Standardization among manufacturers

Imagine trying to fix machinery with no standard bolt and nut sizes! Imagine trying to match farm tractors to implements with no standard pto, hydraulic connectors, drawbar and three point hitch arrangements. Imagine purchasing electrical equipment and appliances if each power company sold power at a different voltage and frequency. Imagine steel design or structural building design if there were no common sizes and strength properties. Standardization among manufacturers is not just important, it is absolutely essential for even a low level of technology in society.

Most standardization among manufacturers in the U.S. is voluntary. Manufacturers realize that widespread public acceptance requires some degree of standardization. Standards are developed through accredited technical societies (such as ASAE). Some trade associations, (such as the Farm and Industrial Equipment Institute) assist the consensus standards development process by identifying needs and submitting proposals to the standards writing organizations. Some standards may be exact-

I BETTER FIGURE OUT HOW TO MAKE
THIS OR LOOK FOR ANOTHER JOB.

ing as is the case with lumber dimensions, steel sizes and stress properties, bolt designs or electric power voltages and wiring methods. Other standards may specify a broad range such as ASAE Standard S203.10, Rear Power Take-Off for Agricultural Tractors which specifies that a drawbar be 330 to 559 mm (13 to 22 in.) above the ground depending on pto type and maximum pto power. Standardization promotes competition. Firms which have a near monopoly or a major product share often resist standardization to reduce competition. This can be both good and bad. By restricting knowledge of planned changes in its product line a company can afford to invest heavily in research and development and charge a premium price to recover its development costs. Similarly, drug companies charge a premium for new drugs to recover their initial development costs. Competitors who do not have the significant research and development costs can often produce some or all of the components more economically. Patents are not always a reliable protection to the product developer because often a competitor can devise a different product which performs the same function in a slightly different manner. Standardization promotes competition which lowers prices and minimizes complacency. Standardization can also make research and development unattractive and, thereby, inhibit technological advance.

Standardization has a typical cycle. When new technology emerges there is little standardization as each entrepreneur develops products independent of others. As the product becomes widely accepted, the number of competing manufacturers decreases, and the manufacturers usually agree to some degree of standardization. Tractor-implement hydraulic couplings are a product example which needs additional efforts to standardize industry wide. Computer languages and computer hardware interconnection methods are areas that are likely to undergo further standardization.

Standards are used to promote safety and to protect the consumer's investment

Think of the lives saved by tractor roll-over protective structures that meet performance standards. Think of the fires prevented and lives saved by requiring electrical grounding and fire detection devices in buildings. Think of the problems with finding drinking water if there were no standards regarding waste disposal and water quality.

Imagine the difficulties you would face trying to select an oil for your car if there were no standards. Imagine your dilemma as a designer or manufacturer if you knew how to produce a safe quality product, but your competitor could produce an unsafe product less expensively that looked like your product.

Standards protect ethical designers, manufacturers and the public

There are two basic types of safety and consumer protection standards: (a) voluntary and (b) mandatory. Voluntary standards include those developed by professional societies such as ASAE, and general standards groups such as ASTM, and ISO. Trade associations such as the Farm and Industrial Equipment Institute (FIEI) develop proposals for standards and work with the standards writing groups to produce standards which meet the needs of all parties involved.

Voluntary standards are usually developed by technical committees (such as the ASAE Loader Committee). The technical committee drafts the standard and votes to approve the standard; then, it is submitted to another review group (the Standards Committee in the case of ASAE). The technical committee members tend to be engineers from manufacturing firms,

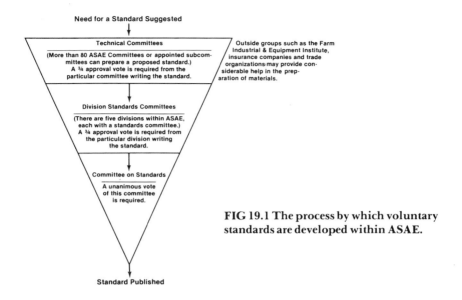

FIG 19.1 The process by which voluntary standards are developed within ASAE.

universities and government with expertise on the particular subject (e.g., loaders). The Standards Committee is a cross-section of experienced agricultural engineers with knowledge of standards and their legal implications.

Voluntary standards are widely accepted by industry for a number of reasons. As the name implies these standards are developed by volunteer panels of experts in the particular subject. Voluntary standards are not really voluntary even though each company has the freedom to choose whether or not to comply. However, failure to comply with voluntary standards developed by accredited groups such as ASAE leaves that company in a much less defensible position should lawsuits arise regarding that aspect of the problem. Therefore, most companies do comply unless they have strong evidence to support their position and are convinced that the product as they designed it is better.

Mandatory standards (regulations) are government required or sanctioned. For example, laws specify the types and quantities of contaminants that a firm can discharge into the environment. An example of "sanctioned" are building requirements which must be met if government money is loaned to purchase the house. A builder need not comply with this standard but then cannot sell the house to a buyer who intends to use government-loaned money.

Mandatory standards can be laws or regulations enforced by virtually any government body. City and county codes may limit

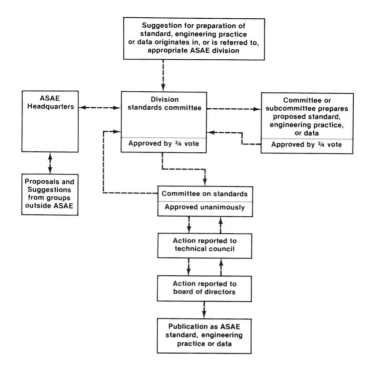

FIG 19.2 The formal voluntary standards procedure of ASAE (courtesy of ASAE).

building and land use through zoning and inspection standards. States may require a professional engineer's stamp of approval for certain types of buildings in the state. The Environmental Protection Agency, Occupational Health and Safety Act, Department of Commerce and National Bureau of Standards are just some of the laws and agencies which develop federal standards.

Simplification is the ultimate in design

Don't ever make the mistake of assuming that your design cannot be simplified in function, form or fabrication. At several points in the design project specifically ask yourself the question, "Can this be done in a simpler way?" Don't be afraid to ask others the same question. They will often produce a response that will trigger a significant simplification after you have analyzed the suggestions. In some companies regular design reviews are conducted, permitting several people to look for design simplications and ways to standardize. Remember, a key factor is to enlist the aid of others to assist you. If you happen to come upon a significant discovery, don't hurry-off as if nothing happened. Use your powers of observation and analysis to their fullest to extract every bit of understanding and simplification that is possible.

Standardization does not imply stagnation

You should always realize that most likely someone or some company is trying to do what you are trying to do, but *better* than you. Designs must be dynamic and constantly changing, not static. These systematic design changes and standardization must be planned. For example, model changes in a product must be carefully planned so that customer-demanded features and changes are provided without unreasonable costs due to frequent design changes. A single, simple engineering change on one prime part would not be sufficient reason to introduce a new model. There is a constant need to balance the benefits of standardization against the hazards of stagnating the design.

References

1. ANSI Standards. Mutivolume set updated annually by the American National Standards Institute.

2. ASAE Standards, Updated annually by the American Society of Agricultural Engineers, St. Joseph, MI. 49085.

3. ASTM Standards. Multivolume set updated annually by the American Society for Testing of Materials.

4. Bellinger, P. 1982. Progress through standards in industry their dynamic future. ASAE Paper 82-5543, ASAE, St. Joseph, MI. 49085.

5. FIEI Guide Lines. Available from the Farm and Industial Equipmant Institute, Chicago, IL

6. General Motors Standards. Three volume set updated annually. Technical Center, Warren, MI 48090.

7. SAE Handbooks. Four volume set updated annually by the Society of Automotive Engineers. Warrendale, PA 15096.

Discussion Problems

1. List and discuss the pros and cons of metric standardization.

2. Discuss how safety standards should be applied to agriculture.

3. Discuss the extent to which computers have been standardized.

Project Problems

1. Can you reduce the number of parts in your present project by standardization. List if you can; explain why not if you can't.

2. Document the impact of safety standards on your present design project.

3. Can you replace any of your manufactured parts in your present project with off-the-shelf components? List them.

Chapter 20
Testing and Evaluation

"Engineering is more experimental evaluation than mathematical calculation."

"Observation, not old age, brings wisdom."

Are you designing a one-time product or a mass-produced product ?

A product which will be mass-produced in a manufacturing plant goes through repeated "design-build-test-evaluate" sequences. The reasons are money and reliability. You cannot afford to over-design beyond a reasonable safety factor, and you need proven product reliability. A one-of-a-kind product, such as a processing plant or a building, goes through only one design-build sequence (hopefully). Testing and evaluating of one-time products is limited. Exceptions are components which are essentially mass produced (e.g., trusses) and design approaches (e.g., Butler Manufacturing's slope-wall building design) which are used in hundreds or thousands of cases. Other types of exceptions are major projects such as dams, bridges, moon rockets and large buildings. They may be tested as models, and certain critical components may be full-scale tested to ensure reliability. A third type of exception is the quality control check. Samples of concrete are collected at construction sites, cured and tested to failure. Surface hardness may be checked, quality may be measured with X-ray techniques and stress concentrations may be examined with photographic techniques.

Theory and calculations put you in the ballpark

That is about all. An engineer's alternatives are often simple. Over-design for a one-of-a-kind product and cut-and-try with mass-produced products. Theory and calculations are important but often only guidelines. Testing and evaluation are essential to develop a reliable, cost-efficient product for mass production. Testing and documentation are needed to prove that the product is safe and reliable. Failure to test and document is professionally unethical and leaves the firm in an indefensible position for any subsequent lawsuits related to a number of issues.

One exception occurs if the product or some aspects of the product are identical or similar to previously or currently manufactured products. There may be enough test history incorporated into a theoretical analysis to allow computer simulation. Obviously, computer simulation is a desirable and inexpensive alternative to actually building and testing a physical model.

There are two major approaches to testing. The first is engineering tests of models, components and material analysis which are used to evaluate the appropriateness of various engineering assumptions, calculations, and predictions. The second is field testing, which means testing the design in situations similar to the intended uses and expected misuses.

Quality control testing

Purchased component check-out is the first consideration in design testing. This may be as simple as visual inspection of the components as they are uncrated. It may be actual operation for products like motors and batteries. Component testing may be complex and include chemical analysis, stress tests, dimensional analysis or thermal tests.

Quality control is another consideration in design, and the means vary widely with the project. A builder will test some trusses to failure to insure that the truss design is suitable for the intended use and to insure quality fabrication. Watershed design is based upon probabilistic recurrence of storm intensities, and thus, quality assurance testing may be extremely difficult. You may sample a fraction of machine components and test to failure to insure reliability. Raw material samples are saved from stock and from construction sites and later checked to insure quality. In most companies product engineering is ultimately responsible for product quality.

Engineering tests are important to insure a properly working design

Similitude (model design theory) is an important subject for the engineer responsible for testing and evaluation. Model testing can be an inexpensive means for evaluating designs. It is also much more complicated than commonly imagined. Seldom do equal-scale reductions of all dimensions and forces yield results similar to those which will occur with full-scale testing. Dimensions in some directions may be scaled by 100; dimensions in other directions by 50 and forces by 20 in order to test a model. Conversely, a model builder may distort the model to simplify model building and then mathematically account for this distortion using similitude techniques.

Similitude is valuable in other ways. Similitude techniques can allow an experimenter to reduce the number of measurements and test cases required to evaluate a design experimentally. To use

BUT THE AUTOMATIC SHUT-OFF WORKED
95% OF THE TIME IN THE LAB.

similitude the relevant variables for the experimental situation are listed. These original variables are expressed in terms of basic dimensions (e.g., mass, length, time, temperature and current). Almost any variable can be expressed as a combination of these dimensions. Variables are then redefined as dimensionless combinations of the original variables involved (e.g., Reynolds Number, which equals mass density times flow velocity times length divided by viscosity). The number of dimensionless variables which must be experimentally evaluated equals the number of original variables minus the number of dimensions.

A second type of engineering testing is experimental analysis of full scale prototypes. Tractor cabs are tested in accordance with ASAE's Roll-Over-Protection Standard (S-383.1). Window infiltration is tested according to ASTM's window insulation standards. Strain gages are applied to a machine, and loads are applied to analyze stresses at critical points. Irrigation sprinklers are mounted at heights typical of in-field conditions, and pressures are varied to evaluate water distribution diameter and uniformity.

Field testing is a requisite for mass-produced products

No matter how carefully lab tests are conceived and conducted, field tests are needed. You can never predict exactly the loads, stresses and environmental conditions to which a product will be exposed. Therefore, even though you do your best to design the product right the first time, don't be surprised when testing shows that improvements are needed. In fact, if your first prototype does not fail under extreme conditions, the product is probably over-designed.

There are four things to try in field testing. First, try the product in the applications for which it was designed. Try to test for worst-case conditions under which you expect it to perform satisfactorily.

Second, try to anticipate the misuses and problem situations in which it may be used. Is the product safe for the operator who misuses it? Do safety devices trigger or shut down the machine when they should — and reliably? Do shear pins and other design-incorporated, product-protection devices work as intended? Many companies have design quality assurance teams which meet regularly to ensure safety standards are met and to determine *fitness for use*.

Third, turn the product over to a test consumer. You cannot perfectly anticipate how a product may be used. You cannot reliably predict the misunderstandings that product users will have. The designer tends to operate the machine correctly. In the field it will not be operated as recommended. That is why it is important to let prospective users test the product without providing them any more training than you will provide when the product is sold on a commercial basis. Sometimes pre-production prototypes are sent out for field testing by customers.

A fourth and very important aspect of testing involves proving reliability. Not only must the product perform satisfactorily during a test, but it must continue to perform over some specified minimum time span. One commonly used measure of this minimum performance time is the mean time between failures (MTBF). For example, MTBF's on combines may be 50 hours while tractors are 200-300 hours. Product testing is required to establish a reliable measure of MTBF's. Sometimes, such testing can be accomplished by monitoring consumer tests while other times these tests are conducted by companies with their own test engineers.

Designing a test procedure

Testing of any kind costs money. It is important to consider carefully the objectives of the tests to be undertaken and record them. Determine the number and type of variables which will be involved in the test. Independent variables are those which the designer has control over and can pre-set at constant or specific values (e.g., ground speed, water pumping rate, structural floor load). Dependent variables are a consequence of the independent variable values and the process involved. Dependent variables are often thought of as the results of the process given a set of independent variable values.

Construct a comprehensive data sheet(s) with sufficient blanks to record all data during the tests after you have carefully reviewed the test objectives and test variables. In complicated or involved situations much of these data may be automatically recorded in electronic storage media. Once the necessary test equipment is assembled, the actual test can be completed.

Don't forget the results

As surprising as it seems many well conceived tests are not conducted through completion! An unanticipated event or surprising occurrence will side-track the engineer. Tests should be carried out to their logical conclusions so that meaningful results can be derived. Often, statistical analysis is needed, and missing replications complicate the process. Carry out the complete test, and record all the data.

Once you have the data, try to condense your test information into a simpler form (e.g., a graph or table). The exercise of condensing the information to only the most relevant information (without discarding the raw data) is critical in helping you understand what you have learned. The condensed data may suggest trends which were masked before by the sheer volume of the raw data! Additionally, the condensed data is a means of explaining your project to others and benefitting from their interpretations and ideas.

Finally, carefully evaluate the data and draw conclusions. One of the conclusions may be that you have conducted the wrong test! If so, use your working results to restructure the test program. Even in testing the design process can be iterative.

Error analysis

Often, results of interest must be calculated from measured variables. How accurate is a calculated result? In general, a calculated result is no more accurate than the least significant number used. For example, if you measure the speed of a machine, it would not be useful to measure either the distance traveled or elapsed time to a different number of significant figures. If both distance and time are measured to three significant figures (i.e., about 0.1% accuracy), then speed can be calculated to three significant figures with approximately similar accuracy.

There is a mathematical basis for obtaining the accuracy of calculated information based on the accuracies of the measured variables used in the formula (Beers, 1957). This method, termed "propagation of error analysis" requires that the independent variable measurement errors be random.

Error is calculated using the equation:

$$E_c^2 = \left(\frac{\partial C}{\partial V_1} \right)^2 E_{V_1}^2 + \left(\frac{\partial C}{\partial V_2} \right)^2 E_{V_2}^2 + \ldots$$

in which:
E_c is the error of the calculated variable C
C is the calculated variable
V_1 is measured variable 1
E_{V_1} is the error of measured variable 1
V_2 is measured variable 2
E_{V_2} is the error of measured variable 2

Caution should be exercised when calculated results require the subtraction of numbers of approximately equal magnitude since this process results in the loss of significant figures. When this will be part of your analysis, you should consider measuring such

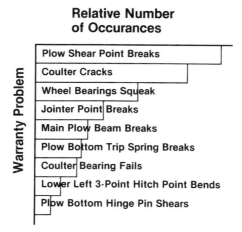

**Relative Number
of Occurances**

Warranty Problem

- Plow Shear Point Breaks
- Coulter Cracks
- Wheel Bearings Squeak
- Jointer Point Breaks
- Main Plow Beam Breaks
- Plow Bottom Trip Spring Breaks
- Coulter Bearing Fails
- Lower Left 3-Point Hitch Point Bends
- Plow Bottom Hinge Pin Shears

FIG 20.1 A Pareto diagram showing the relative failure rates in a moldboard plow.

numbers more accurately (i.e., to more significant figures) than your other measurements.

Product-life testing occurs during the market-life of the product

Eighty percent of the failures are usually the result of twenty percent of the causes. This generalized "80-20 rule" has even wider application than reliability. In the case of students and practicing design engineers this implies that 80% of the work is produced by 20% of the workers! Or for example, 80% of agricultural production is accomplished by 20% of the farmers. In any event, failure is the opposite of reliability, and it is the relative number of failures that occur within each failure category that is important.

A Pareto histogram diagram is a graphical means of showing component failures for a product (Fig 20.1). Bar heights correspond to the number of failures in each category, and these are arranged in declining order of frequency of occurence. Pareto diagrams are useful for planning maintenance and part replacement schedules and as guidelines for establishing warranty policies. They are important guides to the designers of subsequent models and suggest which parts need the most redesign effort.

Pareto diagrams will generally support the "80-20 rule." The obvious conclusion is that if one solves 20% of the design problems they will solve 80% of the complaints. Thus, the design engineer should concentrate on solving these problems first.

References

1. Doebelin, Ernest O. 1983. Mechanical measurements: Application and design. 3rd ed. McGraw-Hill, New York. 876 pp.

2. Mitchell, Bailey. (ed.) 1983. Instrumentation and measurement for environmental sciences. ASAE, St. Joseph, MI. 200 pp.

3. Murphy, G. 1950. Similitude in engineering. John Wiley & Sons. New York.

4. Skoglund, V.J. 1967. Similitude theory and applications. International Textbook, Scranton PA. 320 pp.

Discussion Problems

1. What observations and/or measurements should be recorded in the laboratory to evaluate building trusses supplied by different manufacturers? ASTM requires three test replications; can you explain why?

Project Problem

1. Devise a testing plan for your present project.

2. Conduct an error analysis on a calculated result for your present project.

3. Prepare a data recording sheet for use with your project test program. Arrange for easy, subsequent data processing.

4. Prepare a Pareto diagram for your present project, and try to anticipate the categories of failure as well as their relative frequency.

Part V
Related Design Topics

*"Make no small plans, set no timid goals.
They have not the power to put a gleam in
the eye, to quicken the step and to fire the spirit."*

*"Forewarned is forearmed:
to be prepared is half the battle."*

CHAPTER CONTENTS

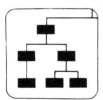

21. Business Styles and Organization Structures
The design engineer must function within an organizational structure. The nature of your position within the organization as well as your success in attaining personal and professional goals will be heavily dependent upon management style and organization.

22. Patents, Trademarks, Copyrights, and Trade Secrets
Intellectual wealth is the product of design engineering. Protection of this property from unauthorized use can be achieved by a number of means that will require the design engineer to interact with the legal profession.

23. Futurology
Fortunes and failures, fame and fool all result from the ability (or inability) to foresee the future. The only thing certain is change. Accept change, think big and enter into the new information era of the "Brain Baron"!

Engineers practice design as part of a larger business environment. An understanding of business structures and the roles of engineers within business can help you be more effective (Chapter 21).

Designs, the products of engineering, are valuable business commodities protected by patents, trade secrets, copyrights and trademarks (Chapter 22). Employers expect to recover the direct and indirect costs of engineering through benefits derived from your novel ideas and problem solutions. Don't be surprised if you are required to sign a loyalty oath or a statement giving all "rights of invention" to your employer as a condition of employment.

Failure to anticipate the future correctly is the principal cause of business stagnation and failure. Engineers, as technical experts, provide their employers insight on the future. Predicting and shaping the future is a most exciting challenge for you (Chapter 23).

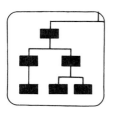

Chapter 21
Business Styles and
Organizational Structures

*"Those who know how, will always have a job
working for those who know why!"*

*"What concerns me is not the way things are,
but rather the way people think things are."*
Epictetus

***Business styles and organization structures are real design
constraints***

Recognizing and understanding the business styles and
structures in your field helps you develop profitable, well-
conceived designs. Failure to understand the relationship between
business and engineering design usually leads to designs which
are never used.

Knowledge of your company's style, formal structure and
informal organization helps you understand the design problem
and know how best to approach the problem in a manner which
maximizes organizational support and minimizes conflict.
Second, knowledge of your company and its competitors helps
you anticipate future products now, in the design stage, and
provides insight that can help you select design specifications
which keep your design competitive. Third, as a design engineer

it is inevitable that you select or consider components from other manufacturers. You need to judge the reliability of these component suppliers, know who can be most helpful in matching the components to your product, understand which companies will help develop a new component design for your application and anticipate supplier support and price changes during your design's life. Lastly, and perhaps most importantly, knowledge of business styles and organizations can help you select a company and job type in which you are happy and effective.

Style and philosophy more than organization structure shape company actions

Deal and Kennedy (1982) classified business style and philo-sophies according to four "corporate cultures." "Individualistic" is the term best describing the first culture discussed by Deal and Kennedy. People are given the latitude to solve problems and good solutions are expected. There is considerable competition within the organization and no real team spirit. Often this is a new firm started by a financier, a developer or an inventor. The starting individual still controls the company. Quick results are expected and long-term research and development are negligible. Individuals are expected to take big risks. Construction, electronics, management consulting, venture capital, advertising and entertainment companies are often this type. Managers of any company tend to have some competitive, individualistic traits, though their organization may not be of that type.

"Work hard, play hard" cultures are characterized by esprit-des-corps and speed. People are expected to get things done fast or they are fired. There is team spirit, and you can expect carry-over into team sports and after-hours parties, both with strong comradery. The weakness of this type of culture is that it is often too shallow and does not take the time to build long-term research and development plans. Firms which sell commodity-like items (i.e., there are competitors trying to sell relatively undifferentiated products) and short-line manufacturers are typically this type. Japanese firms which strive for large-volume and low-price have some of these characteristics. Salesmen and marketing people tend to have these characteristics, though their organization may be more like another culture.

"Bet-your company" cultures are the carefully-planned, research-oriented corporations. Decisions on research and product direction gamble a significant fraction of the organization's future, and such decisions are not made lightly. Millions of dollars are invested in product development without knowing whether the product will succeed; so, the company carefully tracks progress and evaluates whether to continue their commitment at several development stages to compensate for this uncertainty. Team spirit is high, but in a disciplined form with high respect for experience. These firms depend on a continual stream of high-profit margin, new products to succeed. Major manufacturing firms with a reputation for quality (e.g., Caterpillar Tractor Co., Deere and Co., and 3M Co.) typify this culture. Research and development oriented engineers tend to have these characteristics, though their employer company may better fit a different culture.

"Process" cultures are characterized by low-risk, slow-feedback and bureaucracy. Rules and methods may seem more important than results. Heavily regulated industries such as utilities, governmental organizations, banking and accounting firms typify this culture. Most engineers are dissatisfied in this type of culture unless they can determine ways to explore new ideas with minimal interference from the system.

Coherent purpose, not culture type, is important for business success

There are many examples of successful businesses for each of the above "cultures." Success seems most dependent on the individuals who form the organization having an understanding of the organization's purpose. If people in the organization see the same purpose and have a reasonable understanding of acceptable behavior within that organization, the business usually does well.

You, the design engineer, have three reasons for being curious about the corporate cultures of business. First, you are, or will be, an employee, and it is important for your personal happiness and professional development that you work in an organization suited to you. Second, when you identify organizations which seem to have a clear sense of purpose and direction, those firms will probably be reasonable and reliable. If the organization seems confused, expect problems when you must rely on that firm in your design work. Lastly, you can select a general type of firm that is most likely to be receptive to your design needs and tailor your approach to their culture. If you want a standard, low-cost, reliable component, find a work-hard, play-hard company. If you need a new component developed, try a bet-your-company or individualistic firm.

Annual reports, business periodicals and personal contacts provide insight on company styles and structures

Annual reports are required of all publicly-held corporations (i.e., firms traded on a stock exchange). Annual reports provide an overall financial picture and indicate future plans and direction.

Business periodical indices (e.g., Wall Street Journal Index) and investment rating services (e.g., Standard and Poors) provide outside views of companies. Business periodicals and investment rating services are available in nearly all libraries. Trade magazines (Implement & Tractor) are another source of information, often quite detailed, about companies and the industry. Histories, written independently or by company sponsorship, are available for most large companies. Finally, use your personal and professional contacts to learn about a company.

Different ways of classifying firms hiring agricultural engineers

One method is by subject matter: structures and environment, power and machinery, electric power and processing, soil and water or food engineering. Each of these five subject matter areas can be divided into more specific subject matters. Livestock structures, greenhouses, environmental control equipment, waste handling, livestock equipment and rural housing are all subject matter areas within the general structures and environment option.

There are some important general differences among companies in different fields using the above scheme. Farm building firms must be very cost conscious and competitive because many small builders can inexpensively establish themselves as "farm builders." The small builder does not need large financial resources to become a farm builder and often can easily copy ideas without needing to invest heavily in research or development to obtain the ideas. Consequently, some of the large farm builders tend to fit the work-hard, play-hard or the individualistic mold and cannot invest as much as they would like in major, long-term research to develop better building practices.

Large farm machinery requires substantial engineering and financing; so, these firms tend to be research and development oriented. Smaller, less complex machines may be more suited to "work-hard, play-hard" companies.

Food processing and large grain storage facilities tend to be specialized and expensive. Competition is limited by the knowledge and financial requirements. Many of these firms are individualist, and several large, privately-held companies are dominant forces in these fields.

Irrigation firms produce nearly similar machinery which can be easily copied but which involves considerable development costs; so, these firms tend to be secretive regarding current design projects. Similarly the machinery and food processing companies which invest heavily in development are secretive about products under consideration.

Company size is a second way of classifying. Larger companies typically spend more money and time on research and development. They are apt to produce as many components as possible themselves. Larger companies tend to be cautious, requiring more extensive testing, more reviews and more time to design a product. Larger companies tend to produce a wider range of products.

Original equipment manufacturer (OEM) versus component supplier firm is a third classification method. Most firms do not fit completely into either category. OEM firms have larger sales and marketing groups and are well-known. They require a larger price markup over the manufactured cost to service. Component firms tend to specialize in limited areas. For example, there are fewer than 10 pto manufacturing firms and all are virtually unknown except to engineers who design pto driven equipment. There are generally few competitors for the component firms, but quantity and price are essential because the product buyers (OEM firms) are well-informed and cautious.

A fourth categorizing scheme is short-line as opposed to main-line. This category is particularly useful in reference to machinery manufacturers. Short-liners produce a few types of farm implements while main-line firms produce a complete line of implements and farm tractors. Short-liners are usually small to moderate-sized firms, relatively independent, and perhaps a division of a large firm. Short-liners can take a product from the idea stage to a commercially available product quickly. They do not have the time or resources to conduct long-running development projects. Short-liners often specialize in putting a package of "off-the shelf" components together with most components purchased from component supplier firms. Some short-liners have most product sales within one geographic region, while others specialize in an unusual, highly-specific product line (e.g., tomato pickers).

Firms may be organized by function or by product

Most firms are organized by a combination of product lines and job functions. Product line organization means that a separate group within the company is completely responsible for each separate product. In other words, group A in the company is responsible for everything from planning to sales for the silage wagons product line. Group B is responsible for everything from planning to sales of the manure spreaders product line, etc.

Functional organization arrangement means personnel are grouped by job type. In other words, engineering is responsible for design and testing of all products (e.g., silage wagons and

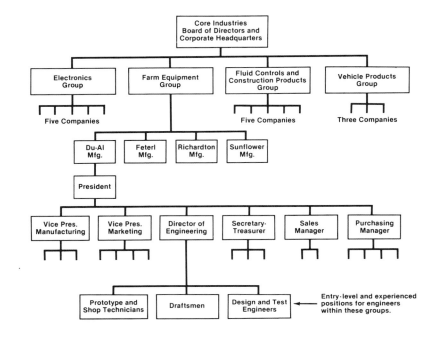

FIG 21.1 Partial corporate structure for Core Industries and its wholly-owned division, DuAl Manufacturing. Note that DuAl is a functionally organized division within a product organized parent company.

manure spreaders); sales is responsible for distribution and marketing of all products, etc.

Seldom are companies organized purely by function or product line. Most firms use a matrix structure — if not formally, then informally. Teams composed of representatives from several functional groups cooperate under the direction of a group leader to develop new products and to evaluate existing products.

Fig 21.1 is a typical flow chart for a medium or small manufacturing firm. Some large firms have relatively independent divisions which are essentially medium-sized firms managed by one board of directors. Other large firms consolidate certain job functions for the entire corporation (Fig 21.2). Different divisions operate independently except where coordination with one of the overall corporate departments is necessary.

Positions may be organized by line or staff

Line versus staff positions are analogous to product versus function in the organization of firms. Line departments are directly involved with production. Most engineering, plant

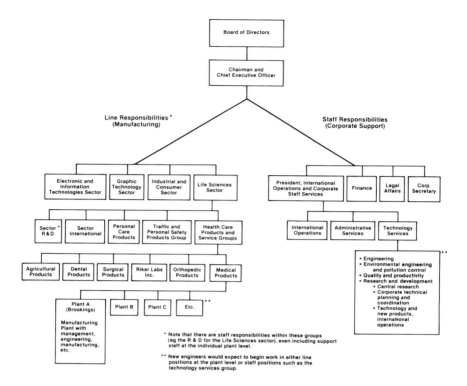

FIG 21.2 Partial corporate structure for 3M Co., a Fortune 100 firm with large corporate staff and a large, multi-layered manufacturing organization (Courtesy of 3M Co.).

management and sales jobs are line positions. Staff positions are functionally organized and used to support the line positions. Research and development, planning and legal departments often serve the entire corporation. Staff people contribute indirectly to production.

In a university structure faculty, department heads, deans, and the president are the line structure. Student records, student advisors, counseling, maintenance, fund raising, etc. are staff departments which contribute to the quality of the university but are not directly responsible for teaching, research or extension. Teaching, research and extension are the line functions of the university. Without the line positions the staff positions would have little meaning.

Advancement in a company is usually through a combination of line and staff positions. People in line positions typically advance slowly but gain valuable experience on the actual product manufacture and sales. Staff positions expose a younger engineer to the methods of top-level executives and give a broader view of the company. Companies must be careful to keep a clear view of their goals (i.e., line position work), and an engineer who wishes to advance into top managment should strive also to maintain a balance between line and staff assignments.

The six engineering job roles

Most engineers are hired to do one or more of six basic functions. These functions are listed in the same order that product development typically occurs (e.g., it begins with planning and ultimately the manufactured product is sold). Engineers in all of these functions interact with personnel from a variety of other job functions (Fig 21.3).

Planning — Overall corporate goals and direction are defined and agreed upon by a group composed of top-level management. Functions of planning are recommending future product development and design directions, guiding changes in market orientation and production locations, changing corporate organizational structures and philosophies appropriate for changing business climates, and budgeting funds for current and future needs. Some companies have a formal staff department which prepares recommendations for review by the corporate officers while others rely solely on committees involving managers and other company personnel.

Engineering, marketing, financial and legal experts provide and help evaluate ideas as part of the planning process. Engineers in formal planning groups are often advanced-degreed technical experts or product managers with business administrative backgrounds. Few beginning engineers are hired into planning departments.

Research and Development (R & D) — R & D explores and develops new product concepts, technologies for improving product quality and/or the economics of manufacturing and new applications for existing products. Corporate R & D is generally more applied and product-oriented (contrasted with university and government research which tends more toward basic science), but many companies invest significantly in basic research to assure that they remain at the forefront of technology related to their products. Corporate R & D also differs from university R & D in that secrecy is maintained and engineering researchers work closely with marketing people. Profit through innovation, not knowledge advancement, is the motivation for United States' companies to invest approximately 5% of sales into R & D.

Often R & D is organizationally separate from production

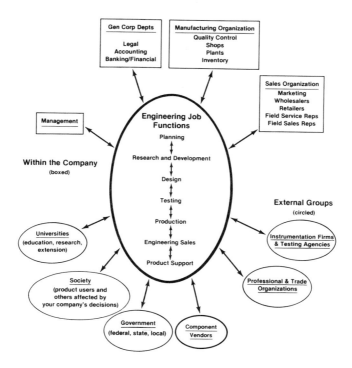

FIG 21.3 Engineering job functions and the people they work with both within a company and outside.

divisions in a company. R & D may function as a consulting group, quite independently from product lines of the company, working on contracts from government and other corporations as well. Engineers and scientists in R & D tend to be those with strong technical abilities and advanced degrees.

Design — Design is responsible for product design and detailed specification. Requests for a new product or for revision of an existing product usually originate from sales or planning groups, and the design engineers have the responsibility to help define the request into a practical possibility and then to develop the design. Engineers (beginning and experienced), draftsmen and technicians work in design and usually are associated with a particular product line or division. In a large corporation there may be separate design groups at each plant site. Testing, sales, manufacturing, R & D and sometimes outside consultants work cooperatively with design on most major projects.

Testing — Testing and design are often combined in small companies, but in large companies they tend to be separated. The test engineer is responsible for instrumenting and testing design prototypes. Testing is composed of engineers and technicians. Usually, testing is smaller than design because one test engineer can test several design engineers' prototypes. Testing is an excellent starting job for an engineer because the engineer learns the companies' product lines and the competitor product lines quickly. The test engineer then understands the weaknesses which need improvement. Design engineers may spend years on one component and not know the strengths and weaknesses of the overall design.

Production — Production is responsible for product manufacturing and usually includes manufacturing engineers, skilled shop foremen, quality control engineers and accounting people. Agricultural engineers may start in this group and often continue as manufacturing engineers. In small companies, production is often part of design and becomes the new engineer's responsibility.

Quality assurance and quality control are testing-related job titles used by many companies. Testing engineers may be working in the R&D, design, or production phases of product introduction. The greatest numbers are responsible for verifying the quality of components and of the final product.

Sales Engineering — This group usually sells components to OEM's or sells to wholesaling firms. This is not a retail sales job. Sales engineering is responsible for solving problems in the field for customers, recommending proper application and maintenance for the product and, of course, selling. Sales engineers, like test engineers, learn the product line quickly and identify problems. Sales is an excellent starting job for learning about the company and for high personal earnings potential. It may be difficult to develop and use technical abilities; however, sales may be a good path to management.

References

1. Deal, T. and A. A. Kennedy. 1982. Corporate culture: The rites and rituals of corporate life. Addison Wesley, Reading MA. 232 pp.

2. Nilsson, W. D. and P. E. Hicks. 1981. Orientation to professional practice. McGraw Hill, New York. 372 pp.

Chapter 22
Patents, Trademarks, Copyrights, and Trade Secrets

*"Engineers are paid for **using** their brains, not **having** brains."*

"Money never starts an idea; it is the idea which starts the money."

The ultimate products of brainpower are intellectual wealth

Design engineers produce intellectual wealth. New products, concepts and compositions are "intellectual property" and can be protected by patents, trademarks, trade secrets or copyrights. Intellectual property rights are protected by law to encourage invention.

Invention differs from innovation in that invention is the process of conceiving a new process or product while innovation is introducing (marketing) the new process or product to mankind. Invention is of no monetary value unless part of the larger innovation process. Intellectual property laws protect both inventors and innovators. Inventors may license their intellectual property to others or market their invention directly while restraining others from making or selling the invention. Innovators may buy a right to make, sell or use the invention and be protected from competitors.

Engineers benefit because business can afford to hire engineers as inventors with some assurance of protecting the products or processes invented by the engineers. Society benefits because business can afford to make the investments in research, development and design which ultimately lead to new and better products.

The process of innovation can last several years, cost millions of dollars and involve several companies (or individuals)—each contributing in significant ways. It is important to define and protect intellectual property as possessions to facilitate this innovative process. Engineer W may devise a new product, Company X may reduce this new product concept to a practical design, Company Y may manufacture the resulting product and Company Z may be the marketing firm. Patents, trademarks, trade secrets and copyrights provide the legal means of defining intellectual property which can then be treated as possessions.

Legal protection of intellectual property does not guarantee financial success

Inventors may be ahead of their time. The cotton picker was invented more than 20 years before it was accepted. Wind turbine patents protect designs that may not be commercially feasible until long after the patent rights expire.

Intellectual property rights are protected only through suit by the party who holds the intellectual property rights against the party "alleged to be infringing on those intellectual property rights." Lawsuits are expensive and may not be worth the expense. Competitors may develop ways to produce nearly similar products without infringing on intellectual property rights. Often it is unclear whether the alleged offender is really infringing on the intellectual property holder's rights. Ultimately these legal matters must be decided in a court of law.

The concept of patents dates to the 15th century

The whole notion of protecting an inventor's right to remuneration for an invention which benefits the public dates to the 15th century in Italy and to the early 1600's in England and may well be the tap root of the industrial revolution. Prior to this time there existed largely the "haves" and the "have nots." If you were part of the power structure you simply took what you wanted without compensation to the owner. Periodically, the "have nots" would rise up, over-throw the oppressors and then become the new "haves."

In 1624, England passed the Statute of Monopolies which outlawed Royal Monopolies and granted patents to the true and rightful owner. Thus, for the first time in history, society was in a position to reward, in general, any inventor who was clever enough to devise methods or means that were particularly useful to society. The English patent philosophy, as well as English law, followed the early settlers to this country. The U.S. Patent Office was formed on the basis of the powers given to Congress by Article 1, Section 8, of the U.S. Constitution "to promote the progress of science and useful arts by securing for limited times for authors and inventors the exclusive right to their respective writings and discoveries." The first U.S. Patent was granted on July 31, 1790 to Samuel Hopkins for a new potash manufacturing process, while in the present series the first serially numbered patent, no. 1, was granted to John Ruggles for his locomotive steam engine on July 13, 1836. Fig. 22.1 is the first page of U.S. Patent No. 3985263 and illustrates the essential nature of the patent contract.

Preparing for a patent application should begin with accurate records during the early design phases

The process of writing a patent application begins long before the preparation of the actual document. As in the case of any legal matter, it is always wise to consult a registered patent practitioner at an early stage of the patent process.

A laboratory notebook, routinely kept and updated, bound with pages consecutively numbered and used, usually forms the first written documentation as to the nature of the invention which has occurred and the exact time of conception. One or more pages should give an overview of the invention, including sketches. These pages should be dated and signed by the inventors, thus identifying the inventors and establishing a conception date. Two witnesses should also be present to sign and date the pages under the heading "Witnessed and Understood," after, of course, you have explained the concept to them. The laboratory notebook is also a means of recording and witnessing performance data and proof of reduction to practice.

An alternative method to establish a recorded date is to submit an informal disclosure directly to the U.S. Commerce Department Patent and Trademark Office, Washington, DC, 20231. Under the "Disclosure Documents Program" the patent office will receive and keep on file disclosure documents submitted by inventors for a limited period (2 years), and the recorded receipt date can be used as proof of conception date for the subject invention. No patent rights or priority is obtained, however.

Neither of the above disclosure methods constitutes public disclosure, an important concept in U.S. and foreign patent law. Public disclosure of an invention prior to filing a patent

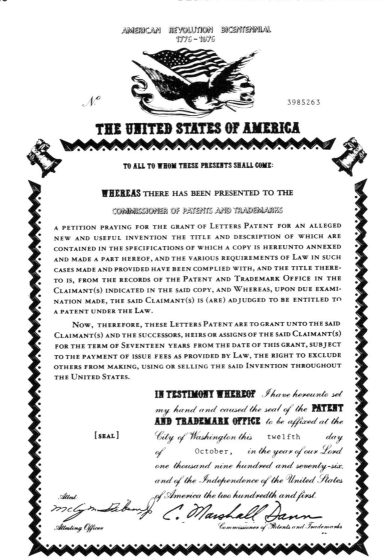

FIG 22.1 The first page of U.S. Patent No. 3,985,263.

application in a foreign country generally voids the patentability in foreign countries. However, U.S. patent laws provide for a one-year delay from the time of public disclosure until a U.S. patent application is filed. Public disclosure can be made, for example, by giving an oral/visual report in a meeting to which the public has access, a newspaper report, a TV news-spot, or a

United States Patent [19]   [11]   3,985,263

Rohrbach et al.   [45]   Oct. 12, 1976

[54] **APPARATUS AND METHOD FOR METERING PARTICLES**

[75] Inventors: **Roger P. Rohrbach; Kun Ha Kim,** both of Raleigh, N.C.

[73] Assignee: **Research Corporation,** New York, N.Y.

[22] Filed: **Apr. 5, 1972**

[21] Appl. No.: **241,328**

[52] U.S. Cl. 221/1; 221/278; 259/36; 302/26

[51] Int. Cl.² **B65G 51/02**

[58] Field of Search 221/278, 1; 302/21, 302/22, 25, 17, 26, 32; 259/4, 36

[56]   **References Cited**
         UNITED STATES PATENTS

1,616,547   2/1927   Pontoppidan 259/36

3,039,531	6/1962	Scott	221/278 X
3,457,691	7/1969	Rogge	221/278 X
3,637,108	1/1972	Loesch et al	221/211
3,697,050	10/1972	Stanley	259/4

Primary Examiner—Robert B. Reeves
Assistant Examiner—David A. Scherbel
Attorney, Agent, or Firm—Cooper, Dunham, Clarke, Griffin & Moran

[57]   **ABSTRACT**

Apparatus and method for metering particles involving circulating particles through a passage, retaining a particle in a particle retention chamber that is part of the passage, and ejecting the retained particle from the particle retention chamber. Particle circulation and retention and ejection are accomplished by fluid flows within the passage.

34 Claims, 8 Drawing Figures

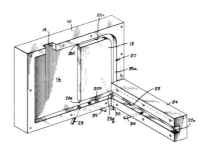

FIG 22.2 The second page of U.S. Patent No. 3,985,263. Often this page will contain sufficient information for the practitioner to understand the true nature of the invention.

technical paper at an engineering society meeting. Thus, the timing of the public disclosure is important and can be made prematurely by a number of means.

U.S. patent laws define the mechanics of patent application

Application for a patent is made to the Commissioner of Patents and Trademarks and includes: (a) an oath or declaration, (b) written specifications, (c) drawings and (d) filing fees. The oath or declaration of the applicant is required by law, and in this the inventors (or inventor) must declare that they believe themselves to be the first, original and true inventors of the subject matter of the application. The basic filing fee can be as much as $300 which entitles the applicant to present twenty (20) claims, including not more than three in independent form.

Additional fees for late or amended filing of certain documents are payable, also. Furthermore, there are patent issue fees ranging from $250 to $500, post-issue fees of from $40 to $1500, patent application processing fees for extension of time from $20 to $750, document supply fees and international application, filing and processing fees. A patent is valid for 17 years after date of issue.

The specifications are generally given by the following in their preferred order (Fig. 22.2):

1. Title of invention including inventor's name, citizenship and residence.

2. Cross-references to any related applications.

3. Abstract of the disclosure.

4. Brief summary of the invention including any related prior art.

5. Brief description of any included drawings.

6. Detailed description of the invention.

7. Claims.

In general, the specifications must set forth the precise invention for which a patent is sought. It must describe completely the specific embodiment and disclose the principle of operation. The writing of claims should never be attempted without the assistance of a skilled practitioner.

The preparation of patent drawings is a highly specialized task. The exact specifications for drawings can be obtained from Title 37 Code of Federal Regulations, Section 1.84, "Standards for Drawings." The requirements relating to drawings are strictly enforced. Drawings submitted, but not conforming to these standards, are examined, but new or corrected drawings will be required later.

Conducting a patent search

The Patent and Trademark Office maintains patent depositories throughout the United States in various university and public libraries. As a patent depository, the library maintains a backfile of all patents and design patents on microfilm, has a complete set of the *Official Gazette*, which is the announcement journal for new patents, and maintains a set of the searching aids necessary for completing a patent search.

With over 4 ½ million United States patents classified into approximately 600 major technological classes and over 112,000 sub-classes, it is important to note that U.S. Patent Depository Libraries now have direct telephone line access to the Patent and Trademark Data Base through the Classification and Search Support Information System, (CASSIS). Patent Depository

Libraries are open to the public. Trained librarians are available to assist you in using the patent collections and all search aids, but they do not conduct patent searches for patrons.

CASSIS can assist your patent search in the following six ways and is presently provided at no cost to the patron:

1. **Original and cross-reference classifications of a patent:** Given a patent number, CASSIS will display all its locations in the U.S. Patent Classification System (PCS) —the world's most comprehensive system for categorizing patented technology.

2. **All patents assigned to a classification:** Given a technology as described by a PCS classification, CASSIS will display all patents assigned to that classification, with the newest patents shown first. Thus, patents relating to a particular technology can be identified.

3. **Classification titles:** CASSIS will display PCS classification titles three ways, as described below, and permit the user to alternate between them while staying focused on a particular classification.

—**Page display**: shows the titles as they appear in the official Manual of Classification. Once a classification has been selected, the system automatically generates a page display with the chosen classification as the starting point and focus.

—**Coordinate display**: shows only those classifications which (a) are in the same broader technological category and (b) have the same "level of indentation" (detail) as the one selected. This permits faster browsing of classification titles by eliminating the need to read unnecessary detail until an interesting title is found.

—**Full title display**: brings together, in one display, the title of a chosen classification along with the titles of all broader category classifications to which it relates. This permits quick and complete retrieval of all pertinent title information on any classification.

4. **Search of key words in classification titles:** Given key words, CASSIS will identify all classifications whose full titles contain those words. Furthermore, classifications whose titles contain specified words may be excluded. This permits fast, automatic searching of over 112,000 classification titles to identify those of interest.

5. **Search of key words in patent abstracts:** Given key words, CASSIS will identify patents whose abstracts contain those words or stems. A ranked list of the classifications of those patents is created to identify those areas most directly related to the subject matter of search interest.

6. **Search of classification index terms:** Given subject terms, CASSIS will search the alphabetical list of subject headings of the

Index to the U.S. Patent Classifications to identify the classifications containing the subject matter of interest.

The public search room in the U.S. Patent Office in Washington, D.C. maintains a hard copy collection of patents filed by class and subclass, making searching relatively easy. Patent depository libraries use CASSIS to produce a list of patent numbers in each class and subclass. Each patent must then be located in either the Official Gazette or the patent microfilmed collection, both of which are organized numerically by patent number. A thorough search of the patent literature can be a very long and difficult job.

"Patented" gives you the exclusive right to make, sell, or use

No one else can make, sell or use your patented invention without your permission. This means that you are civilly liable for damages if you build and use someone else's patented invention, even if you only use it yourself. When you sell your patented product, you are licensing the purchaser to use that one product. You can, additionally, sell the exclusive or nonexclusive right to another firm for them to build and sell your invention.

A patentee, or rightful licensee under a patent, is required to mark the articles with the word "patent" followed by the number of the patent. Failure to mark may result in the patentee's inability to recover damages from an infringer unless the infringer was duly notified of the infringement and continued to infringe after notice. It is also worth noting that marking an article as "patented" when it is not is against the law and subjects the offender to a penalty.

The words "patent pending" or "patent applied for" have no legal effect, but serve to give notice that an application is in process with the U.S. Patent Office. Thus, infringement during this period cannot technically occur since there is no patent in force. Use of "patent pending" (or similar phrases) is illegal if used to misrepresent. You, a designer, should heed "patent pending" because you may have to quit using your design if it infringes on the patent which may be granted to someone who has a patent application pending.

Design patents and plant patents differ from utility patents

Utility (conventional) patents last for 17 years and may be obtained for "new and useful processes , machines, manufacturing methods, compositions of matter or any new and useful improvements thereof." "New and useful" means not patented, previously invented nor obvious to those skilled in the field. "New and useful" also means of value for a legal purpose. "Improvements thereof" means you can patent an improvement of yours or someone else's patented invention. Note that you can't patent methods of doing business, abstract ideas, basic laws of nature or knowledge.

According to the law, a novel design may be patented. Design patents only cover the appearance and not the structural or utilitarian features of an item, and only one claim is permitted. Design patents are issued for 14 years.

The law also provides for patenting any plant material that has been asexually reproduced from any distinct and new variety of plant other than a tuber-propagated plant or a naturally occurring plant found in an uncultivated state. The only plants covered by the term "tuber-propagated" are the Irish potato and the Jerusalem artichoke. Since a plant patent is granted on the entire plant, only one claim is permitted.

While one would expect the resultant life forms created as a result of genetic engineering efforts to be the subject of plant patents such is not the case. In the U.S. Supreme Court decision, Diamond v. Chakrabaity, the court held patent law as sufficiently broad to include man-made life forms as patentable, provided all other patentability conditions were met and that simply being alive did not preclude its patentability as a "new and useful process, machine, manufacturing method, or composition of matter, or any new and useful improvements thereof." Therefore, the results of genetic engineering can be protected by utility patents.

Trademarks

As the word implies, a trademark is a distinctive mark used to distinguish goods in trade from other manufacturers. The word trademark is also the generic term used to refer to all four legally defined marks: trademarks, service marks, certification marks, and collective marks. Trademarks are used in commerce to distinguish one manufacturer's goods from another. Often, trademarks are the company's initials, a simple geometric shape or pattern that the manufacturer wants the public to use to recognize their product.

Service marks are used to identify suppliers of similar services like banks, hotels, restaurants, etc. Certification marks are used by businesses that perform, for example, standardization or safety checks. Collective marks are those marks used to identify a collection of individuals who share common goals like the ASAE octagon or the 4-H clover.

Trademarks which are used in interstate or foreign commerce may be renewably registered for periods of 20 years with the patent and trademark office. Trademarks remain in effect as long as they continue to be used.

Copyrights

Copyright law includes a wide variety of intellectual property such as books, periodicals, drama, musicals, maps, artistic drawings, photographic prints, pictorial illustrations, photoplays, motion pictures, and musical compositions on mechanical instruments. Electronic circuits and computer software are also protected by copyright law. A copyright can presently be obtained for the life of the author plus 50 years.

Like patents, copyrights do not cover ideas. You obtain a copyright on the collection of words, or artistic form of a drawing used to *express* the idea, not the idea itself. Both published and unpublished works may be copyrighted, but copyrights to published works may be lost as soon as it is published if a claim to those rights has not been asserted by publication with the statutory notice in the form of "Copyright © 19xx, by I .M. Author, All Rights Reserved."

To obtain a certificate of copyright, the applicant must submit copies of the material to the Register of Copyrights, Library of Congress, Washington, D.C. 20540. The submitted material must contain the applicants claim to copyright.

Trade secrets

While patent law has evolved to encourage the disclosure to the public of new and improved technology, no law requires disclosure. Indeed, you can devise or invent a new process (often the subject of trade secrets) and simply choose to keep that new process a secret. There are many well-known foods whose ingredients are secret (e.g., Coca-Cola). Software can also be developed and imbedded in an integrated circuit such that it can be maintained as a trade secret.

Needless to say, trade secrets are difficult to maintain in large companies. Trade secrets do, however, have value in the legal system and an employee who steals and passes on a trade secret can be sued for doing so. Companies who steal trade secrets from other companies may be civilly and/or criminally liable for doing so.

References

1. Kinney and Lange. 1984. Overview of intellectual property laws for business lawyers. Kinney and Lange, Minneapolis, MN.

2. Joenk, R.J., Editor. 1982. Patents and patenting for engineers and scientists. IEEE, 345 E 47th, New York, 10017. 105 pp.

3. U.S. Department of Commerce. "General information concerning patents" Washington, D.C. 20231.

Chapter 23
Futurology

"Too frequently we ask ourselves only what should happen next? We do not look far enough down the years, visualize what should happen ultimately, then work backward to the present as well as forward from where we are now in developing our plans." Wortman and Cummings

"Problems represent challenges; challenges are opportunities; opportunities are the vehicle to success."

Engineers create the future

Technology — more than laws, business mergers and high finance together — forms the future. Laws, mergers and finance influence which organizations do the work and who reaps the benefits. They may speed, slow or guide technology in a nation. But on a world scale, engineers guide the future more than any other group. The engineering profession faces an exciting responsibility!

Your success as an engineer rests on your ability to anticipate future needs and then to develop creative solutions to those needs. Success in a business rests on the ability of its people to anticipate

CHECKING THE NORTH 40

future needs and provide solutions. As an engineer you have a critical role, in cooperation with other groups in your organization, to identify these problems and develop solutions. Fortunes and failures, fame and fool, all result from the ability (or inability) to foresee the future. Yet we can never know the future.

We can use knowledge and techniques to give us clues about the future. Here are six suggestions for studying the future: (a) think big, (b) ask questions, (c) look at resources and needs, (d) forget economics, (e) do not simply extrapolate the present and (f) understand the technology adaptation process.

Think big

Think big, which means, "Be creative on a global scale." Let your imagination run wild! Dream, and do not let "minor" technical or economic practicalities inhibit your thinking. Such details are important and are the day-to-day work for most engineers. For anticipating the future, though, it is important that you look for the broader perspective, assuming that the details can be worked out as needed.

Do not confuse thinking big with "gigantic corporations" and "omni-present government." Organizational size and type will have less to do with the future than the societal needs and the available avenues for solutions. Conversely, do assume that the organization size and structure can be formed, if needed, for an important project (e.g., space exploration, multinational pollution control strategies, etc.).

Ask questions

Remember the earlier chapters of this book that stressed the concepts of formulating clear and concise problem *definitions*. It is in the problem definition that the solution is born. No problems are solved until defined.

Consider bioengineering as an example. The real excitement about bioengineering is that problems are being defined and formulated for today's engineers and researchers that weren't even considered several years ago. For example, can you design a corn plant to be a nitrogen fixer? Are 1.5 m tall hogs genetically possible? Is it possible for a single mouse to have 4 genetic parents? Once asked, these and similar questions will be the catalysts needed for engineers and researchers to develop solutions. No problem is solved without first asking the defining problem question. How, when, where, why and what are still the most important questions to be asked, and these can be tools to help you conceive new ideas for the future.

Look at resources and needs

Look at resources and needs from a macro perspective. These can be related in a form analogous to a chemical reaction equation (Fig 23.1). Energy, land, raw materials, labor and the cumulative effects of labor (technology) are the resources available to meet our needs and wants. Our needs and wants are food, energy, manufactured goods and services which include medical care, schools, entertainment and governmental institutions. The social and biological environment affects and is affected by our efforts to meet our needs and wants using available resources. These system effects are important because a means of meeting our needs and wants is unacceptable if it destroys the environment for future generations or if it disrupts society more than it helps society.

Energy, land and physical resources are remaining nearly constant; though, clearly our resources are being dispersed in

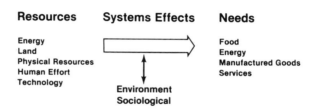

FIG 23.1 The economic equation in generic form.

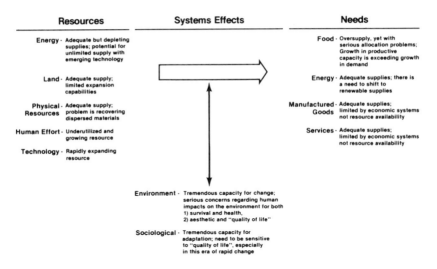

FIG 23.2 The economic equation—assessment of the current situation.

what today is often an irretrievable fashion (Fig 23.2). Labor resources are growing, though not uniformly. Most importantly, the human resource of accumulated knowledge (both technological and social) is growing dramatically and is likely to expand our ability to use other resources which were previously under-utilized (e.g., the biological capabilities of land and new organisms, space, physical resources sorted from low concentrations, nuclear and solar energy, etc.).

Needs and wants are increasing dramatically as the world population grows and the less developed countries improve living standards (Fig 23.2). Energy, land and raw material resources available to meet these needs are not increasing, and, often, accessibility for needy countries is being more limited. Meanwhile, the environment and social systems are heavily taxed by the population and the quantities of material and energy resources consumed meeting current needs and wants. Tremendous interrelated, environmental, social and political challenges face engineers and other leaders (Fig 23.2). Human efforts and technology are our hope for the future—they are the only resources that are growing!

Applying the resources and needs equation to the current United States agricultural situation can be helpful (Fig 23.3). It appears that production capacity will grow more rapidly than U.S. food needs plus our ability to export food products. This suggests that viewing agriculture as a source of renewable energy,

Resources	Systems Effects	Needs
Capacity for expansion of agricultural output is considerable based on emerging technologies and adequate supplies of the other resources. This is supported by recent growth in the number of countries which are net agricultural exporters and by the fact that governments support agricultural product prices because of this oversupply.		Near term opportunities for using the excess food production capacity of agriculture are as a renewable source of energy or as materials for manufacturing.
	Soil losses are serious both for the land productivity and for water pollution. Food quality is growing in importance. Living space, entertainment, and environmental preservation are important concerns. Quality of life for people is a major problem, accentuated by the rate of change in society.	

FIG 23.3 Using the economic equation to understand trends in agricultural production.

a resource for manufacturing and a way of providing a better life will be important for predicting changes that will occur in U.S. agriculture during the next 25 years.

Forget economics

The most common argument against change is: it is uneconomical. People have said that since money was invented. Many important changes appear uneconomical when first conceived. Only after considerable research, development and achievement of volume production do such changes become really economical. Farm computers and calculators, center-pivot irrigation machines, fan-ventilated confinement buildings, automatic controls and motor-driven, bulk-grain conveying equipment appeared uneconomical for most agricultural applications as late as the 1950's.

The problem with looking at economics to predict technology is that economics is a "means to an end," not the "end." Economics is simply a means for allocating resources to satisfy needs and wants. Whether socialistic, capitalistic or some combination of the two, economics ultimately reflects the needs, wants and abilities of people plus the supply of resources. If a method or technology is developed which better utilizes resources to attain needs or wants, the economic system can be adjusted to encourage this technology. The speed and success of the change may be limited by people's abilities to adjust the economic system.

Once you have a sense of needed direction, *then* face the key economic problem. That problem is how to work within (or fine-tune) the economic system to achieve the desired end. Common methods for fine-tuning the economic system are: government support of research according to perceived needs, selective taxes or tax breaks and laws which prohibit or require certain actions believed to be in the public interest.

Do not simply extrapolate the present

The temptation is great and the logic compelling. Energy consumption in the U.S. grew about 4% annually through the 1960's and 1970's and was highly correlated with economic growth. Governmental and industrial leaders passionately argued that attempts to reduce this growth through conservation were futile and would cause our economy to collapse. Yet, in the early 1980's energy consumption growth slowed, actual energy consumption declined, and the economy did not collapse; rather, the economy shifted and experienced growth. Since then, energy prices have fluctuated as has economic activity, with little apparent cause-effect relationship.

If our ancestors in 1900 tried to predict the future by extrapolation of the past into the future they would have reached some interesting conclusions. First, we needed to work on better draft horse varieties for more efficient farming. Second, the U.S. would have a colossal food shortage by the mid-1900's because our agriculture simply could not feed the population of this country. The list goes on. Hybrid crop varieties with tripled yields, computers, television, automatic machine guidance, and electronic controls could scarcely be imagined. In fact, your parents may have learned to calculate using a slide rule because the $15 hand held calculator we use cost millions of dollars and occupied an entire room.

The point of this is that technological advances cannot be predicted by extrapolation. Advances are certain; the type of advances and the directions they will take are not certain. Imagination plus a careful look at resources and future needs can help.

Understand the "technology adaptation process"

Technology adaptation usually proceeds in a chain-like fashion beginning with the development of the scientific and theoretical foundation (Fig 23.4). This knowledge leads to engineering ideas for applying that scientific knowledge to solve problems. At this time the ideas are usually uneconomical and technically underdeveloped for all problems. The next step is application of the idea to the field most suited and most in need of the technology.

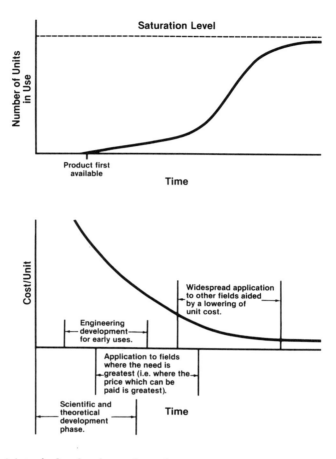

FIG 23.4 A typical technology adaptation curve.

The final step is utilization of the now mass-produced, well-developed technology in the host of peripheral fields.

An example of this process is the electronics field. During the first half of the 20th century, scientists and engineers slowly, painstakingly developed the chemistry, physics, electronic and processing theory and technologies which made solid-state electronics a technical possibility. During the 1950's and 1960's electronics developed explosively as they were applied to the conventional electrical equipment, leading to the development of computers and better electronic controls. We are now in an advanced phase of electronic technology development. Mass production has reduced costs and increased the reliabilities dramatically. Electronics are now applied to livestock ventilation, tractor carburetion and performance monitoring, irrigation system

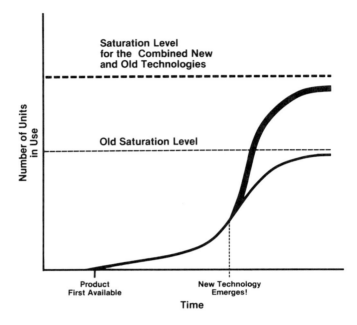

FIG 23.5 The influence of a new development with its new technology adaptation cycle on an in-progress technology adaptation cycle. Note: new development may have a negative impact (not shown) or a positive impact on the older technology.

guidance and control, grain bin moisture measurement, dairy herd management and a variety of other applications which were not traditionally electrical engineering fields. In fact, rudimentary knowledge of electronics is essential for all engineering fields.

Of course, new developments will continue in electronics. Each significant new development starts a similar technology adaptation process (Fig 23.5). The new development may replace or enhance the older developments. Most areas of technology have several developments, in some phase of the technology adaptation process, which cumulatively suggest where and how that technology will be applied.

The trick in using this technology adaptation process to predict the future is to identify those developments which are in the scientific idea or early adaptation phases. Consider genetic engineering. Present applications are limited to high value uses such as medicine, but this looks promising for replacing the high-energy physical and chemical processes currently used to distill alcohol, convert soybeans to oil, desalinate water and purify wastes. Consider agricultural residues. Agricultural residues are used now for energy on a limited basis, but they look promising as a manufacturing and energy resource — providing we can develop the right collection procedures, processing alternatives and applications.

We are living in dynamic times

These are transitory times. Scientific and engineering knowledge, expanding exponentially, is propelling us out of the manufacturing or industrial era. Look around you and see the signs of change. We struggle with information overload, not information availability, as we shuffle through rooms full of computer-generated and retrieved data on bearing lubrication. We live in a global economy where news of a government leader's illness in Australia is transmitted within minutes via satellite to even the most sparsely populated regions, and then affects stock prices. Teamwork is imperative as we face the growing complexity of technology and realize that we must work together on a world scale or risk nuclear war.

The scientific barriers separating agricultural food resources from energy and manufacturing raw materials are crumbling. The whole concept of agriculture will change when we can "manufacture" food in an industrial building by combining minable raw materials, and conversely, can "grow" on farms a great array of energy and manufacturing raw resources. Tomorrow's agriculture will be shaped by the currently-vague concepts of biotechnology and genetic engineering that are roaring ahead, fueled by record levels of venture capital and new ideas.

History provides an example of transitory times during the late 18th and early 19th centuries as we moved from an "agricultural era" to this "manufacturing era." Such change is troubling because values, institutions, career avenues and life styles are in turmoil. New businesses spring up and others fade away or adapt. Whole career options disappear and unheard of options emerge. Who even imagined being a computer programmer in 1950?

Transitory times are also a rare and exciting opportunity! Without a doubt, there are tremendous opportunities for starting new businesses. People with vision and the desire to implement their visions can more easily do so. Several of the largest international companies did not exist 25 years ago and are built upon electronics, computer and other technologies known only in this century.

The 21st century will be the era of the "Brain Barons"

Many experts agree that we are stepping into an information

era where knowledge is king. Of course that does not mean we will abandon manufacturing any more than the move into the manufacturing era meant that we would abandon agricultural food production. Rather it means that information will be the most important ingredient for success in business or government. Land barons dominated most of history by controlling land, the key ingredient of the agricultural era. Capital barons dominated the manufacturing era by controlling the money needed to build, operate and increase the productivity of industry. Brain barons will monopolize the future by their abilities to obtain, sort, interpret and apply knowledge. The brain factories (i.e., colleges and universities) must increase internal productivity to insure an adequate supply of brain barons.

If you doubt such change is happening, look at growth of research parks and incubation centers. State and local government leaders are spending millions of dollars to set up these centers, frequently tying them to universities which have strong engineering and science programs. Business leaders are seeing innovation and knowledge as their hope for the future and are responding by allowing greater freedom of approach in research and development, by providing far greater financial support to research and by implementing financial incentive programs which encourage enterpreneurship ("intrapreneuring") within companies. Industrialized nations, groping with the issue of how their workers can compete with workers earning less than one-tenth as much in developing countries, are concluding that knowledge (new technology) is the major ingredient in a solution.

Robots, electronic controls and sensors, lasers, smart microorganisms and a host of other new technologies looming on the horizon are reshaping manufacturing and agriculture. Will we be jaded by technological abundance and potential or will we be excited about the prospects, celebrating the changes? Will we destroy ourselves and tear apart the social fabric of the world or will we capitalize on the opportunities to make this a better world? Certainly, there are tremendous technical and societal challenges confronting us as we make this transition.

What are the challenges facing agricultural engineers ?

Challenges facing agricultural engineers are to: (a) produce more food, and in a greater variety, (b) provide improved food storage and more efficient distribution systems, (c) produce biologically the energy and raw materials for manufacturing, (d) minimize or reduce energy consumption in agriculture, (e) increase the profitability of agriculture, (f) improve and protect the environment, (g) promote change in socially desirable and acceptable ways and (h) develop new technologies and draw on technologies from other fields to make this a "better" world. Pull yourself out of the confusion of the present as you look to the future. There will be dramatic changes; things technically and economically infeasible today will be commonplace tomorrow.

Following are some predictions by the authors designed to pique your imagination and to encourage you to develop your own ideas:

1. Information sorting and organization will become increasingly important. Consequently, people will pay for information sorting. Use of consultants with a specialized expertise will be more widespread.

2. Biological and microbiological processing will replace chemical/mechanical processing as the principal means for converting biological products to a more desired form. Waste handling practices and energy from biomass will be revolutionized.

3. Agriculture will be the principal source of raw materials for manufacturing, replacing metals and other mined materials.

4. Recycling scarce resources will outstrip mining as a source for new raw materials.

5. Research and education will become more important. People will need more formal education, and they will use continuing education opportunities on a more frequent basis.

6. Numbers of women in agricultural engineering will continue to increase, and the participation by women in the professional and scientific fields will also increase. This will change lifestyles and work patterns in all fields.

7. Mass communication equipment will favor population dispersion because there no longer will be the need for many traditionally city firms to locate in large cities.

8. Water use and water quality will become the number one resource issue — at least in the western United States.

9. Steel and lumber will no longer be the principal building materials for agricultural facilities and equipment. A variety of new materials will emerge.

10. Engineering design will become increasingly complex. A variety of specialists will be needed for most problems. The ability to work with and coordinate people will be essential to the engineering designer.

References

1. Naisbett, J. 1982. Megatrends: Ten new directions transforming our lives. Warner Books, New York, NY. 290pp.

2. Coates, J. 1983. Personal correspondence with J.F. Coates Inc., 3738 Kanawha Street, N.W., Washington, DC 20015.

3. Peters, T.J. and R.H. Waterman, Jr. 1982. In search of excellence. Harper & Row, New York. 360 pp.

4. Isaacs, G. 1983. Agricultural engineering in a changing world. *Agricultural Engineering*, 64(8):16-18.

APPENDIX I
Code of Ethics for Engineers

Preamble

Engineering is an important and learned profession. The members of the profession recognize that their work has a direct and vital impact on the quality of life for all people. Accordingly, the services provided by engineers require honesty, impartiality, fairness and equity, and must be dedicated to the protection of the public health, safety and welfare. In the practice of their profession, engineers must perform under a standard of professional behavior which requires adherence to the highest principles of ethical conduct on behalf of the public, clients, employers and the profession.

I. FUNDAMENTAL CANONS
Engineers, in the fulfillment of their professional duties, shall:
1. Hold paramount the safety, health and welfare of the public in the performance of their professional duties.
2. Perform services only in areas of their competence.
3. Issue public statements only in an objective and truthful manner.
4. Act in professional matters for each employer or client as faithful agents or trustees.
5. Avoid improper solicitation of professional employment.

II. RULES OF PRACTICE
1. Engineers shall hold paramount the safety, health and welfare of the public in the performance of their professional duties.

(a) Engineers shall at all times recognize that their primary obligation is to protect the safety, health, property and welfare of the public. If their professional judgment is overruled under circumstances where the safety, health, property or welfare of the public are endangered, they shall notify their employer or client and such other authority as may be appropriate.

(b) Engineers shall approve only those engineering documents which are safe for public health, property and welfare in conformity with accepted standards.

(c) Engineers shall not reveal facts, data or information obtained in a professional capacity without the prior consent of the client or employer except as authorized or required by law or this Code.

(d) Engineers shall not permit the use of their name or firm name nor associate in business ventures with any person or firm which they have reason to believe is engaging in fraudulent or dishonest business or professional practices.

(e) Engineers having knowledge of any alleged violation of this Code shall cooperate with the proper authorities in furnishing such information or assistance as may be required.

2. Engineers shall perform services only in the areas of their competence.

(a) Engineers shall undertake assignment only when qualified by education or experience in the specific technical fields involved.

(b) Engineers shall not affix their signatures to any plans or documents dealing with subject matter in which they lack competence, nor to any plan or document not prepared under their direction and control.

(c) Engineers may accept assignments and assume responsibility for coordination of an entire project and sign and seal the engineering documents for the entire project, provided that each technical segment is signed and sealed only by the qualified engineer who prepared the segment.

3. Engineers shall issue public statements only in an objective and truthful manner.

(a) Engineers shall be objective and truthful in professional reports, statements or testimony. They shall include all relevant and pertinent information in such reports, statements or testimony.

(b) Engineers may express publicly a professional opinion on technical subjects only when that opinion is founded upon adequate knowledge of the facts and competence in the subject matter.

(c) Engineers shall issue no statements, criticisms or arguments on technical matters which are inspired or paid for by interested parties, unless they have prefaced their comments by explicitly identifying the interested parties on whose behalf they are speaking, and by revealing the existence of any interest the engineers may have in the matters.

4. Engineers shall act in professional matters for each employer or client as faithful agents or trustees.

(a) Engineers shall disclose all known or potential conflicts of interest to their employers or clients by promptly informing them of any business association, interest, or other circumstances which could influence or appear to influence their judgment or the quality of their services.

(b) Engineers shall not accept compensation, financial or otherwise, from more than one party for services on the same project, or for services pertaining to the same project, unless the circumstances are fully disclosed to, and agreed to, by all interested parties.

(c) Engineers shall not solicit or accept financial or other valuable consideration, directly or indirectly, from contractors, their agents, or other parties in connection with work for employers or clients for which they are responsible.

(d) Engineers in public service as members, advisors or employees of a governmental body or department shall not participate in decisions with respect to professional services solicited or provided by them or their organizations in private or public engineering practice.

(e) Engineers shall not solicit or accept a professional contract from a governmental body on which a principal or officer of their organization serves as a member.

5. Engineers shall avoid improper solicitation of professional employment.

(a) Engineers shall not falsify or permit misrepresentation of their, or their associates' academic or professional qualifications. They shall not misrepresent or exaggerate their degree of responsibility in or for the subject matter of prior assignments. Brochures or other presentations incident to the solicitation of employment shall not misrepresent pertinent facts concerning employers, employees, associates, joint venturers or past accomplishments with the intent and purpose of enhancing their qualifications and their work.

(b) Engineers shall not offer, give, solicit or receive, either directly or indirectly, any political contribution in an amount intended to influence the award of a contract by public authority, or which may be reasonably construed by the public of having the effect or intent to influence the award of a contract. They shall not offer any gift, or other valuable consideration in order to secure work. They shall not pay a commission, percentage or brokerage fee in order to secure work except to a bona fide employee or bona fide established commercial or marketing agencies retained by them.

III. PROFESSIONAL OBLIGATIONS

1. Engineers shall be guided in all their professional relations by the highest standards of integrity.

(a) Engineers shall admit and accept their own errors when proven wrong and refrain from distorting or altering the facts in an attempt to justify their decisions.

(b) Engineers shall advise their clients or employers when they believe a project will not be successful.

(c) Engineers shall not accept outside employment to the detriment of their regular work or interest. Before accepting any outside employment they will notify their employers.

(d) Engineers shall not attempt to attract an engineer from another employer by false or misleading pretenses.

(e) Engineers shall not actively participate in strikes, picket lines, or other collective coercive action.

(f) Engineers shall avoid any act tending to promote their own interest at the expense of the dignity and integrity of the profession.

2. Engineers shall at all times strive to serve the public interest.

(a) Engineers shall seek opportunities to be of constructive service in civic affairs and work for the advancement of the safety, health and well-being of their community.

(b) Engineers shall not complete, sign, or seal plans and/or specifications that are not of a design safe to the public health and welfare and in conformity with accepted engineering standards. If the client or employer insists on such unprofessional conduct, they shall notify the proper authorities and withdraw from further service on the project.

(c) Engineers shall endeavor to extend public knowledge and appreciation of engineering and its achievements and to protect the engineering profession from misrepresentation and misunderstanding.

3. Engineers shall avoid all conduct or practice which is likely to discredit the profession or deceive the public.

(a) Engineers shall avoid the use of statements containing a material misrepresentation of fact or omitting a material fact necessary to keep statements from being misleading; statements intended or likely to create an unjustified expectation; statements containing prediction of future success; statements containing an opinion as to the quality of the Engineers' services; or statements intended or likely to attract clients by the use of showmanship, puffery, or self-laudation, including the use of slogans, jingles, or sensational language or format.

(b) Consistent with the foregoing, Engineers may advertise for recruitment of personnel.

(c) Consistent with the foregoing, Engineers may prepare articles for the lay or technical press, but such articles shall not imply credit to the author for work performed by others.

4. Engineers shall not disclose confidential information concerning the business affairs or technical processes of any present or former client or employer without his consent.

(a) Engineers in the employ of others shall not without the consent of all interested parties enter promotional efforts or negotiations for work or make arrangements for other employment as a principal or to practice in connection with a specific project for which the Engineer has gained particular and specialized knowledge.

(b) Engineers shall not, without the consent of all interested parties, participate in or represent an adversary interest in connection with a specific project or proceeding in which the Engineer has gained particular specialized knowledge on behalf of a former client or employer.

5. Engineers shall not be influenced in their professional duties by conflicting interests.

(a) Engineers shall not accept financial or other considerations, including free engineering designs, from material or equipment suppliers for specifying their product.

(b) Engineers shall not accept commissions or allowances, directly or indirectly, from contractors or other parties dealing with clients or employers of the Engineer in connection with work for which the Engineer is responsible.

6. Engineers shall uphold the principle of appropriate and adequate compensation for those engaged in engineering work.

(a) Engineers shall not accept remuneration from either an employee or employment agency for giving employment.

(b) Engineers, when employing other engineers, shall offer a salary according to professional qualifications and the recognized standards in the particular geographical area.

7. Engineers shall not compete unfairly with other engineers by attempting to obtain employment or advancement or professional engagements by taking advantage of a salaried position, by criticizing other engineers, or by other improper or questionable methods.

(a) Engineers shall not request, propose, or accept a professional commission on a contingent basis under circumstances in which their professional judgment may be compromised.

(b) Engineers in salaried positions shall accept part-time engineering work only at salaries not less than that recognized as standard in the area.

(c) Engineers shall not use equipment, supplies, laboratory, or office facilities of an employer to carry on outside private practice without consent.

8. Engineers shall not attempt to injure, maliciously or falsely, directly or indirectly, the professional reputation, prospects, practice or employment of other engineers, nor indiscriminately criticize other engineers' work. Engineers who believe others are guilty of unethical or illegal practice shall present such information to the proper authority for action.

(a) Engineers in private practice shall not review the work of another engineer for the same client, except with the knowledge of such engineer, or unless the connection of such engineer with the work has been terminated.

(b) Engineers in governmental, industrial or educational employ are entitled to review and evaluate the work of other engineers when so required by their employment duties.

(c) Engineers in sales or industrial employ are entitled to make engineering comparisons of represented products with products of other suppliers.

9. Engineers shall accept personal responsibility for all professional activities.

(a) Engineers shall conform with state registration laws in the practice of engineering.

(b) Engineers shall not use association with a nonengineer, a corporation, or partnership, as a "cloak" for unethical acts, but must accept personal responsibility for all professional acts.

10. Engineers shall give credit for engineering work to those to whom credit is due, and will recognize the proprietary interests of others.

(a) Engineers shall, whenever possible, name the person or persons who may be individually responsible for designs, inventions, writings, or other accomplishments.

(b) Engineers using designs supplied by a client recognize that the designs remain the property of the client and may not be duplicated by the Engineer for others without express permission.

(c) Engineers, before undertaking work for others in connection with which the Engineer may make improvements, plans designs, inventions, or other records, which may justify copyrights or patents, should enter into a positive agreement regarding ownership.

(d) Engineers' design, data, records, and notes referring exclusively to an employer's work are the employer's property.

11. Engineers shall cooperate in extending the effectiveness of the profession by interchanging information and experience with other engineers and students, and will endeavor to provide opportunity for the professional development and advancement of engineers under their supervision.

(a) Engineers shall encourage engineering employees' efforts to improve their education.

(b) Engineers shall encourage engineering employees to attend and present papers at professional and technical society meetings.

(c) Engineers shall urge engineering employees to become registered at the earliest possible date.

(d) Engineers shall assign a professional engineer duties of a nature to utilize full training and experience, insofar as possible, and delegate lesser functions to subprofessionals or to technicians.

(e) Engineers shall provide a prospective engineering employee with complete information on working conditions and proposed status of employment, and after employment will keep employees informed of any changes.

"By order of the United States District Court for the District of Columbia, former Section 11(c) of the NSPE Code of Ethics prohibiting competitive bidding, and all policy statements, opinions, rulings, or other guidelines interpreting its scope, have been rescinded as unlawfully interfering with the legal right of engineers, protected under the antitrust laws, to provide price information to prospective clients, accordingly, nothing contained in the NSPE Code of Ethics, policy statements, opinions, rulings, or other guidelines prohibits the submission of price quotations or competitive bids for engineering services at any time or in any amount."

STATEMENT BY NSPE EXECUTIVE COMMITTEE

In order to correct misunderstandings which have been indicated in some instances since the issuance of the Supreme Court decision and the entry of the Final Judgment, it is noted that in its decision of April 25, 1978, the Supreme Court of the United States declared: "The Sherman Act does not require competitive bidding."

It is further noted that as made clear in the Supreme Court decision:

1. Engineers and firms may individually refuse to bid for engineering services.

2. Clients are not required to seek bids for engineering services.

3. Federal, state, and local laws governing procedures to procure engineering services are not affected, and remain in full force and effect.

4. State societies and local chapters are free to actively and aggressively seek legislation for professional selection and negotiation procedures by public agencies.

5. State registration board rules of professional conduct, including rules prohibiting competitive bidding for engineering services, are not affected and remain in full force and effect. State registration boards with authority to adopt rules of professional conduct may adopt rules governing procedures to obtain engineering services.

6. As noted by the Supreme Court, "nothing in the judgment prevents NSPE and its members from attempting to influence governmental action..."

NOTE:

In regard to the question of application of the Code to corporations vis-a-vis real persons, business form or type should not negate nor influence conformance of individuals to the Code. The Code deals with professional services, which services must be performed by real persons. Real persons in turn establish and implement policies within business structures. The Code is clearly written to apply to the Engineer and it is incumbent on a member of NSPE to endeavor to live up to its provisions. This applies to all pertinent sections of the Code.

NSPE Publication No. 1102 as revised, January, 1985.

APPENDIX II
Organizations with activities related to Agricultural Engineering

AGRICULTURAL SOCIETIES

Animals

American Feed Manufacturers Assoc., Oakley M. Ray, Pres. 1701 N. Fort Meyer Drive, Arlington, VA 22209 (703) 524-0810

American Society of Animal Science, Claude J. Cruse, 309 W. Clark St. Champaign, IL 61820 (217) 356 3182

American Veterinary Medicine Asso., D.A. Price, Exec. VP 930 N Meacham Rd., Schaumburg, IL 60196 (312) 885-8070

Dairy and Food Industries Supply Assoc., Inc., Fred J. Greiner, Chair., 6245 Executive Blvd., Rockville, MD 20852 (301) 984-1444

National Pork Producers Council, Orville K. Sweet, Exec. VP P.O. Box 10383, Des Moines, IA 50306 (515) 223-2600

National Cattleman's Assoc., John Meetz, Exec. VP, 1301 Pennsylvania Ave, NW Suite 300 Washington, DC 20004 (202) 347-0228

Poultry Science Association, Claude J. Cruse, Bus. Mgr. 309 W. Clark St., Champaign, IL 61820 (217) 356-3182

Biotechnology

Alliance for Engineering in Medicine and Biology, Patricia Horner, Exec. Dir. 1101 Connecticut Ave., NW Suite 700 Washington, DC 20036 (202) 857-1199

American Society for Microbiology, Michael I. Goldberg, Exec. Dir. 1913 Eye St. Washington, DC 20006 (202) 833-9680

Economics and Management

American Association of Agricultural Economists. There is no association headquarters — the presidency and journal editorship rotate with each election.

American Society of Farm Managers and Rural Appraisers, T. Jan Wiseman, Exec. VP 950 S. Cherry Suite G-16 Denver, CO 80222 (303) 758-3531

National Council of Farmer Cooperatives, Wayne A. Boutwell, Pres. 1800 Massachusetts Ave. N.W., Washington, DC 20036 (202) 659-1525

Southern Association of Agricultural Scientists, Leon McGraw, Sec. 1068 Terrace Acres Auburn, AL 36830 (205) 887-5652

Plants

American Forage and Grassland Council, J. Kenneth Evans, Exec. Dir. 2021 Rebel Rd. Lexington, KY 40503 (606) 278-0177

American Society for Horticultural Science, Cecil Blackwell, Exec. Dir. 701 North Saint Asaph St., Alexandria, VA 22314 (703) 836-4606

American Society of Agronomy, Rodney A. Briggs, Exec. VP 677 S. Segoe Rd. Madison, WI 53711 (608) 274-1212

Entomological Society of America, W. Darryl Hansen, Exec. Dir. 4603 Calvert Rd., Box AJ College Park, MD 20740 (301) 864-1334

Fertilizer Institute, The, Gary D. Meyers, Pres., 1015 18th N.W. St. Washington, DC 20036 (202) 861-4900

Soil Science Society of America, Inc., Rodney A. Briggs 677 S. Segoe Rd. Madison, WI 53711 (608) 274-1212

Weed Science Society of America, Claude J. Cruse, Exec. Sec. 309 W. Clark St. Champaign, IL 61820 (217) 356-3182

General

American Farm Bureau Federation, Robert B. Delano, Pres. 225 Touhy Ave., Park Ridge, IL 60068 (312) 399-5700

Agricultural Research Institute, Paul T. Truitt, Exec. VP Room 835 Joseph Henry Bldg., 2100 Pennsylvania Ave. N.W., Washington, DC 20037

American Society of Agricultural Consultants, Frand Frazier, Exec. VP, Suite 470, Enterprise Center, 8301 Greensboro Dr., McLean, VA 22102 (703) 356-2455

Council for Agricultural Science and Technology, Charles A. Black, Exec. VP, 250 Memorial Union, Iowa State University, Ames, IA 50011 (515) 294-2036

National Council of Farmer Cooperatives, Wayne A. Boutwell, Pres. 1800 Massachusetts Ave. N.W., Washington, DC 20036 (202) 659-1525

Southern Association of Agricultural Scientists, Leon McGraw, Sec. 1068 Terrace Acres, Auburn, AL 36830 (205) 887-5652

AGRICULTURAL ENGINEERING PRODUCTS

Buildings and HVAC

American Society of Heating, Refrigerating and Air-Conditioning Engineers, Inc., Frank M. Coda, Exec. VP 1791 Tulle Circle NE, Atlanta, GA 30329.

Farmstead Equipment Assoc., a Council of the FIEI, James H. Ebbinghaus, Sec., 410 N. Michigan Ave., Chicago, IL 60611 (312) 321-1470

International Silo Assoc., J. T. Knight, Pres. 815 Office Park Rd., Suite 2, West Des Moines, IA 50265 (515) 225-0643

Metal Building Manufacturers Assoc., Charles M. Stockinger, Gen. Mgr. 1230 Keith Bldg., Cleveland, OH 44115 (216) 241-7333

National Frame Builders Assoc., J. T. Knight, Pres. 815 Office Park Rd., Suite 2 West Des Moines, IA 50265 (515) 225-0643

Food, Feed & Processing

Conveyor Equipment Manufacturers Assoc., Raymond J. Lloyd, Exec. VP 152 Rollins Ave., Suite 208, Rockville, MD 20852 (301) 984-9080

Crop Dryer Manufacturers Council, A Council of the FIEI. James H. Ebbinghaus, Secretary, 410 N. Michigan Ave., Chicago, IL 60611 (312) 321-1470

Grain Bin Manufacturers Council, a Council of the FIEI, James H. Ebbinghaus, Secretary, 410 N. Michigan Ave., Chicago, IL 60611 (312) 321-1420

League for International Food Education, Albert Meisel, Exec. Dir. 915 15th St. NW Rm 915, Washington, DC 20005 (202) 331-1658

Milking Machine Manufacturers Council, a Council of the FIEI, James H. Ebbinghaus, Sec., 410 N. Michigan Ave., Chicago, IL 60611 (312) 321-1470

National Electrical Manufacturers Assoc., Bernard H. Falk, Pres. 2101 L St., N.W. Washington DC 20037 (202) 457-8400

Land and Water

American Water Resources, Association, Kenneth D. Reid, Exec. Dir. 5410 Grosvenor Ln., Suite 220 Bethesda, MD 20814 (301) 493-8600

American Water Works Assoc., David B. Preston, Exec. Dir. 6666 W. Quincy Ave., Denver, CO 80235 (303) 794-7711

International Commission of Irrigation and Drainage, U.S. National Committee, Larry D. Stephens, executive secretary P.O. Box 15326, Denver, CO 80215

International Water Resources Assoc., Glenn E. Stout, Exec. Dir. 208 North Romine University of Illinois Urbana, IL 61801 (217) 333-0536

Irrigation Assoc., The, Walter D. Anderson, Exec. Dir. Suite 310, 13975 Connecticut Ave. Silver Springs, MD 20906

Land Improvement Contractors of America, Gene A. Honn, Exec. VP 1300 Maybrook Drive, Box 100 Maywood, IL 60153 (312) 344-0700

National Association of Conservation Districts, Charles L. Boothby, Exec. VP, Suite 1105, 1025 Vermont Ave., N.W. Washington, DC 20005 (202) 347-5995

Soil Conservation Society of America, The, Walter N. Peechatka Exec. VP., 7515 N.E. Ankeny Rd. Ankeny, IA 50021 (515) 289-2331

Water Systems Council, Pamela Frazen, Exec. Dir., 221 N. LaSalle St., Chicago, IL 60601 (312) 346-1600

Machinery

Auger and Elevator Manufacturers Council, a Council of the FIEI, James H. Ebbinghaus, Sec., 410 N. Michigan Ave. Chicago, IL 60611 (312) 321-1470

Construction Industry Manufacturers Assoc., Fred J. Braod, Exec. VP, Marine Plaza-1700, 111 E. Wisconsin Ave., Milwaukee, WI 53202 (414) 272-0943

Farm and Industrial Equipment Institute, Emmett Barker, Pres., 410 N. Michigan Ave., Chicago, IL 60611 (312) 321-1470

Farm Equipment Manufacturers Association, Robert K. Schnell, Exec. VP 243 N. Lindberg Blvd., St. Louis, MO 63141 (314) 991-0702

Mid-West Retail Farm Equipment Assoc., LeRoy F. Barry, Exec. VP 4331 N. 65th St., Omaha, NE 68104

National Sprayer and Duster Association, a Council of the FIEI,Richard Howell, Sec., 410 N. Michigan Ave. Chicago, IL 60611 (312) 321-1470

Nebraska Board of Tractor Test Engineers, G. W. Steinbruegge, Chair. Agricultural Engineering Dept., University of Nebraska Lincoln, NE 68503

Outdoor Power Equipment Institute, Inc., Dennis C. Dix, Exec. Dir. Suite 700, 1901 L St., N.W. Washington, DC 20036 (202) 296-3484

Society of Automotive Engineers, Joseph Gilbert, Exec. VP 400 Commonwealth Dr., Warrendale, PA 15096 (412) 776-4841

Southern Farm Equipment Manufacturers, Betty Lynskey, Adm. Sec. 6510 Arlington Dr. Dunwoody, GA 30338 (404) 393-3330

Tillage Equipment Council, a Council of the FIEI, James H. Ebbinghaus, Sec., 410 N. Michigan Ave. Chicago, IL 60611 (312) 321-1470

ENGINEERING INPUTS

Instruments

Instrument Society of America, Glenn F. Harvey, Exec. Dir. P.O. Box 12277, 67 Alexander Dr. Research Triangle Pk., NC 27709 (919) 549-8411

Machine & Equipment Components

Air Movement and Control Assoc., Edward A. Cruse, Exec. VP, 30 W. University Dr. Arlington Heights, IL 60004 (312) 394-0150

American Chain Assoc., Raymond J. Lloyd, Exec. Sec. 152 Rollins Ave., Suite 208 Rockville, MO 20852 (301) 984-9080

American Concrete Pipe Association, Richard E. Barnes, Pres. 8320 Old Courthouse Rd., Vienna, VA 22180 (703) 821-1990

American Gear Manufacturers Assoc., William W. Ingraham, Exec. Dir., Suite 1000, 1901 N. Fort Myer Dr. Arlington, VA 22209 (703) 525-1600

Anti-Friction Bearing Manufacturers Association, Inc., James J. Whitsett, Pres., Crystal Gateway One, Suite 704 1235 Jefferson Davis Hwy, Arlington, VA 22202 (703) 979-1261

Engine Manufacturers Assoc., Thomas C. Young, Exec. Dir., 111 E. Wacker Dr., Chicago, IL 60601 (312) 644-6610

Fluid Power Society, Harry Holsten, Pres. 3333 N Mayfair Rd., Milwaukee, WI 53202 (414) 778-3377

Illuminating Engineering Society, Rogers B. Finch, Exec. VP 345 E. 47th St., New York, NY 10017 (212) 705-7926

National Academy of Sciences, Philip M. Smith, Exec. Officer Constitution Ave., N.W., Washington DC 20418 (202) 334-2000

National Clay Pipe Institute, E. Jack Newbould, Pres. 1015 15th St. NW Suite 1250 Washington, SC 20005 (202) 789-1630

National Fluid Power Assoc., James L. Morgan, Pres. 3333 N. Mayfair Rd., Milwaukee, WI 53222 (414) 778-3344

Tire and Rim Assoc., J.F. Pacuit, Exec. VP 3200 W. Market St., Akron, OH 44313 (216) 836-5553

Manufacturing Methods

American Welding Society, Paul W. Ramsey, Exec. Dir. P.O. Box 351040, 550 Le Jeune Rd., NW Miami, FL 33135 (305) 443-9353

International Association of Milk, Food and Environmental, Sanitatians, Kathy Hathaway, Exec. Sec. P.O. Box 701, Ames, IA 50010 (515) 232-6699

Association of Rotational Molders, Pamela Frazen, Exec. Dir. 221 N. LaSalle St., Chicago, IL 60601 (312) 346-1600

Steel Joist Institute, E.T.E. Sprague, Mng. Dir. 1205 48th Ave N, Suite A, Myrtle Beach, SC 29755 (803) 449-0487

Wire Reinforcement Institute, William V. Wagner, Jr., Pres. 8361A Greensboro Dr. McLean, VA 22102 (703) 790-9790

Materials

Aluminum Association, The, John C. Bard, Pres. 818 Connecticut Ave., N.W., Washington DC 20006 (202) 862-5100

American Concrete Institute, George F. Leyh, Exec. Dir. P.O. Box 19150, Redford Station, Detroit, MI 48219 (313) 532-2600

American Institute of Steel Construction, Neil W. Zundel, Pres. 400 N. Michigan Ave, 8th Floor, Chicago, IL 60611 (312) 670-2400

American Institute of Timber Construction, Russel P. Wibbens, Exec. VP. 333 W. Hampden Ave., Englewood, CO 80110 (303) 761-3212

American Iron and Steel Institute, Robert B. Peabody, Pres. 1000 16th St., N.W., Washington DC 20036 (202) 452-7100

American Plywood Association, William T. Robison, Pres. 1191 A St., Box 11700, Tacoma, WA 98401 (206) 565-6600

Forest Products Research Society, Arthur B. Brauner, Exec. VP 2801 Marshall Court, Madison, WI 53705 (608) 231-1361

National Forest Products Assoc., David Stahl, Pres., 1619 Massachusetts Ave., N.W., Washington, DC 20036 (202) 797-5800

National Precast Concrete Association, Robert W. Walton, Exec. VP. 825 E. 64th St., Indianapolis, IN 46220 (317) 253-0486

Portland Cement Association, Richard Reuss, Pres. 5420 Old Orchard Rd., Skokie, IL 60077

Rubber Manufacturers Association, The, Donald G. Brotzman, Pres. 1400 K St., NW, Washington, DC 20005 (202) 682-4800

ENGINEERING ISSUES

Education

Accreditation Board for Engineering and Technology, David R. Reyes-Guerra, Exec. Dir. 345 E. 47th St. (212) 705-7685

American Association for Vocational Instructional Materials, W. H. Parady, Exec. Dir. Agricultural Engineering Center University of Georgia, Athens, GA 30602 (404) 542-2586

American Society for Engineering Education, W. Edward Lear. Exec. Dir. Suite 200, 11 Dupont Circle, N.W., Washington DC 20036 (202) 293-7080

National Institute for Certification in Eng. Tech., John D. Antrion, Gen. Mgr. 1420 King St., Alexandria, VA 22314 (703) 684-2835

National Council of Engineering Examiners, Roger B. Strieklin, Jr., Exec. Dir. P.O.Box 1686, Clemson, SC 29633 (803) 654-6824

Energy

American Petroleum Institute, Charles J. DiBona, Pres. 2101 L St., N.W., Washington, DC 20037 (202) 682-8000

Edison Electric Institute, William McCollam, Jr., Pres. 1111 19th St., N.W., Washington DC 20036 (202) 828-7400

Electric Power Research Institute, Marina Mann, Dir. Inf. Services, Box 10412, Palo Alto, CA 94303 (415) 855-2000

Electrical Generating Systems Marketing Association, Tony Ravcci Exec. Dir. P.O. Box 9257, Coral Springs, FL 33065 (305) 755-2677

Food and Energy Council, Kenneth L. McFate, Exec. Mgr., 409 Vandiver West, Suite 202, Columbia, MO 65202

Gas Research Institute, 8600 West Bryn Mawr Ave., Chicago, IL (312) 399-8100

National LP-Gas Association, J.D. Capps, Exec. VP, 1301 W. 22nd St., Oak Brook, IL 60521 (312) 986-4800

National Rural Electric Cooperative Association, Robert Bergland Exec. VP, 1800 Massachusetts Ave., N.W., Washington DC 20036 (202) 857-9500

Environment

Air Pollution Control Assoc., G. Steve Hart, Exec. VP P.O. Box 2861, Pittsburg, PA 15230 (412) 621-1090 National Water

Well Assoc., Inc., Dr. Jay H. Lehr, Exec. VP 500 W. Wilson Bridge Rd., Worthington, OH 43085 (614) 846-9355

Water Quality Association, Douglas R. Oberhamer, Exec. Dir. 4151 Naperville Rd., Lisle, IL 60532 (312) 369-1600

Safety and Liability

American Insurance Assoc., T. Lawrence Jones, Pres. 85 John St., New York, NY 10038 (212) 669-0400

American Society of Safety Engineers, Judy T. Neel, Exec. Dir. 850 Busse Highway, Park Ridge, IL 60068 (312) 692-4121

Human Factors Society, The Marian G. Knowles, Exec. Adm. P.O. Box 1369, Santa Monica, CA 90406 (213) 394-1811

National Fire Protection Association, Robert W. Grant, Pres. Batterymarch Park, Quincy, MA 02210 (617) 770-3000

National Institute for Farm Safety, David Baker, Sec-Tres. 2601 Rose Ct. Columbia, MO 65202 (413) 882-2731

National Safety Council, T. C. Gilehrest, Pres. 444 N. Michigan Ave., Chicago, IL 60611 (312) 527-4800

Umbrella Standards Groups

American National Standards Institute, Donald L. Peyton, Pres. 655 15th N.W. Suite 300, Washington, DC 20005 (202) 639-4090

American Society for Testing and Materials, William T. Cavanaugh,Pres. 1916 Race St., Philadelphia, PA 19103 (215) 299-5400

Umbrella Technical Groups

Accreditation Board for Engineering and Technology, David R. Reyes-Guerra, Exec. Dir., 345 E. 47th St. New York, NY 10017 (212) 705-7685

American Association for the Advancement of Science, William D. Carey, Exec. Off., 1333 H.SE., N.W., Washington, DC 20005

American Association of Engineering Societies, Daniel DeSimone, Exec. Dir., 345 E. 47th St., New York, NY 10017 (212) 705-7840

National Academy of Sciences, Philip Smith, Pres. 2101 Constitution Ave., N.W., Washington, DC 20418 (202) 334-2000

National Society of Professional Engineers, Donald G. Weinert, Exec. Dir. 1420 King St., Alexandria, VA 22314 (703) 684-2800

Scientific Manpower Commission, Ms. Betty M. Vetter, Exec. Dir. 1776 Massachusetts Ave., N.W., Washington, DC 20036 (202)223-6995

ENGINEERING PROFESSIONAL SOCIETIES
(Discipline-Oriented)

American Institute of Chemical Engineers, J. Charles Forman Exec. Dir., 345 E. 47th St., New York, NY 10017 (212) 705-7338

American Society of Agricultural Engineers, J.L. Butt, Exec. VP, 2950 Niles Rd., St. Joseph, MI 49085 (616) 429-0300.

American Society of Civil Engineers, Edward P. Frang, Exec. Dir., 345 E. 47th St., New York, NY 10017 (212) 705-7496

American Society of Mechanical Engineers, The, Paul Allmendirge United Engineering Center, 345 E. 47th St., New York, NY 10017 (212) 705-7722

Institute of Electrical and Electronics Engineers, Inc., Eric Herz, Exec. Dir., 345 E. 47th St., New York, NY 10017 (212) 705-7950

FOREIGN-BASED ORGANIZATIONS

CEMA, European Committee of Association of Manufacturers of Agricultural Machinery, 19 rue Jacques Binger, Paris 17E, France

CIGR, International Commission of Agricultural Engineering, M.A. Carlier, Sec. Gen., 17 rue de Javel, 75015 Paris, France

COPANT, Pan American Standards Commission, Beatriz Ghirelli de Ciaburri, Sec. Gen., Avda, Pte, Roque Saenz Pena 501, Piso 7 - Office 716, Buenos Aries, Argentina

Canadian Society of Agricultural Engineering, Bob Jung, Sec., Suite 907, 151 Slater St., Ottawa, Ontario, Canada K1P 5H4

European Committee of Association of Manufacturers of Agricultural Machinery, CEMA, 19 rue Jacques Bingen, Paris 17, France

IAMFE, International Association of Mechanization of Field Experiments, Egil Yjord, Pres., LT1, 1432 Aas-NLH, Norway

International Commission of Agricultural Engineering, CIGR, M.A. Carlier, Sec.Gen., 17 rue de Javel, 75015 Paris, France

International Organization for Standardization, 150 J.G. Allardyc, Dir. Tech. Coor., 1 rue de Varembe, 1211 Geneva 20, Switzerland

OECD, Organization for Economic Cooperation and Development, Chateau de la Muette, 2 rue Andre Pascal, Paris 16E, France

National Research Council of Canada, William G. Schneider, Pres., Montreal Rd., Ottawa, Ontario, Canada K1A 0R6

GOVERNMENT AGENCIES

Department of Agriculture, Clarence Becker, Agricultural Engineering Program Manager for USDA-Cooperative States Research, 15th and Independence Ave. SW, Washington, DC 20251 (202) 447-5680

Department of Energy, John S. Herrington, Off. of Sec., Rm. 7a-257, 1000 Independence Ave., SW, Washington, DC 20585 (202) 252-6210

Environmental Protection Agency, Harvy Pipper, Dir. Grants Admin., SW 257, 401 M Street SW, Washington, DC 20460

National Bureau of Standards, Tech. Inf. Off., Room E128. Bldg. 101, Gaothersburg, MD 20899 (301) 921-2318

National Science Foundation, Carl Hall, Asst. Dir. Directorate for Engineering, Washington, DC 20550 (202) 357-7717

APPENDIX III
Engineering Forms and Formats

1. Product development forms.
   (a) Project definition, 282
   (b) Marketing analysis, 283
   (c) Engineering analysis, 284
   (d) Production analysis, 285
   (e) Financial analysis, 286
2. Project scheduling forms.
   (a) Task definition, 287
   (b) Task schedule, 288
   (c) Budget sheet, 289
3. Patent disclosure form, 290-293
4. Drawing plate example formats.
   (a) With revision record, back of book
   (b) With revision record and bill of materials list, back of book

PROJECT DEFINITION

Project title _____
_____
_____
_____

Person(s) originating request: _____
_____
_____

Date needed for completion: _____

General project description (i.e. define objectives and criteria in a general sense and ideas for product in a general sense):

_____
_____
_____
_____
_____
_____
_____
_____
_____
_____

Rationale for development request (i.e. history, present status, anticipated need, current and anticipated competitive situation and other pertinent information):

_____
_____
_____
_____
_____
_____
_____
_____
_____
_____
_____
_____
_____
_____
_____
_____
_____
_____

Signature: _____   Date: _____
    Project Engineer

MARKETING ANALYSIS

Project Title: _____

Importance of project: _____

Priority relative to other projects: _____

Estimated total market for next five years:

     Units/Year _____ _____ _____ _____ _____
     $ Sales/Year _____ _____ _____ _____ _____

Ranking of factors important for market acceptance:

____ Cost ____ Quality/Reliability ____ Features ____ Service ____ Promotion

Notes on competition: _____

Effects on current products sales: _____

Target list price: _____ Range: _____ to _____

Estimated product life (to next basic redesign): _____

Anticipated model variations: _____

Optional accessories: _____

Promotional requirements: _____

Remarks: _____

Signature: _____ Date: _____
     Vice President of Marketing

ENGINEERING ANALYSIS

Project Title: _____

_____

Time requirements:
    Design calendar months: _____   Design person-months: _____
    Test calendar months: _____   Test person-months: _____

Outside consultant needs: _____

_____

_____

Lab test needs: _____

_____

_____

Field test needs: _____

_____

_____

Approval body requirements (eg. Underwriters Laboratory, Gas Appliance
Laboratory): _____

_____

_____

Estimated costs*:   Design personnel _____ $ _____
                     Test personnel _____ $ _____
                     Consultants _____ $ _____
                     Design travel, supplies
                     and equipment _____ $ _____
                     Approval body costs _____ $ _____
                     Total: _____ $ _____

Cost/unit product: _____

Remarks: _____

_____

_____

_____

_____

_____

_____

_____

*All costs would include overhead costs appropriate to company

Signature: _____   Date: _____
          Vice President of Engineering

PRODUCTION ANALYSIS

Project Title: _____

_____

Additional machinery and tooling required: _____

_____
_____
_____
_____
_____
_____

Building modifications: _____

_____
_____
_____
_____
_____
_____

Production engineering: hours: _____, $_____
Tooling: lead time: _____, $_____
Building modification: lead time: _____, $_____
Machinery & equipment purchased: lead time: _____, $_____

Total: lead time: _____, $_____

Remarks: _____

_____
_____
_____
_____
_____
_____
_____
_____
_____
_____
_____
_____
_____
_____

Signature: _____ Date: _____
          Vice President of Manufacturing

FINANCIAL ANALYSIS

Project Title: _____

Initial Costs: Marketing: $_____
                Engineering: $_____
                Production: $_____
                Interest: $_____
                Other: $_____
     Total investment: $_____

Estimated annual cost of initial investment: _____

_____
_____
_____
_____

Profit Analysis:

Annual volume _____

    Unit sale price to
       distributors . . . . $_____   Ann. income . . . . $_____
    Unit manufactured costs . . . . $_____   Ann. manu. cost . . . . $_____
    Unit selling costs . . . . $_____   Ann. sales cost . . . . $_____
    Unit investment costs . . . . . . $_____   Ann. investment cost . . . . $_____

    Unit before tax profit . . . . $_____   Ann. before tax profit . . . . $_____

Projected rate of return on investment: _____

Cash Flow:

	Year 1	Year 2	Year 3	Year 4	Year 5	Year 6	Year 7
Income							
Expenses							
Annual return							
Cumulative return							
Cumulative rate of return of investment							

Signature: _____   Date: _____
        Vice President of Finance

TASK DEFINITIONS

oject Title: _____

_____

ask Schedule Activity: _____

ıb tasks:

Task	Deadline	Person Responsible

Signature: _____ Date: _____

ask Schedule Activity: _____

ıb tasks:

Task	Deadline	Person Responsible

Signature: _____ Date: _____

ask Schedule Activity: _____

ub tasks:

Task	Deadline	Person Responsible

Signature: _____ Date: _____

288

TASK SCHEDULE

Project Title: _____

Task Number	Week Number																				Critical Deadlines	Hours Required
	1	2	3	4	5	6	7	8	9	10	11	12	13	14	15	16	17	18	19	20		
1																						
3																						
4																						
6																						
7																						
8																						
9																						
10																						
11																						
12																						
13																						
14																						
15																						
16																						
17																						
18																						
19																						
20																						

Signature: _____ Date: _____

Project Engineer

BUDGET SHEET

Project Title: _____

_____

Task No.	Personnel	Supplies		Phone	Travel	Equipment	Total
		Office	Mechanical				

Remarks: _____

_____

_____

_____

Signature: _____   Date: _____

Project Engineer

PATENT DISCLOSURES FORM

I. Descriptive

1. Title of invention _____

2. Brief description. Is the invention a new process, composition o
matter, a device or one or more products? A new use for, or a
improvement to, an existing product or process? Explain fully.

_____

_____

_____

_____

_____

_____

_____

_____

Use additional sheets to elaborate, or attach descriptive materials.

3. From the description, pick out and expand on novel and unusua
features. How does the invention differ from present technology? Wha
problems does it solve, or what advantages does it possess?

_____

_____

_____

_____

_____

_____

_____

_____

4. If not indicated previously, what are possible uses for the invention? In addition to immediate applications, are there other uses that might be realized in the future?

5. Does the invention possess disadvantages or limitations? Can they be overcome? How?

6. Enclose sketches, drawings, photographs and other materials that help illustrate the description. (Rough artwork, flow sheets, Polaroid photographs and penciled graphs are satisfactory as long as they tell a clear and understandable story.)

II. Other Pertinent Data

1. Are there publications—theses, reports, preprints, reprints, etc.—pertaining to the invention? Please list with publication dates, and attach copies insofar as possible. Include manuscripts for publication (submitted or not), news releases, feature articles and items from internal publications.

a. _____

b. _____

c. _____

d. _____

2. Are laboratory records and data available? Give reference numbers and physical location, but do not enclose.

_____

_____

_____

3. Are related patents or other publications known to the inventor? Please list.

_____

_____

_____

_____

4. Date, place, and circumstances of first public disclosure.

_____

_____

_____

_____

5. Was the work that led to the invention sponsored? If yes, attach copy of contract or agreement if possible, and fill in the appropriate blanks below.

    a. Title of Government agency _____

       Contract No. _____

    b. Name of industrial company _____

    c. Name of university sponsor _____

    d. Other sponsor(s) _____

6. Any commercial interest shown at this stage? Name companies and specific persons if possible.

_____

_____

_____

   a. Do you know of other qualified firms? Please list. _____

_____

7. Name(s) and title(s) of inventor(s)

   a. _____

   b. _____

   c. _____

   (Contact for more data _____ Telephone _____)
                                  (name)

8. Mailing address for inventor(s) _____
                                    (department and institution)

_____
   (street and number)   (city and state)   (zip code)

9. Signature(s) of inventor(s) and date

   a. _____(date) _____

   b. _____(date) _____

   c. _____(date) _____

0. Institutional representative _____
                                (please type name and title)

_____(date) _____
        (signature)

_____ Telephone _____
   (department and institution)

_____
   (street and number)   (city and state)   (zip code)

APPENDIX IV
Annotated Bibliography

ASAE. 1985. **Standards, 32nd ed**. American Society of Agricultural Engineers, St. Joseph, MI.

ASAE's standards making procedure is defined, members of standards-developing technical committees are named and standards currently being revised or developed are noted. Materials are classified as "standards," "tentative standards," "engineering practices" or "data" depending on the content. There are six major subject areas: (a) general agricultural engineering, (b) properties of materials, (c) agricultural equipment, (d) powered lawn and garden equipment, (e) structures, livestock and environment and (f) soil and water.

ASHRAE. 1985. **Fundamentals Handbook**. American Society of Heating, Refrigerating and Air-Conditioning Engineers, Atlanta, GA.

The ASHRAE publishes a five-volume series of handbooks related to heating, ventilating, refrigerating and air conditioning. Thermal/air quality environmental needs for people, plants, animals, numerous types of equipment and processes are defined.

Barker vs Lull. 1978. **Product Liability Reports**, Commerce Clearing House Inc., 4025 W. Peterson Ave., Chicago, Illinois 60646, No. 382, Feb. 16.

This landmark case clarified the definition of strict liability law as it relates to a design defect. The injured party does not need to prove that product is "unreasonably dangerous," rather: (a) that it failed to perform as safely as an ordinary consumer would expect in reasonably foreseeable use or (b) that the design caused injury and the manufacturer cannot prove that the benefits outweigh the risks of such design.

Beers, Y. 1957. **Introduction to the Theory of Error**. Addison-Wesley Publishing Co., Reading, MA 65 pp.

This brief book describes the theory and method of propagation of error analysis. The reader can learn how to calculate the error in calculated variables based upon the values measured, the defining equation(s) and the measurement accuracy for each variable.

Bennett, E., J. Degan, and J. Spiegel. (ed.) 1963. **Human Factors in Technology**. McGraw-Hill, New York, N.Y. 685 pp.

This is a compilation of information prepared for the Human Factors Society, by 53 human factors experts. Most of the data included are applicable today. Emphasis is on the application of human factors to specific classes of equipment (e.g., automobile design and radiation environments) or to unusual situations (e.g., sensory supplementation for handicapped and response to vibration).

Bonoma, T.V. and Dennis P. Slevin. 1978. **Executive Survival Manual**. CBI Publishing Boston. 234 pp.

This book presents an interesting and refreshing look at managing not only your job but also your life. Ways to identify stress and means for developing action plans to reduce and manage stress are described in an easy-to-read book.

Boyd, T.A. 1957. **The Professional Amateur, The Biography of Charles F. Kettering,** Dutton, New York. 242 pp.
    Kettering was one of the greatest and most famous engineers of the 20th century. The author describes Kettering's engineering philosophy and capsulizes his accomplishments in an entertaining fashion.

Buhl, H.R. 1960. **Creative Engineering Design**. Iowa State University Press, Ames, IA. 195 pp.
    Buhl, a mechanical engineer, views design in an entertaining fashion. He stresses techniques and philosophies for being more creative, illustrating them with cartoons. Creativity is applied to define the problem, conceive a solution and sell the result.

Burgess, John A. 1984. **Design Assurance for Engineers and Managers.** Marcel Dekker, Inc., New York. 303pp.
    This book provides the necessary background to establish an effective system of managing design teams to produce designs that result in meeting product quality requirements. It proposes a total quality control of design to prevent the production of defective products. A chapter on design of engineering computer software is included.

Crosby, P. 1972. **The Art of Getting Your Own Sweet Way**. McGraw-Hill, New York. 182 pp.
    Phil Crosby is a successful business manager and quality control expert. This book explains the importance of defining clearly the problem and describes the difficulties that occur when seemingly simple problems are not clearly defined. "Have an ironclad contract that spells out the objectives specifically and the terms by which success and failure will be measured," advises Crosby.

Deal, T. and A.A. Kennedy. 1982. **Corporate Cultures: The Rites and Rituals of Corporate Life**. Addison Wesley, Reading, MA. 232pp.
    Healthy organizations typically have a strong corporate value system which is clearly understood by all employees. That corporate culture may be *tough guy, macho, 'work hard-play hard, bet your company* or *process*. A new employee should look for an organization's values and decide whether they are compatible with personal values.

Dieter, G. 1983. **Engineering Design — A Materials and Processing Approach.** McGraw-Hill, Inc., New York. 592 pp.
    Dieter emphasizes the subjects of: (a) material selection, (b) modeling, optimization and statistical techniques and (c) product liability and associated methods for evaluating reliability and maintaining quality. These emphasized topics are integrated into a detailed explanation of design, particularly as appropriate to machine design engineers.

Faupel, Joseph H. and Franklin E. Fisher. 1981. **Engineering Design — A Synthesis of Stress Analysis and Materials Engineering, 2nd Ed**. John Wiley and Sons, New York. 1056 pp.
    Detailed mathematical analysis procedures for metal and plastic materials in design are described. The authors deal with the practical aspects of calculating stress and behavior of fabricated parts, considering the effects of stamping, shearing and drilling on materials.

French, T.E., C.J. Vierck and Robert J. Foster. 1986. **Engineering Drawing and Graphic Technology, 13th Ed**. McGraw-Hill, New York, 737 pp.
Sufficient detail and drafting methods and standards are presented to serve as a practical alternative to the American National Standards Institute's various standards on drafting. The authors include numerous illustrations of industry drafting. Drafting methods for welds, tolerances, fasteners, gears, pipes, electrical and electronics, structures and maps are discussed in considerable detail.

Girard, J. and S. Brown. 1977. **How to Sell Anything to Anybody**. Warner Books, New York, N.Y., 238 p.
Automobile salesman Joe Girard explains how he earned the worlds record in car sales. Emphasize *win-win* for the buyer and seller or any success will be short-lived; develop a system for finding prospects and recording their needs; encourage prospects to talk and sell to their needs and wants. Most importantly, remember that selling continues after the sale through support and service — a good salesman would **never** "sell a refrigerator to an eskimo."

Hammer, W. 1972. **Handbook of Product Safety**. Prentice Hall, Englewood Cliffs, N.J. 351 pp.
Hammer, a manufacturing engineer, discusses liability laws, safety programs and risk assessment in manufacturing settings. The book is an excellent safety reference for employee safety. It does not discuss product liability where people use an engineer's product outside the manufacturing plant.

Hill, P. 1970. **The Science of Engineering Design**, Holt, Rinehart and Winston, New York. 372 pp.
Hill discusses the design stages in depth (Chapter 3) and PERT/CPM methods with excellent examples (Chapter 7). An extensive annotated bibliography of design texts is included in this book. Forty eight design problems and case histories are included, some with considerable detail.

Hillier, Fredrick S. and Gerald J. Lieberman. 1974. **Operations Research**, Holden-Day, San Francisco, 800 pp.
A well-accepted textbook in operations research. This book will serve as a good reference for linear programming using the simplex method, network analysis using PERT/CPM, probablistic models, queueing theory, reliability and decision analysis. Advanced material is also included on mathematical programming techniques.

IES. 1981, 1984. **Lighting Handbooks — Applications (1981) and References (1984)**. Illuminating Engineering Society, New York, 505 and 482 pp., (respectively).
The IES prepares handbooks on lighting methods, lighting practices, and the response of people, plants, and animals to light. The spectral distribution and intensity associated with commercially available types of lighting are explained.

Jensen, C. and J.D. Helsel. 1985. **Engineering Drawing and Design, 3rd ed**. McGraw-Hill, New York, 788 pp.
The authors detail and provide examples of engineering drawing and specifications practices. Special emphasis is on machinery manufacturing methods, with a major part on fastening and forming and a second on mechanical and fluid power transfer. Tolerancing and material analysis are discussed in advanced topics.

Joenk, R.J., Editor. 1982. **Patents and Patenting for Engineers and Scientists**. IEEE, New York.
An excellent collection of papers by patent lawyers, patent examiners and engineers on a wide variety of issues related to patents and the patenting process.

Jones, J.C. 1980. **Design Methods — Seeds of Human Futures, 2nd ed**. Wiley & Sons, New York. 407 pp.
  An English engineer, artist and playwrite composed this book advocating design on a global scale (i.e., not restricted to an engineering approach). Jones recommends experimentation, open-mindedness and intuition as design tools. According to Jones, scientists describe and explain phenomena that exist, designing experiments to check hypotheses. Artists work solely in the present, acting on imagination. Designers work in the future, trying to anticipate problems and devise solutions.

Krutz, Gary, Lester Thompson and Paul Claar. 1984. **Design of Agricultural Machinery**. John Wiley & Sons, New York. 472 pp.
  Designed as a college senior text as well as a reference for practicing design engineers, this book contains well-developed material on combined stress analysis, fatigue analysis, finite element analysis, statistical tolerance design, mechanical power transmission, gear analysis and hydraulic design.

Leech, D.J. 1972. **Management of Engineering** . Wiley and Sons, London. 258 pp.
  A British industrialist explains the role of engineers and the importance of economical solutions clearly and concisely. Management refers to self-management and team work as well as to supervising others. Leech stresses the importance of defining the problem, breaking it into manageable steps and then carefully and systematically working toward a solution. The customer often does not know what he really wants; so, the engineer must work carefully with the customer to identify the real problem.

Love, Sydney F. 1980. **Planning and Creating Successful Engineered Designs**. Van Nostrand Reinhold Company, New York. 260 pp.
  The four concerns of engineering design teams are effectively developed: schedule, cost, results and organization. Love includes ways to calculate present worth of any design feature. He explains how to define project objectives and determine design requirements. A chapter on CPM/PERT is also included.

Meredith, Dale D., K.W. Wong, R.W. Woodhead, and R.H. Wortman. 1985. **Design and Planning of Engineering Systems, 2nd ed**. Prentice Hall, Englewood Cliffs, N.J. 367 pp.
  This book is a civil engineering text which emphasizes design related to large-scale public and private works (e.g., water treatment plants, transportation syatems, waste treatment plants and commercial buildings). Planning, defining, systems modeling, optimizating and decision making methods are explained.

Mitchell, Bailey (ed). 1983. **Instrumentation and Measurement for Environmental Sciences, 2nd ed**. American Society of Agricultural Engineers, St. Joseph, MI. 200 pp.
  Several ASAE committee members cooperated to prepare this instrumentation handbook which describes sensors, data acquisition and analysis for agricultural applications. This is particularly relevant to agricultural engineers because it discusses the measurement methods and procedures commonly used for bio-environmental applications.

Naisbett, J. 1982. **Megatrends: Ten New Directions Transforming Our Lives**. Warner Books, New York, N.Y. 290 pp.
  Best-selling author and futurologist John Naisbett defines 10 major trends which he believes are the most important factors now shaping the world. These range from the advent of high technology to growth in human interaction (high tech — high touch) and from population shifts to growth of multi-lingualism in nations. Naisbett suggests that we will be most successful if we try to work with these trends rather than try to fight them.

Nilsson, W.D. and P.E. Hicks. 1981. **Orientation to Professional Practice**. McGraw Hill, New York, N.Y. 372 pp.

These consulting engineers spent a major portion of their technical careers in the computer industry and universities, respectively. Their book emphasizes four major topics: (a) career planning and job seeking, (b) effectiveness in the business work environment through understanding of corporate structures and competency in formal and informal presentations, (c) professional ethics and product safety and (d) professional development through self-evaluation and participation in technical societies and course-work.

Ostrofsky, Benjamin. 1977. **Designing, Planning and Development Methodology**. Prentice-Hall, Inc., Englewood Cliffs, New Jersey. 401 pp.

In a series of flow charts throughout his book, Ostrofsky presents the design process and then discusses the major diagram blocks in subsequent chapters. Several chapters are devoted to development of candidate systems (solutions) based upon design criteria and the subsequent formal optimization within and among candidate systems.

Peters, T.J. and R.H. Waterman, Jr. 1982. **In Search of Excellence**. Harper & Row, New York. 360 pp.

Written by Stanford Business School professors as an analysis of successful business management practices, this book also provided insight on how to manage companies for the future. Companies are successful because they adapt to the future.

Pitts, G. 1973. **Techniques in Engineering Design**. Halsted Press — a Division of John Wiley and Sons, Inc., New York. 154 pp.

The basic design philosophy is outlined. Optimization of design decisions, including linear programming methods, are employed.

Pollack, H.W. 1968. **Manufacturing and Machine Tool Operations**. Prentice Hall, Englewood Cliffs, N.J. 593pp.

Pollack describes and graphically illustrates metal-working manufacturing machinery and processes. The reader need not have manufacturing or machine tool experience to understand this material, which makes the book an excellent reference for the design engineer.

Richey, C.B., Paul Jacobson and Carl W. Hall. 1961. **Agricultural Engineers Handbook**. McGraw-Hill, New York. 880 pp.

This book contains a wealth of basic information about agricultural engineering design topics written in a concise, clear and analytic approach. Students with little or no experience in production agriculture would find this book useful.

Roebuck, J.A., Jr., K.H.E. Kroemer, and W.G. Thomson. 1975. **Engineering Anthropometry Methods**. Wiley & Sons, New York, N.Y. 459 pp.

This one book, in a nine volume series on human factors, describes the methods used to measure human anthropometric data and presents a limited amount of actual data. Data collection methods for special applications related to vehicle, space-craft and special clothing are discussed.

Schey, John A. 1977. **Introduction to Manufacturing Processes**. McGraw-Hill, New York. 392 pp.

This manufacturing process textbook focuses on design as affected by manufacturing and differs from conventional manufacturing processes texts in that it is not a "how to" manual of manufacturing techniques. Materials science principles are explained in practical terms.

Schwartz, D.J. 1965. **The Magic of Thinking Big**. Simon and Schuster, New York, N.Y., 192 pp.
   Success, whether in business or personal relationships, is influenced primarily by attitudes — attitudes of self confidence, willingness to dream and sincere interest in other people. Action and goal-setting, not excuses and meandering, are particularly emphasized.

Shoup, Terry E., Leroy S. Fletcher and Edward V. Mochel. 1981. **Introduction to Engineering Design with Graphics and Design Projects**. Prentice-Hall, Englewood Cliffs, N.J. 391 pp.
   This book was prepared as a first year textbook and is available in paperback. The latter chapters contain an excellent presentation of the practical elements of engineering graphics along with a number of useful appendixes on screw-threads and fasteners, standard symbols, anthropometric data and economic data.

Skoglund, V.J. 1967. **Similitude Theory and Applications**. International Textbook, Scranton, PA, 320 pp.
   Similitude theory is a means of scientifically reducing the number of tests needed to develop equations defining the inter-relationships among variables. Similitude is also the theory used to scale models for experimental purposes, whether these be similar or distorted. This powerful tool is frequently used for fluids, heat transfer, electrical and particle movement applications.

Strunk, W. Jr. and E.B. White. 1979. **The Elements of Style, 3rd ed**. Macmillan Co., New York. 85 pp.
   This classic writing reference is a superb example of clarity in writing. The authors review: elementary grammatical rules for writing, common grammatical errors, principles of composition and word choice for effective communication.

Tichauer, E.R. 1978. **The Biomechanical Basis of Ergonomics**. John Wiley and Sons, New York. 99 pp.
   Tichauer describes peoples' capabilities in work environments based upon energetic, dynamic and physiological principles. The objective is to aid the equipment designer in determining what is physically possible and reasonable for workers.

Toastmasters International. 1984. **Communication and Leadership Program**. Toastmasters International, Box 10400, Santa Ana, CA 92711, 71 pp.
   Toastmasters International is a world-recognized organization which helps members develop speaking abilities (prepared and extemporaneous), improve interpersonal relationships, build management skills and learn how to be a more effective meeting participant. The Communication and Leadership Manual encourages the user to practice gestures, vocal variety, word usage, persuasiveness and inspiration through progressive speeches. Advanced manuals oriented to managers, sales people, professional speakers, debaters and others encourage further development of communication talent.

Todd, Alden, 1972. **Finding Facts Fast.** William Morrow and Company, New York. 109 pp.
   Todd writes a handbook on how to find material about a subject. His approach is general, like that of a detective or investigative reporter, but the detail and methodology apply to engineering well.

Townsend, R. 1970. **Up the Organization**. A.A. Knopf, New York. 202 pp.
Townsend is an iconoclastic manager who brought Avis Rent-A-Car from near bankruptcy to a strong number 2 position with his unorthodox management style. This book is easy and entertaining reading. He encourages one to focus on and define the real problem, and his succinct style provides an excellent example.

Von Oech, Roger. 1983. **A Whack on the Side of the Head: How to Unlock Your Mind for Innovation**. Warner Books, New York, N.Y. 141 pp.
Creativity is developed through self-management and practice. Von Oech's entertaining writing style and cartoons make this easy reading, yet it is filled with ideas and examples on how to think creatively.

Woodson, Wesley E. 1981. **Human Factors Design Handbook: Information and Guidelines for the Design of Systems, Facilities, Equipment, and Products for Human Use**. McGraw-Hill, New York. 1047 pp.
This handbook provides a general reference to key human factors questions and human-product interface design suggestions in a form that engineers can utilize with minimal searching or study.

Yankee, H.W. 1979. **Manufacturing Processes**. Prentice-Hall, Englewood Cliffs, N.J. 765 pp.
Metal cutting, shaping, casting, forming, treatments and coatings are emphasized in this clear description of basic metal manufacturing processes. Numerous pictures and illustrations aid the reader who is not expected to be familiar with manufacturing methods. One chapter is devoted to plastics manufacturing.

APPENDIX V—English/Metric Conversion

PREFERRED UNITS FOR EXPRESSING PHYSICAL QUANTITIES *

1. Quantities are arranged in alphabetical order by principal nouns. For example, surface tension is listed as tension, surface.
2. All possible applications are not listed, but others such as rates can be readily derived. For example, from the preferred units for energy and volume the units for heat energy per unit volume, kJ/m³, may be derived.
3. Conversion factors are shown to seven significant digits, unless the precision with which the factor is known does not warrant seven significant digits.

Quantity	Application	From: Old Units	To: SI Units	Multiply By:
Acceleration, angular	General	rad/s²	rad/s²	
Acceleration, linear	Vehicle	(mile/h)/s	(km/h)/s	1.609 344*
	General (includes acceleration of gravity)#	ft/s²	m/s²	0.304 8*
Angle, plane	Rotational calculations	r (revolution)	r (revolution)	
		rad	rad	
	Geometric and general	° (deg)	°	
		' (min)	° (decimalized)	1/60*
		' (min)	'	
		" (sec)	° (decimalized)	1/3600*
		" (sec)	"	
Angle, solid	Illumination calculations	sr	sr	
Area	Cargo platforms, roof and floor area, frontal areas, fabrics, general	in.²	m²	0.000 645 16*
		ft²	m²	0.092 903 04*
	Pipe, conduit	in.²	mm²	645.16*
		in.²	cm²	6.451 6*
		ft²	m²	0.092 903 04*
	Small areas, orifices, cross section area of structural shapes	in.²	mm²	645.16*
	Brake & clutch contact area, glass, radiators, feed opening	in.²	cm²	6.451 6*
	Land, pond, lake, reservoir, open water channel (Small)	ft²	m²	0.092 903 04*
	(Large)	acre	ha	0.404 687 3(d)
	(Very Large)	mile²	km²	2.589 998
Area per time	Field operations	acre/h	ha/h	0.404 687 3
	Auger sweeps, silo unloader	ft²/s	m²/s	0.092 903 04*
Bending Moment	(See Moment of Force)			
Capacitance, electric	Capacitors	μF	μF	
Capacity, electric	Battery rating	A·h	A·h	
Capacity, heat	General	Btu/°F	kJ/K†	1.899 101
Capacity, heat, specific	General	Btu/(lb·°F)	kJ/(kg·K)†	4.186 8*
Capacity, volume	(See Volume)			
Coefficient of Heat Transfer	General	Btu/(h·ft²·°F)	W/(m²·K)†	5.678 263
Coefficient of Linear Expansion	Shrink fit, general	°F⁻¹, (1/°F)	K⁻¹, (1/K)†	1.8*
Conductance, electric	General	mho	S	1*
Conductance, thermal	(See Coefficient of Heat Transfer)			
Conductivity, electric	Material property	mho/ft	S/m	3.280 840
Conductivity, thermal	General	Btu·ft/(h·ft²·°F)	W/(m·K)†	1.730 735
Consumption, fuel	Off highway vehicles (See also Efficiency, fuel)	gal/h	L/h	3.785 412
Consumption, oil	Vehicle performance testing	qt/(1000 miles)	L/(1000 km)	0.588 036 4
Consumption, specific, oil	Engine testing	lb/(hp·h)	g/(kW·h)	608.277 4
		lb/(hp·h)	g/MJ	168.965 9
Current, electric	General	A	A	
Density, current	General	A/in.²	kA/m²	1.550 003
		A/ft²	A/m²	10.763 91
Density, magnetic flux	General	kilogauss	T	0.1*
Density, (mass)	Solid, general; agricultural products, soil, building materials	lb/yd³	kg/m³	0.593 276 3
		lb/in.³	kg/m³	27 679.90
		lb/ft³	kg/m³	16.018 46
	Liquid	lb/gal	kg/L	0.119 826 4
	Gas	lb/ft³	kg/m³	16.018 46
	Solution concentration	----	g/m³, mg/L	----
Density of heat flow rate	Irradiance, general	Btu/(h·ft²)	W/m²	3.154 591††
Consumption, fuel	(See Flow, volume)			
Consumption, specific fuel	(See Efficiency, fuel)			
Drag	(See Force)			
Economy, fuel	(See Efficiency, fuel)			

*Reprinted from ASAE Engineering Practice: ASAE EP285.6

PREFERRED UNITS FOR EXPRESSING PHYSICAL QUANTITIES (cont'd)

1. Quantities are arranged in alphabetical order by principal nouns. For example, surface tension is listed as tension, surface.
2. All possible applications are not listed, but others such as rates can be readily derived. For example, from the preferred units for energy and volume the units for heat energy per unit volume, kJ/m³, may be derived.
3. Conversion factors are shown to seven significant digits, unless the precision with which the factor is known does not warrant seven digits.

Quantity	Application	From: Old Units	To: SI Units	Multiply By:
Efficiency, fuel	Highway vehicles			
	economy	mile/gal	km/L	0.415 143 7
	consumption	—	L/(100 km)	§
	specific fuel consumption	lb/(hp·h)	g/MJ	168.965 9
	Off-highway vehicles			
	economy	hp·h/gal	kW·h/L	0.196 993 1
	specific fuel consumption	lb/(hp·h)	g/MJ	168.965 9
	specific fuel consumption	lb/(hp·h)	kg/(kW·h)§§	0.608 277 4
Energy, work, enthalpy, quantity of heat	Impact strength	ft·lbf	J	1.355 818
	Heat	Btu	kJ	1.055 056
		kcal	kJ	4.186 8*
	Energy usage, electrical	kW·h	kW·h	
		kW·h	MJ	3.6
	Mechanical, hydraulic, general	ft·lbf	J	1.355 818
		ft·pdl	J	0.042 140 11
		hp·h	MJ	2.684 520
		hp·h	kW·h	0.745 699 9
Energy per area	Solar radiation	Btu/ft²	MJ/m²	0.011 356 528
Energy, specific	General	cal/g‡	J/g	4.186 8*
		Btu/lb	kJ/kg	2.326*
Enthalpy	(See Energy)			
Entropy	(See Capacity, heat)			
Entropy, specific	(See Capacity, heat, specific)			
Floor loading	(See Mass per area)			
Flow, heat, rate	(See Power)			
Flow, mass, rate	Gas, liquid	lb/min	kg/min	0.453 592 4
		lb/s	kg/s	0.453 592 4
	Dust flow	g/min	g/min	
	Machine work capacity, harvesting, materials handling	ton (short)/h	t/h, Mg/h**	0.907 184 7
Flow, volume	Air, gas, general	ft³/s	m³/s	0.028 316 85
		ft³/s	m³/min	1.699 011
	Liquid flow, general	gal/s (gps)	L/s	3.785 412
		gal/s (gps)	m³/s	0.003 785 412
		gal/min (gpm)	L/min	3.785 412
	Seal and packing leakage, sprayer flow	oz/s	mL/s	29.573 53
		oz/min	mL/min	29.573 53
	Fuel consumption	gal/h	L/h	3.785 412
	Pump capacity, coolant flow, oil flow	gal/min (gpm)	L/min	3.785 412
	Irrigation sprinkler, small pipe flow	gal/min (gpm)	L/s	0.063 090 20
	River and channel flow	ft³/s	m³/s	0.028 316 85
Flux, luminous	Light bulbs	lm	lm	
Flux, magnetic	Coil rating	maxwell	Wb	0.000 000 01*
Force, thrust, drag	Pedal, spring, belt, hand lever, general	lbf	N	4.448 222
		ozf	N	0.278 013 9
		pdl	N	0.138 255 0
		kgf	N	9.806 650
		dyne	N	0.000 01*
	Drawbar, breakout, rim pull, winch line pull[*], general	lbf	kN	0.004 448 222
Force per length	Beam loading	lbf/ft	N/m	14.593 90
	Spring rate	lbf/in.	N/mm	0.175 126 8
Frequency	System, sound and electrical	Mc/s	MHz	1*
		kc/s	kHz	1*
		Hz, c/s	Hz	1*
	Mechanical events, rotational	r/s (rps)	s⁻¹, r/s	1*
		r/min (rpm)	min⁻¹, r/min	1*
	Engine, power-take-off shaft, gear speed	r/min (rpm)	min⁻¹, r/min	1*
	Rotational dynamics	rad/s	rad/s	
Hardness	Conventional hardness numbers, BHN, R, etc., not affected by change to SI.			

PREFERRED UNITS FOR EXPRESSING PHYSICAL QUANTITIES (cont'd)

1. Quantities are arranged in alphabetical order by principal nouns. For example, surface tension is listed as tension, surface.
2. All possible applications are not listed, but others such as rates can be readily derived. For example, from the preferred units for energy and volume the units for heat energy per unit volume, kJ/m³, may be derived.
3. Conversion factors are shown to seven significant digits, unless the precision with which the factor is known does not warrant seven digits.

Quantity	Application	From: Old Units	To: SI Units	Multiply By:
Heat	(See Energy)			
Heat capacity	(See Capacity, heat)			
Heat capacity, specific	(See Capacity, heat, specific)			
Heat flow rate	(See Power)			
Heat flow - density of	(See Density of heat flow)			
Heat, specific	General	cal/g‡	kJ/kg	4.186 8*
		Btu/lb	kJ/kg	2.326*
Heat transfer coefficient	(See Coefficient of heat transfer)			
Illuminance, illumination	General	fc	lx	10.763 91
Impact strength	(See Strength, impact)			
Impedance, mechanical	Damping coefficient	lbf·s/ft	N·s/m	14.593 90
Inductance, electric	Filters and chokes, permeance	H	H	
Intensity, luminous	Light bulbs	candlepower	cd	1*
Intensity, radiant	General	W/sr	W/sr	
Leakage	(See Flow, volume)			
Length	Land distances, maps, odometers	mile	km	1.609 344*‖
	Field size, turning circle, braking distance, cargo platforms, rolling circumference, water depth, land leveling (cut and fill)	rod	m	5.029 210 ‖
		yd	m	0.914.4
		ft	m	0.304 8*
	Row spacing	in.	cm	2.54*
	Engineering drawings, product specifications, vehicle dimensions, width of cut, shipping dimensions, digging depth, cross section of lumber, radius of gyration, deflection	in.	mm	25.4*
	Precipitation, liquid, daily and seasonal, field drainage (runoff), evaporation and irrigation depth	in.	mm	25.4*
	Precipitation, snow depth	in.	cm	2.54*
	Coating thickness, filter particle size	mil	μm	25.4*
		μin.	μm	0.025 4*
		micron	μm	1*
	Surface texture Roughness, average	μin.	μm	0.025 4*
	Roughness sampling length, waviness height and spacing	in.	mm	25.4*
	Radiation wavelengths, optical measurements (interference)	μin.	nm	25.4*
Length per time	Precipitation, liquid per hour	in./h	mm/h	25.4*
	Precipitation, snow depth per hour	in.h	cm/h	2.54*
Load	(See Mass)			
Luminance	Brightness	footlambert	cd/m²	3.426 259
Magnetization	Coil field strength	A/in.	A/m	39.370 08
Mass	Vehicle mass, axle rating, rated load, tire load, lifting capacity‡‡, tipping load, load, quantity of crop, counter mass, body mass general	ton (long)	t, Mg**	1.016 047
		ton (short)	t, Mg**	0.907 184 7
		lb	kg	0.453 592 4
		slug	kg	14.593 90
	Small mass	oz	g	28.349 52
Mass per area	Fabric, surface coatings	oz/yd²	g/m²	33.905 75
		lb/ft²	kg/m²	4.882 428
		oz/ft²	g/m²	305.151 7
	Floor loading	lb/ft²	kg/m²	4.882 428
	Application rate, fertilizer, pesticide	lb/acre	kg/ha	1.120 851
	Crop yield, soil erosion	ton (short)/acre	t/ha**	2.241 702
Mass per length	General, structural members	lb/ft	kg/m	1.488 164
		lb/yd	kg/m	0.496 054 7
Mass per time	Machine work capacity, harvesting, materials handling	ton (short)/h	t/h, Mg/h**	0.907 184 7
Modulus of elasticity	General	lbf/in.²	MPa	0.006 894 757
Modulus of rigidity	(See Modulus of elasticity)			
Modulus, section	General	in.³	mm³	16 387.06
		in.³	cm³	16.387 06
Modulus, bulk	System fluid compression	psi	kPa	6.894 757
Moment, bending	(See Moment of force)			
Moment of area, second	General	in.⁴	mm⁴	416 231.4
		in.⁴	cm⁴	41.623 14

PREFERRED UNITS FOR EXPRESSING PHYSICAL QUANTITIES (cont'd)

1. Quantities are arranged in alphabetical order by principal nouns. For example, surface tension is listed as tension, surface.
2. All possible applications are not listed, but others such as rates can be readily derived. For example, from the preferred units for energy and volume the units for heat energy per unit volume, kJ/m³, may be derived.
3. Conversion factors are shown to seven significant digits, unless the precision with which the factor is known does not warrant seven digits.

Quantity	Application	From: Old Units	To: SI Units	Multiply By:
Moment of force, torque, bending moment	General, engine torque, fasteners, steering torque, gear torque, shaft torque	lbf·in.	N·m	0.112 984 8
		lbf·ft	N·m	1.355 818
		kgf·cm	N·m	0.098 066 5*
	Locks, light torque	ozf·in.	mN·m	7.061 552
Moment of inertia, mass	Flywheel, general	lb·ft²	kg·m²	0.042 140 11
Moment of mass	Unbalance	oz·in.	g·m	0.720 077 8
Moment of momentum	(See Momentum, angular)			
Moment of section	(See Moment of area, second)			
Momentum, linear	General	lb·ft/s	kg·m/s	0.138 255 0
Momentum, angular	Torsional vibration	lb·ft²/s	kg·m²/s	0.042 140 11
Permeability	Magnetic core properties	H/ft	H/m	3.280 840
Permeance	(See Inductance)			
Potential, electric	General	V	V	
Power	General, light bulbs	W	W	
	Air conditioning, heating	Btu/min	W	17.584 27
		Btu/h	W	0.293 071 1
	Engine, alternator, drawbar, power take-off, hydraulic and pneumatic systems, heat rejection, heat exchanger capacity, water power, electrical power, body heat loss	hp (550 ft·lbf/s)	kW	0.745 699 9
Power per area	solar radiation	Btu/ft²h	W/m²	3.154 591
Pressure	All pressures except very small	lbf/in.² (psi)	kPa	6.894 757
		in.Hg (60 °F)	kPa	3.376 85
		in.H₂O (60 °F)	kPa	0.248 84
		mmHg (0 °C)	kPa	0.133 322
		kgf/cm²	kPa	98.066 5
		bar	kPa	100.0*
		lbf/ft²	kPa	0.047 880 26
		atm (normal = 760 torr)	kPa	101.325*
	Very small pressures (high vacuum)	lbf/in.² (psi)	Pa	6 894.757
Pressure, sound level	Acoustical measurement-When weighting is specified show weighting level in parenthesis following the symbol, for example dB(A).	dB	dB	
Quantity of electricity	General	C	C	
Radiant intensity	(See Intensity, radiant)			
Resistance, electric	General	Ω	Ω	
Resistivity, electric	General	Ω·ft	Ω·m	0.304 8*
		Ω·ft	Ω·cm	30.48*
Sound pressure level	(See Pressure, sound, level)			
Speed	(See Velocity)			
Spring rate, linear	(See Force per length)			
Spring rate, torsional	General	lbf·ft/deg	N·m/deg	1.355 818
Strength, field, electric	General	V/ft	V/m	3.280 840
Strength, field, magnetic	General	oersted	A/m	79.577 47
Strength, impact	Materials testing	ft·lbf	J	1.355 818
Stress	General	lbf/in.²	MPa	0.006 894 757
Surface tension	(See Tension, surface)			
Temperature	General use	°F	°C	$t_{°C} = (t_{°F} \cdot 32)/1.8$*
	Absolute temperature, thermodynamics, gas cycles	°R	K	$T_K = T_{°R}/1.8$*
Temperature interval	General use	°F	K†	$1 K = 1 °C = 1.8 °F$*
Tension, surface	General	lbf/in.	mN/m	175 126.8
		dyne/cm	mN/m	1*
Thermal diffusivity	Heat transfer	ft²/h	m²/h	0.092 903 04
Thrust	(See Force)			
Time	General	s	s	
		h	h	
		min	min	
	Hydraulic cycle time	s	s	
	Hauling cycle time	min	min	

PREFERRED UNITS FOR EXPRESSING PHYSICAL QUANTITIES (cont'd)

1. Quantities are arranged in alphabetical order by principal nouns. For example, surface tension is listed as tension, surface.
2. All possible applications are not listed, but others such as rates can be readily derived. For example, from the preferred units for energy and volume the units for heat energy per unit volume, kJ/m³, may be derived.
3. Conversion factors are shown to seven significant digits, unless the precision with which the factor is known does not warrant seven digits.

Quantity	Application	From: Old Units	To: SI Units	Multiply By:
Torque	(See Moment of force)			
Toughness, fracture	Metal properties	ksi·in.$^{0.5}$	MPa·m$^{0.5}$	1.098 843
Vacuum	(See Pressure)			
Velocity, angular	(See Velocity, rotational)			
Velocity, linear	Vehicle	mile/h	km/h	1.609 344*
	Fluid flow, conveyor speed, lift speed, air speed	ft/s	m/s	0.304 8*
	Cylinder actuator speed	in./s	mm/s	25.4*
	General	ft/s	m/s	0.304 8*
		ft/min	m/min	0.304 8*
		in./s	mm/s	25.4*
Velocity, rotational	(See Frequency)			
Viscosity, dynamic	General liquids	centipoise	mPa·s	1*
Viscosity, kinematic	General liquids	centistokes	mm²/s	1*
Volume	Truck body, shipping or freight, bucket capacity, earth, gas, lumber, building, general	yd³	m³	0.764 554 9
		ft³	m³	0.028 316 85
	Combine harvester grain tank capacity	bushel	L	35.239 07
	Automobile luggage capacity	ft³	L	28.316 85
	Gas pump displacement, air compressor, air reservoir, engine displacement			
	Large	in.³	L	0.016 387 06
	Small	in.³	cm³	16.387 06
	Liquid - fuel, lubricant, coolant, liquid wheel ballast	gal	L	3.785 412
		qt	L	0.946 352 9
		pt	L	0.473 176 5
	Small quantity liquid	oz	mL	29.573 53
	Irrigation, reservoir	acre·ft	m³	1 233.489‖
			dam³	1.233 489‖
	Grain bins	bushel (U.S.)	m³	0.035 239 07
Volume per area	Application rate, pesticide	gal/acre	L/ha	9.353 958
Volume per time	Fuel consumption (Also see Flow)	gal/h	L/h	3.785 412
Weight	May mean either mass or force—avoid use of weight			
Work	(See Energy)			
Young's modulus	(See Modulus of elasticity)			

*Indicates exact conversion factor.

†In these expressions K indicates temperature intervals. Therefore K may be replaced with °C if desired without changing the value or affecting the conversion factor. kJ/(kg·K) = kJ/(kg·°C).

‡Not to be confused with kcal/g. kcal often called calorie.

§Convenient conversion: 235.215 ÷ (mile per gal) = L/(100 km).

‖Official use in surveys and cartography involves the U.S. survey mile based on the U.S. survey foot, which is longer than the international foot by two parts per million. The factors used in this standard for acre, acre foot, rod are based on the U.S. survey foot. Factors for all other old length units are based on the international foot. (See ANSI/ASTM Standard E380-76, Metric Practice).

#Standard acceleration of gravity is 9.806 650 m/s² exactly (Adopted by the General Conference on Weights and Measures).

**The symbol t is used to designate metric ton. The unit metric ton (exactly 1 MG) is in wide use but should be limited to commercial description of vehicle mass, freight mass, and agricultural commodities. No prefix is permitted.

††Conversions of Btu are based on the International Table Btu.

‡‡Lift capacity ratings for cranes, hoists, and related components such as ropes, cable chains, etc., should be rated in mass units. Those items such as winches, which can be used for pulling as well as lifting, shall be rated in both force and mass units for safety reasons.

§§ASAE S209 and SAE J708. Agricultural Tractor Test Code, specify kg/(kW·h). It should be noted that there is a trend toward use of g/MJ as specified for highway vehicles.

INDEX

Action plan, 60
Advanced design topics, 231
Agricultural engineering
  challenges facing, 262
  future of, 253
  job roles, 240
  organizations, 273
  predictions for, 263
Agricultural firms classified, 236
Analysis, 135
  error, 228
  estimating market size for cost, 184
  factors to consider in an economic, 193
Anthropometry, 152
APL, 36, 43
Assembly Parts List, 36, 37
  example, 37

Bibliography, 295
"Bracketing" design parameters, 136
"Brain Barons"
  the era of, 261
Brainstorming, 95
  morphological approach, 96
Budget
  cash flow, 192
  example form for research and development, 189
  project, 188
Business styles, 233
  classified, 234

CAD, 35, 208
CAE, 35
CAM, 35, 208
Cash flow
  typical product, 194
Code of ethics, 265
Component and supplier selection, 197
Component suppliers, 187
  multi-source when possible, 200
Computer models
  limitations in design, 139
Computer-aided design, 35
Concept testing, 147
Conspectus sketch, 147
Copyrights, 243, 252
Cost estimating, 183
Costs
  effect of technology on unit production, 260
  manufacturing, 209
  of manufacturing, 186
  of materials, 185
CPM, 117-123
  example flow diagram, 121

CPM/PERT
  example, 121
Creativity, 93, 254
  common characteristics of, 98
  defined, 94
  enhancing your, 95
  environment for, 100
  in the design process, 94
  match and complement your talents, 99
  seeking help for, 98
Criteria for materials selection, 160
Critical path method, 117

Data
  example form to gather time and motion, 153
  human body size, 152
  sources of material properties, 162
Deadlines
  progress reports and, 32
Decision matrix
  example of, 128
Decisions
  characteristics of good, 129
Delays
  caused by indecision, 127
Design
  a people process, 73
  final, 133
  getting started, 67
  iterative process of, 68
  philosophy of, 71
  team approach, 29
  technical analysis within, 131
  truisms of problem solving in engineering, 78
Design changes
  on parts drawings, 43
Design criteria
  determining, 81
  example, 144
  example check list, 88
  quantification of, 87
  versus design objectives, 87
"Design defect", 178
Design engineer
  being an effective, 19
Design engineering functions
  example, 115
Design engineers
  are generalists, 29
  as salesmen, 59
Design notebook, 245
  example, 144
  versus design criteria, 87

Design of
air jet blueberry drier, 144
animal restraining head-gate, 137
low pressure sprinkler nozzle, 88
moldboard plow, 81
poles for pole buildings, 136
self-feeding sorghum mill, 139
solar grain drier, 140
tractor cab door, 152
tractor cab noise levels, 155
tractor seats, 155
Design problems
are complicated, 76
break into small pieces, 91
have multiple solutions, 75
Design process
illustrated, 69
Designs
skills used in selling your, 61
Dimensioning
example drawing, 41
Drawing
example engineering parts, 39
Drawings, 35

Economic feasibility, 184
effect of taxes upon, 192
Economics
in the future, 256
Electrical symbols
table, 41
Engineering change notice, 44
example, 44
Engineering design constraints, 73
Engineering drawings, 37
Engineering organizations, 273
Engineering variables
"bracketing" of, 136
need for comprehensive list of, 140
Enthusiasm
in design, 93
Equations
Darcy-Weisbach, 138
for calculating the value of money,
191
for estimating product cost for
propagation of error, 228
limitations in design, 138
Error analysis, 228
Ethics
in the practice of engineering, 165, 265

Factors of safety, 165
Failure modes and effect analysis,
166, 175
Failures
learn from, 77
Fault, 176

Human factors engineering, 151

Illustrations
examples of, 55, 56, 57, 58
Information finding, 103
library reference section, 105
personal contacts, 110
Innovation, 243
"intellectual property", 243
Invention, 243

Liability, 165
as a civil case, 178
"design defect", 178
design record requirements, 179
misconceptions, 179
negligence, 177
product, 177
professional, 177

Machine Design Magazine, 162
Manufacturing
capabilites, 203
generalized design rules that
influence, 212
Manufacturing considerations, 203
Manufacturing process
classified, 212
Market size estimating, 184
Material properties data, 162
Materials selection, 160
Metric conversion tables, 303
Money
equations for calculating value of, 191
equations fo estimating selling price,
185
Motivation, 59, 62
of others, 31
psychology of, 63
three myths about, 62

Occupational Safety and Health Act, 155
Optimal solutions, 76
Organizational structures, 233
business, 233

Pareto histogram, 229
example for a moldboard plow, 229
Patent
plant, 250
Patent application
writing of, 245
"Patent pending", 250
"Patented", 250
Patents, 188, 218, 243
brief history of, 244
conducting a search of, 248
public disclosure, 246
witnesses, 245
PERT, 117-127
example flow diagram, 125
Positions classified
line versus staff, 238

Positive work environment, 64
Prices
    establishing retail and manufactured, 185
    from OEM's, 187
Prime part
    example drawing, 39
Prime parts, 36
Problem definition
    expect changes in, 89
Problems
    creative, 90
    define in writing, 85
    factual, 90
    judicial, 90
    list engineering variables to define, 85
Product safety, 165
Product claims
    be careful of, 199
Product development, 131
Product directories, 197
Product liability
    as a civil case, 178
    design record requirements, 179
    misconceptions, 179
Product life testing, 229
Production volume
    effects upon design, 223
Professionalism, 181
Profitability, 183
Progress
    difficulty of achieving true, 64
Project scheduling, 113, 118
Propagation of error, 228
Psychological factors, 155
Purchased parts, 162

Quality assurance, 210
Quality control, 210

References
    list of non-undergraduate textbook references, 141
    style of, 50
Reports
    executive summary, 61
    oral, 52
    outline for technical, 49
    status, 61
Responsibility
    delegating, 31
Roles
    of analysis and systhesis, 131

Safety, 165
    factors of, 166
    product, 165
    tests for, 179
Salesman
    attributes of a good, 60
Salesmen
    telephoning and talking with, 200

Selling price, 185
Simplification, 215
Simplifying assumptions, 139
Site visits, 97
Speaking, 47
    deficiencies, 47
Specifications, 35
Standard items, 36
Standardization, 215
    for product safety, 219
    reasons for, 215
    voluntary, 219
Standards
    development of, 219
    mandatory, 219
    voluntary, 219
Synthesis, 143
    central issues in project, 144
    of alternative analysis scenarios, 144

Taxes
    effect upon economic feasibility, 192
Team effectiveness, 29
    inhibition of, 31
Technical report writing, 48
Technology adaptation, 258
Testing, 223
    field, 226
    planning for, 224
    procedures for, 227
    product life, 229
    quality control, 224
    results from, 227
    similitude, 225
Tests
    engineering, 225
Time
    management of, 19
Time and motion studies, 153
    example results, 153
Tolerancing
    costs of, 209
Trade secrets, 188, 243, 252
Trademarks, 243, 251

User considerations, 151
    not related directly to humans, 156

Value of money over time, 190
Visual aids, 54
    examples of, 55, 56, 57, 58

Weldment
    example drawing, 43
Weldments, 36, 40
Writing, 47, 48
    a proposal, 51
    deficiencies, 47
    in your design notebook, 52
    technical paper, 49
    technical report, 48

1   7   8

A

B

C

D

E

| | CODE OR DRWG. NO. | REMARKS |

F

CUST. REF.

'ISE SPECIFIED TOLERANCE TO BE ±

SCALE

G

CHANGE

DATE

MATERIAL | SIZE | PART NO

CE
ED

.6)

NS ARE IN

DATE	DRAWN	PART NO.
DATE	DATE	
	CHK'D	
DATE	SCALE	SHEET	OF